MW00620825

An

Intimate Note

to the

Sincere Seeker

Gurudev Sri Sri Ravi Shankar

Sri Sri Publications Trust, India

An Intimate Note to the Sincere Seeker
Daily Knowledge Sutras by Gurudev Sri Sri Ravi Shankar

1st Edition December 2008
Copyrights Sri Sri Publications Trust, 2008

Published by:

THE ART OF LIVING
Sri Sri Publications Trust
Art of Living International Centre,
21st KM, Kanakapura Road, Udayapura, Bangalore – 560082
Email: info@srisripublications.com
Website: www.sattvastore.com
Toll Free: 1800-258-8888

ISBN: 978 9380592787

Layout by: Sri Sri Publications Trust

Printed in India by: Pentaplus Printers Pvt. Ltd., Bangalore - 44

Contents

1. This Begins a New Practice   1

2. Close to the Master   2

3. Prarabdha Karma and Sanchita Karma   3

4. Only Speak Knowledge; Find Comfort in Conflicts   4

5. Master is the Door   5

6. Doubt   6

7. Fire   7

8. Habits and Vows   8

9. Dealing with Blame   9

10. Today is Krishna's Birthday: Birth of the Centre of Attraction   10

11. Asuya and Anasuya   11

12. The Love of the Ignorant, the Anger of the Enlightened   13

13. A Liar is Innocent   14

14. Be a Gopal   15

15. Silence   16

16. The Big Mind   17

17. The Only Thing You Must Remember   18

18. Freedom and Discipline   19

19. Discipleship Ends   20

20. Sakha: Your Reliable Sense   21

21. Scepticism   23

22. Shaucha and Ashaucha   24

23. Boredom and Sadhana   25

24. Who Are You: Brahma, Vishnu, Shiva - or Guru?   26

25. How to Maintain Intimacy   27

26. All are searching for sweets   28

27. Overcoming Events   29

28. The Washing Machine   30

29. Divine is All Celebration   31

30. New Year's Celebration   32

31. Wrapping Paper   33

32. Is Guru Satisfied or Unsatisfied?   34

33. Advice from Hawaii   35

34. The Most Beautiful Spot in the Universe   36

35. Indebtedness or Abundance?   37

36. Abiding in the Self   39

37. Knowledge and Faith   40

38. Respect   41

39. Desire and Joy 43
40. Faith and Love 44
41. Questions & Dealing with Desire 46
42. Blame and Misery 48
43. Attachments 49
44. Vivek 50
45. Words 51
46. Karma 53
47. Sanyas & Your Associations 54
48. Illusion 55
49. Self 56
50. Enlightenment 57
51. Samadhi 58
52. What You Know 59
53. Seva is Saviour 60
54. When We are Joyful 62
55. Judgments and Good Company 64
56. God is a Thorough Businessman 66
57. Surrender and Responsibility 67
58. Respect Everybody as You Respect Me 69
59. Doing versus Happening 70
60. Don't Be Grateful! 71
61. Faith, Devotion and Meditation 73
62. Infinite Patience and Smart Shopping 75
63. Surrender, Shame and Shyness 77
64. Special... or Ordinary? 78
65. Whether You Win or Lose 80
66. The Well-Baked Pot 81
67. The Fall that Rises 82
68. Which is more expensive: your smile or your anger? 83
69. The Perfect Balance 86
70. The Nine Nights of Navaratri 87
71. Celebrating the Silence 88
72. Sincerity and Blessings 89
73. In the Solitude of the Self 90
74. See the Divine 91
75. Annihilate Conflict 92
76. Desire and Prayerfulness 93
77. Faith and Happiness 94

78. How to Deal with Rude Behaviour   95

79. Pleasure   97

80. The Five Aspects of the Universe   98

81. Self-Reliance and Surrender   99

82. New Year's Celebration   100

83. Padmanabha: the Lotus Navel   101

84. Bhakti   103

85. Accept the World at Its Worst   104

86. Indigestion of Knowledge   105

87. Unknown Knowledge   106

    The Little Monster in My Head   107

    The Divine Mirror   108

    Hopeless   109

    Breath: Doorway to Silence   110

    Unending Wealth   111

    Why are you still frustrated?   112

    The Perfect Plan   113

    Guru is not who you think he is!   114

    The Roller Coaster   114

    Note from a Devotee   115

    Where is He?   116

    Faith of the Faithful   117

    The Music of Life   118

    Gossip   119

    Nonviolence and Gratitude for Cats   120

88. Be Loved   121

89. Seva Blessings   122

90. Share Your Joy   123

91. Angels   125

92. The Eleventh Commandment   126

93. A Friend is an Enemy, an Enemy is a Friend   127

94. Simple or Complex?   128

95. Expand Your Vices   129

96. The Primal Instinct   130

97. Satsang is Shelter   131

98. Three Kinds of Love   132

99. What enhances your beauty?   134

100. Drop Your Self-image   135

101. The World Belongs to You   136

102. Dedication and Commitment 138
103. The Way Out of Sorrow 139
104. The Divine Beyond Time 140
105. Every Stone is Precious 141
106. Sensitivity and Strength 142
107. The Personal and the Impersonal 143
108. The Golden Veil 145
109. With Whom Are You At Ease? 146
110. Let Love Be 147
111. Make Everything Personal and Universal 148
112. On Respect 149
113. Sacrifice 150
114. Window Shutters 151
115. Raksha Bandhan 152
116. Truth Once Found 153
117. A Big Dilemma 155
118. How to Get Centred 156
119. The Five Insights 157
120. Five Signs of the Satguru 158
121. Six Signs of a Seeker 159
122. Yagyas 160
123. God as a Child 161
124. Feel Blessed 162
125. Diwali 163
126. Love is Your Very Existence 165
127. Your Expressions of Love 166
128. Ego 168
129. Memory 169
130. Intellect 170
131. Time and Mind 172
132. Faces of Infinity 173
133. Celebration and the Christmas Tree 174
134. A Wise Person is Happy Even in Bad Times 176
135. You are Pure Electricity 177
136. Politics 178
137. Tolerance and Acceptance are Not Virtues 180
138. False Security 182
139. Organisation and Devotion 183
140. When a Mistake is Not a Mistake 184

141. Respect 186
142. Shiva and Vashi 187
143. Formality and Cordiality 188
144. You are the Tenth 189
145. Inside Out 190
146. Dreams 192
147. Impression and Expression 193
148. Tarka, Vitarka and Kutarka 195
149. Softness and Forcefulness 196
150. Do Not Follow Me 197
151. Confusion and Decision 198
152. You are Privileged 199
153. The Value of Chanting 200
154. Intensify Your Longing 201
155. Faith is Your Wealth 202
156. Who Wakes Up First? 204
157. Breaking Beyond the Rational Mind 206
158. If You Cannot Meditate - Be Stupid! 207
159. Give Away Your Rights 208
160. Generosity is a Quality of Spirit 209
161. The Path of Love is Surrender 210
162. It Takes Courage to Say "I Am" 211
163. Do You Know I Have No Mercy? 212
164. Ego Is Only an Atom 213
165. Loyalty 214
166. Do You Love Someone Because They Are Great or Unique? 215
167. Singing, Communication And Ego 216
168. Expansion of Consciousness is Peace 218
169. Dependence, Independence, Interdependence And Oneness 219
170. Rest And Activity 221
171. Do It Until You Become It ! 222
172. Silence 223
173. Do Not Correct Your Mistakes! 224
174. Yagna 225
175. The Different Kinds of Understanding 226
176. The Cause of Return 228
177. Appreciation 230
178. What Are the Signs of Love? 231
179. The Purpose of Life 232

180. Austerity   233
181. Focus And Expansion   234
182. Sublimating Lust   235
183. Uncertainty   237
184. Organisation   239
185. Recycling and Hygiene   240
186. Bliss   242
187. Do You Test God, or Does God Test You?   244
188. Welcoming And Resisting   245
189. Stimulating the Soul   246
190. Stretching the Emptiness   247
191. Love's Wisdom   248
192. Becoming Defenceless   249
193. Diksha   250
194. Love And Lust   251
195. Doubt And Closeness   253
196. Intelligence   254
197. Attaining Self - Knowledge   255
198. You And Your Time   256
199. A Prayer   257
200. The Noise of Nonviolence   258
201. Life Is Too Short; Life Is Eternal   259
202. A Deep Rest   260
203. Blessing   261
204. Shortcut !   262
205. Faith; Nature of Consciousness   263
206. Success   264
207. Message   265
208. Blessed Are Those Who Are Bored   266
209. Religion And Politics   267
210. Love And Renunciation   268
211. Change and Love   270
212. Thank Superficially   271
213. Satyam Param Dhimahi   272
214. Guru Is The Goal   273
215. How to Conquer Jealousy or Envy   274
216. Anu Vrat   276
217. Knowledge As A Burden   277
218. Protection And Transformation   278

219. Who Wins? 279
220. Two Anecdotes 280
221. Compassion And Karma 281
222. Negativity Needs An Anchor 282
223. Life Is A War 283
224. Spirituality And Celebration 284
225. Sound Faith 285
226. Always? 286
227. Being In Utter Love 287
   Homage to Amma 288
228. Death And Spirituality 289
229. Aggression As A Way To Overcome Depression 290
230. Think Fresh 291
231. The Five Secrets 292
232. The Wisdom Of Secrets 293
233. Intention 294
234. The Nature Of The Five Senses Is Knowledge 295
235. Five Factors That Influence The Mind 296
236. Reasons To Be With A Guru 298
237. Evolution: Not Part Of The Self 299
238. Varieties Of Spirit 300
239. The Problem's Tail 301
240. Do Not Worship Or Idolize 302
241. Feel The Pinch 303
242. Skill In Praising 305
243. News Flood 306
244. Form And Formless, Aggression And Intuition 308
245. The Goal Of All Answers 309
246. Surrender 310
247. How To Handle Feverishness 311
248. How Does A Desire Arise? 312
249. Ram Navami 313
250. Desire Kills Joy And All Desires Aim For Joy 314
251. You Are Nothing 315
252. Desire For Truth 316
253. Seekers Beware 317
254. Is The Guru Responsible? 318
255. Life Without Wisdom Is Incomplete 319
256. Education 320

257. Truth 321
258. I Am Neither Honest Nor Humble 322
259. How To Deal With Humiliation 323
260. Legends 324
261. Arguments And Wrong Action 325
262. Virtues 326
263. Action and Reaction 327
264. Technology 328
265. Love - The Question of an Answer 329
266. Conflict and Innocence 330
267. Problems? One More 331
268. Do Not Make a Mistake by Pointing Out Mistakes 332
269. Wise Are the Ones Who Make You Crave for the Divine 333
270. Do You Have to be Thankful and Feel Obliged? 334
271. Divine Love and the Complaining Face 335
272. The Devotee Becomes God 336
273. Devotion is Steeped in Mystery 337
274. Perfection is the Nature of the Enlightened 338
275. Ignorance of Your Capability Can Expand You 339
276. Love is the Shadow of the Self 340
277. Are You a Tourist or a Pilgrim? 341
278. The Bodhi Tree 342
279. Nimit - Instrument of the Divine 343
280. The Problem's Solution 345
281. Sacredness and You 346
282. I am God 348
283. Atheism is Not a Reality 350
284. Atheism 352
285. To Say "Sorry" is a Good Mistake 354
286. Kick the Ball and Be in the Goal 355
287. "Important" and "Unimportant" 356
288. Worship - A Sign of Maturity 357
289. The Kumbha Mela 358
290. The Other Side of Friendliness 360
291. Longing Itself is Divine 362
292. Back to Space 363
293. Passion and Self-Reliance 365
294. The Other Side of Fear - The Usefulness of Fear 366
295. The Other Side of Ego 368

296. The Paradox of Sacrifice   369
297. Divine in the Form and Formless   370
298. Strength and Subordination   371
299. Commitment and Convenience   373
300. Dealing with Blame and Accusation   375
301. Self-Confidence and Ambition   377
302. The Dangers of Belongingness and Advantages of Obligations   378
303. Prestige and Honour - Your Golden Cage   380
304. Life is a Dream, a Burden or a Joke   381
305. Reason and Faith   382
306. Doing Trivial Things   383
307. Joy and Sorrow   384
308. Deep Rest and Bliss   385
309. Five Types of Restlessness   386
310. Tendencies and Influences   388
311. Authenticity and Skilfulness   389
312. Time, Space and Mind   391
313. Mistakes   392
314. The Great Pleasure of Rest   393
315. Worry & Feelings   394
316. Who is Pleasing Whom?   395
317. Two Perspectives of the Guru   396
318. Love & Authority   397
319. Ganesha   398
320. Hungry for Power   399
321. You & Ownership   400
322. Reverence & Ownership   401
323. War : The Worst Act of Reason   402
324. Terrorism : the Cause & the Remedy   404
325. How to Deal With Anxiety   406
326. Is War Violence or Nonviolence?   408
327. Honey   409
328. Drop Your Intentions   410
329. Aishwarya & Madhurya   411
330. Volunteer   412
331. Adulation   414
332. Seva   415
333. Confidence With Humility: the Rarest Combination   416
334. Dreaming the Impossible   417

335. Respect & Ego   418

336. Maya   419

337. Letting Go of Control   420

338. Memory: a Hindrance & a Blessing   421

339. Don't be Perturbed by Foolishness   422

340. Glory & Dispassion (Vaibhav & Vairagya)   423

341. Where Dispassion is Detrimental!   424

342. Business & Spirituality   425

343. The Subtle Truth About Virtues   426

344. Humour & Humiliation   427

345. Love & Truth   429

346. An Awkward Situation   430

347. The True Yajña   432

348. Your Nature is Shiva   433

349. Praise the Fools   434

350. What Makes a Real Holiday?   435

351. Wake up & Slow Down   436

352. Communism & Spirituality   437

353. Was Buddha an Atheist?   438

354. The Strength of Commitment   439

355. Two Types of Knowledge   440

356. Friendship for a Cause   441

357. Three Types of Dispassion   442

358. Faith & Alertness   443

359. Enthusiasm & Dispassion   444

360. Guru Tidbits   445

361. Nigraha, Agraha, Satyagraha & Duraagraha   446

362. Wake Up & Transcend   447

363. Know Your Group Type   448

364. Creativity   449

365. 'Free Will And Destiny   450

Message For The New Millennium   451

Wisdom For Organisers   452

Words are too small to convey the Truth
Yet they can trigger the flames of wisdom,
Shower comfort on the intense longing,
Raise cheers of joy and make you
Know I treasure your love for me.

Like God his creation,
The root its trunk,
Unknown, unheard, unseen,
In the silent chamber of heart
I am in you as you,
You are in me as me.

Ha! What a blessing!

- Gurudev Sri Sri Ravi Shankar

Since June, 1995, people around the world eagerly await the Knowledge from Gurudev each week. It started out as a simple note from the Master; later, devotees began to add a weekly "news flash" to carry a fragrance of the events surrounding Gurudev on his extensive travels.

People from various countries assist Gurudev with transcribing, translating, and transmitting the Weekly Knowledge. Next week it could be you.

This first volume contains the Weekly Knowledge from June 21, 1995 through June 13, 1996.

1. THIS BEGINS A NEW PRACTICE

This begins a series of weekly notes of Knowledge from Gurudev Sri Sri Ravi Shankar.

> *Beyond an event is Knowledge.*
> *Beyond an object is Infinity.*
> *Beyond a person is Love.*

Knowledge is beyond events. Every event colours your awareness in some way: pleasure, pain, joy, sorrow, anger, jealousy. Each event gives you a false notion of what reality is. Truth is beyond all the colours of particular events.

Behind every object is infinity. Objects are limited and changing, yet they exist in infinite space that never changes. Reduce any object to atoms; you will find that within each atom is contained infinite space. Beyond all objects is infinity.

Beyond each person is love. A personality changes. A body, a mind, a complex of behaviours is always changing. Beyond each personality there is unchanging love; love is what you are. When you lose your self, you'll find your Self!

The event behind the event is Knowledge. The object behind the object is infinity. The person behind the person is love.

Maya – delusion – is when you are stuck in events, personalities, or objects. *Brahman* – divine consciousness – is seeing beyond all these.

See? Just a little shift.

2. CLOSE TO THE MASTER

If you're not feeling close to the Master, it's because of you – because of your mind, your ego concepts.

Just being on the levels of formal and informal communication cannot make you feel close. "How are you?" "Where are you going?" "How have you been?" Stop these formal and superficial conversations with the Master. Speak with your heart what is deep in your life, what is important and intimate to you. Don't just say how much the squash costs – 30 cents or whatever.

Share what you have and don't judge, "Oh, this is garbage." The Master is ready to accept garbage of any extent. However you are, he will embrace you. Do not feel shame, shy, or judgmental about yourself.

If you don't feel close to the Master, there's no point in having a Master. He is just another burden to you, and you have enough burdens already. Just say, "Goodbye."

Question: When you play little games with us and push us away, how can we feel close to you?

Gurudev: You should feel more close if you are scolded or ignored, because to ignore somebody takes a lot of effort. When a Master does not even ignore wrapping paper or a flower in a vase, how can he ignore a walking, talking, breathing human being who is connected to him? Once you understand this, you immediately feel close.

Torre: Can we call you every week?

Kenny: Call Gurudev**every week, and if he doesn't answer the phone, then you know you are loved!

Gurudev: Yes, put that in. *(Laughter)*

> You are with the Master to share the joy of the Master, to share the
> consciousness of the Master.
>
> For this, you have to empty your cup of what is already in it.

The Master is ready to share. You have only to share from your side.

---

*Gurudev thought to send out Weekly Knowledge notes, and everyone liked the idea -so this first week he sent two!

**People around the world commonly address Gurudev as Guruji (honoured teacher).

3. Prarabdha Karma and Sanchita Karma

Some *karma* can be changed and some cannot.

When you prepare a dessert, if sugar or *ghee* is too little, you can add more. If some other ingredient is too much, it can all be adjusted and repaired. But once it is cooked, it cannot be reversed.

Milk can become sweet yoghurt or sour yoghurt, and sour yoghurt can be sweetened. But neither can be reversed back to milk.

Sanchita karma can be changed and adjusted by spiritual practices. *Prarabdha karma* cannot be changed. And *Satsang** burns the seed of all negative *karma*s before they are given a chance to sprout.

**The company of the Master; also refers to a group of individuals who come together to celebrate the Knowledge.*

4. ONLY SPEAK KNOWLEDGE; FIND COMFORT IN CONFLICTS

Only speak Knowledge. Don't repeat anything bad that someone tells you about someone. And don't listen to someone who tells you that "so-and-so said such-and-such" about you. When someone comes to tell you such things, discourage them. Don't believe it.

If someone blames you directly, don't believe in what they say. Just know that they are taking away your bad *karma* and let it go. And if you're one of the Master's close ones, you will take all the blame of the world with a smile.

> *When you blame someone,*
> *you take on their bad karma;*
> *When you praise someone,*
> *you take on their good karma;*
> *Surrender both good and bad karma to the Divine – and be free.*

Conflict is the nature of the world; comfort is the nature of the Self. Amidst conflict, find the comfort.

When you are tired of conflicts and the games of the world, get into the comforts of the Self. When you are bored with comfort, get into the games of the world. If you are one of the Master's close ones, you do both simultaneously.

People who love peace do not want to fight, and those who fight do not have peace. What is needed is to be peaceful within and then fight. Just trying to end a conflict only prolongs it.

Instead, face the conflict while seeking the comfort of the Self. Does this ring a bell? This is the whole message of the *Bhagavad Gita - Krishna* tells *Arjuna* to be centred in peace and to fight at the same time.

God is alive in the world and has been putting up with all conflicts throughout the ages. If God can put up with all these conflicts, you can too. And the moment you agree to be with a conflict, it no longer appears as a conflict to you.

The nature of this world is that once you resolve one conflict, another arises. For example, Russia is solved and then Bosnia is in trouble. Or you get a cold, then you get better – then your back hurts, then it gets better. And when your body is fine, then the mind goes. Things in this world run this way, don't they?

Without any intention, misunderstandings simply happen and conflicts arise. It's not up to you to resolve them. Just be with them and be alive!

5. MASTER IS THE DOOR

You are lost on the street. There is rain, thunder, wind and cold; you need shelter. You look around and you find a door. You come to the door because it is more inviting, more charming, more joyful than anything out on the street.

When you enter the door of the Master, you come Home. You see the world from a new perspective. From inside you can still hear the thunder and see the rain, but it no longer disturbs you. Inside there is warmth and security. The world looks much more beautiful – not a nasty place, but a place filled with love, cooperation, compassion. Your fear drops away.

When you can see the whole world through the eyes of the Master, it is a sign that you have come to the Master; you have entered the door. This is the purpose of having a Master.

If you are still seeing the world as before, then you have not yet come to the Master; you are still standing out in the street, cold and wet; you are only looking at the door, you have not yet entered in.

What does it mean to "see through the eyes of the Master"? Just this: Every situation that you face, you are thinking- *If this situation comes in front of the Master, how would he handle it? If this complication comes to the Master, how would he take it? If someone blames the Master, what would he do?*

The key is to feel the Presence of the Master. The Master is the Presence, not a relationship. Relationships can be broken, mended, and broken again. There is craving and aversion in every relationship. This is the wheel of *sansara*, the misery of the world. All relationships go topsy-turvy, whereas the Presence is vast, infinite, stable and centred.

Don't make the Master a worldly relationship. "Oh, he looked at me." "He didn't look at me." "Oh, he said this." "He didn't say that." "Somebody else is close; I am not close." All this garbage comes into it.

Just enter the door of the Master and come Home. Only the Presence of the Master will bring fulfilment to your life – and to all your relationships.

---

*the full moon day in July when one traditionally celebrates and honours the Master.

6. DOUBT

A doubt is a gray area. Gray is something which is neither white nor black. Now, how to solve a doubt?

Accept a doubt as either black or white.

See your doubt as white and there is no doubt. See the doubt as black and accept it. Either way, you accept it and move on.

See someone as either honest or dishonest and accept him. Then your mind is quiet. Then you are not in the gray area of doubt. Have conviction: "He is dishonest and yet he is still part of me. I accept him as he is." That's it. Finished.

Doubt is an unstable state with footing neither on this shore nor that shore. From there tension arises. One way or the other, take a direction and regain your footing.

Have you noticed that you usually doubt only the things that are positive in your life? Negative things you don't doubt. You doubt a person's honesty, and you believe in his dishonesty. When someone is angry with you, you have no doubt about his anger. But when someone says he loves you, a doubt creeps in: Does he really love me? When you are depressed, do you ever think am I really depressed? No, you take your depression as a fact. Yet when you are happy, you doubt: Am I really happy; is this really what I wanted? You doubt that you are capable, but do you ever doubt that you are incapable?

See this tendency to doubt the positive things in your life.
Put doubt in its proper place and doubt the doubts.
Doubt the negative and put your trust more in the positive.

7. FIRE

The senses are like fire. Whatever you put into your senses burns in this fire.

A fire of toxic material creates pollution and bad smell. But if you burn sandalwood, it creates fragrance.

The same fire that supports life can also destroy. A fire can heat your home or burn it down. Celebration happens around a bonfire. Grief happens around the fire of cremation. A burning tyre creates toxic fumes. A *ghee* lamp lights your way and purifies the surroundings.

Does your fire create smoke and pollution – or are you like a camphor flame that creates light and fragrance? A saint creates light and the fragrance of love. He is the friend of life.

A fire that creates light and warmth is of high quality. A fire that creates light and a little smoke is of medium quality. The fire that creates smoke and darkness is of low quality. Learn to distinguish these different fires.

> *When your senses are engaged in goodness, then you will create light and fragrance;*
> *When engaged in impurity, you create smoke and darkness.*

It is *sanyama* that transforms the quality of fire in you. Next week we will discuss *sanyama*.

8. HABITS AND VOWS

How to get rid of *vasanas* (impressions)? This is a question for all those who want to come out of habits.

You want to get rid of habits because they give you pain and restrict you. The nature of a *vasana* is to bother you – bind you – and wanting to be free is the nature of life. When a soul does not know how to be free, it wanders for lifetimes craving freedom.

The way to come out of habits is vows.

A vow should be time-bound. For example, suppose someone says, "I will quit smoking;" but cannot do it. He can take a time-bound vow not to smoke for five days. If someone is used to cursing and swearing, he can take a vow not to use bad language for ten days. Don't take a vow for a lifetime – you will break it immediately! If you happen to break it anyway, don't worry; just begin again. When you fulfil your vow, pick a new starting time and renew it again. Slowly increase the length of your vow until it becomes your very nature.

This is *sanyama*. Everybody is endowed with a little *sanyama*. When the mind falls back into its old patterns, two possibilities can happen. One is, you feel discouraged, you blame yourself, and you feel you have not made any progress. The second possibility is that you see it as an opportunity for *sanyama* and feel happy about it.

Bad habits will clog you and drain your life energy. Without *sanyama*, life will not be happy and disease-free. For example, you know you should not eat three servings of ice cream or eat ice cream every day. If you do, you will get sick. Just give a positive direction to your life energy and you can rise above any habit through *sanyama*.

All those habits that bother you, bind them in vows, in *sanyama*. Take a time-bound vow today and make a note of it. If you break a vow, make a note of it and share the time and date at the next *Satsang*. Continue it again. Tie those habits which bring you pain in *sanyama*.

9. Dealing with Blame

When someone blames you, what do you usually do? You blame them back or you put up a resistance in yourself.

How do you feel when someone blames you? Hurt, unhappy, sad, heavy? This is all because you are resisting! What you resist, persists.

You get hurt because you resist the blame.

Know that when someone blames you, they take away some negative *karma* from you. If you understand this, you will only feel happy about it. .

If you resist when someone blames you, you are not allowing them to take away the negative *karma*. Even if you don't react outwardly, you may still be resisting inside.

Actually it's fine to resist outside, but inside don't resist. You will feel immediately lighter. You can feel happy: Oh, good, somebody is blaming me and taking some of my negative *karma*.

The ignorant person says, "Don't blame me" because it hurts him. An enlightened person also says, "Don't blame me." Do you know why? Because it might hurt you. You can tell someone not to blame you out of anger or out of compassion.

✍ **News Flash:** *Gurudev arrived in Poland for an enchanting course with nearly 400 people. Every eye filled with tears of gratitude. Then Gurudev came to Braunlage, Germany, where more than 200 people are celebrating the silence.*

10. TODAY IS KRISHNA'S BIRTHDAY: BIRTH OF THE CENTRE OF ATTRACTION

Krishna means the most attractive. He is the divinity, the energy, that pulls everything to it. *Krishna* is the formless centre that is everywhere.

Any attraction anywhere comes only from Krishna.

Often people fail to see the spirit behind an attraction and merely hold on to the outer shell. The moment you possess the shell, you will see *Krishna* has played a trick. You will be left empty with the shell in your hands and tears in your eyes.

Don't be tricked by *Krishna* – be clever like *Radha*. *Krishna* could not escape from *Radha*, for her whole world was filled with *Krishna*. If you can see that wherever there is an attraction, there is *Krishna*, then you have become *Radha*. Then you are always in your centre.

The mind moves towards beauty, joy, and truth. So *Krishna* tells *Arjuna*, "I am the beauty in the beautiful, the strength in the strong, the wisdom in the wise." In this way he attracts the mind so that it does not move away from him.

Krishna reveals this Knowledge to *Arjuna* because he is *anasuya*. Next week we will see what *anasuya* is.

11. ASUYA AND ANASUYA

There is a certain mind set that always finds fault even under the best conditions. When you give such a person the best possible things, he finds faults. Even with the ideal companion or the most beautiful painting, he will still find something wrong. This kind of mind set is called *asuya*; it can never know the sacred Knowledge.

Asuya is finding a fault or seeing a malicious intent everywhere. Suppose it is windy and you shut the door, but at that moment someone else was just about to walk in. He will think that the door has been slammed in his face! This is *asuya*.

You have a friendship, and after ten years you find a fault and decide to break it off. Now you do not see any good from that entire relationship. This is *asuya*.

The moment you are out of the spiritual Path, you feel that everything on the Path was all wrong. This is *asuya*.

Asuya is when a child says, "Mother, you don't love me!" The child's vision is wrong; if the mother does not love the child, who will? It frustrates the mother.

Asuya is when someone comes to me and says, "Gurudev, you don't love me!" If I don't love them, forget about it. Who else in the world will? Yet a Master never becomes frustrated.

Knowledge is different at different levels of consciousness. At a particular point you become *anasuya*.

Anasuya means being devoid of fault-finding eyes.

Krishna tells *Arjuna* that he is giving him the Royal Secret because he is *anasuya*: "You are not finding fault in Me, even though you are so close."

From a distance, it is easy to miss a fault in somebody; up close, no fault escapes you. Even craters cannot be seen from afar; up close, even a smooth surface has imperfections. If you are interested only in holes, you will not see the larger dimension of things.

Unless you are devoid of fault-finding eyes, there is no point in giving you Knowledge because it cannot blossom in you.

If a mirror is dusty, you can clean it. But if your eyes have a cataract, any amount of dusting the mirror will not help. You have to remove the cataract. Then you will see that the mirror was already clean.

Asuya – fault–finding eyes, give you the idea, "The whole world is not sharp, the whole world is no good."

Anasuya is knowing, "It is my own vision of the world that is blurred." And once you discover you have the wrong vision, half of the problem has already disappeared.

12. THE LOVE OF THE IGNORANT, THE ANGER OF THE ENLIGHTENED

The love of the ignorant can be harmful, yet even the anger of the Enlightened is not harmful. It can only be good!

We have a school at the ashram in Bangalore. There are 250 children enrolled, but only 200 come to class on any given day. Fifty children don't show up! Why? Because they cry at home, "Mother, I don't want to go to school."

The mother says, "Oh, la la, don't cry...okay." She thinks, "No child in the world is like my child." She gives in to the child and defends him. She does not see the teacher's point of view.

So, what happens? The child grows up spoiled. The child will never learn the alphabet, never learn to read or write. And the mother says, "Oh, never mind, there are sheep to look after and fields to tend." Her love in ignorance has spoiled the child.

On the other hand,

The anger of the Enlightened is a blessing.

The *Puranas* give many instances of this. Once a Master was travelling with a disciple in the middle province of India. Some boys who were rude, rough, and abusive began to throw stones and tease the disciple, calling him names. This went on for some time as the boys followed the Master and the disciple.

They came to a river. The Master and the disciple got into a boat and started to cross. The boys got into another boat which began to sink in the middle of the river.

The Master slapped the disciple across the face. The disciple was so surprised, as he had not said a single word in response to the boys' taunts! He had been such a good disciple and yet the Master had slapped him.

The Master said, "It is your fault. You are responsible for their boat sinking. You did not respond to their abuse. Nature has now punished them in a worse way because you did not have enough compassion to quell their insults."

That slap from the Master took away the *karma* of this event so that it would not be carried into the future of the boys. It also served to take away any little bit of joy the disciple may have felt as he was seeing the boys' boat sink! Thus, it also took away the *karma* of the event for the disciple.

Even the anger of the Enlightened is a blessing!

13. A Liar is Innocent

A dear person whom you trust lies to you and you catch him. What do you feel?

1. Sadness
2. Anger
3. Cheated
4. Disappointment
5. Compassion
6. Let down
7. Loss of respect
8. Wonder
9. Shock
10. Embarrassment

Recently when someone lied to me, I felt happy and more love, for they were not a good liar. Had he been a good liar, he would not have been caught. I thought He is so innocent that he could not even lie properly. He lied and got caught! If he had not been caught, how would ever you know he was a liar?

So... you can never know a good liar.

The person you call a liar is not a good liar... and he is innocent. Isn't he?

And so... (Laugh), you need not go through all the above listed mental gymnastics. Instead melt and dissolve in love.

14. BE A GOPAL

You walk until you come to the ocean. You don't walk or run in the ocean – you float and swim. Like this, once you come to the Master, seeking stops, blossoming begins.

You seek until you Come to the Master.

Seeking is a desire. Desire is a thought. Thoughts are in the mind. The mind is in the Big Mind. The Big Mind in me is love. Emotions are ripples in love. Love is all Knowledge. Every atom of the Big Mind is crammed with Knowledge. Knowing this, you stop seeking.

You are Knowledge. Every atom in you is shimmering with Knowledge. In Sanskrit, this is called go. Go has four meanings:

- Knowledge

- Movement

- Achievement

- Freedom or liberation

Pal means friend or protector – one who takes care of you. Be a *Gopal* *(go-pal)*; be a friend in Knowledge. Often you become friends by:

- Gossiping about negative things

- Complaining

- Similar cravings or aversions

- Common enemies or common problems

- Common goals or common addictions

You become friends with someone because you have something in common. But coming together in Knowledge is rare.

Be a friend in Knowledge. Uplift each other in Knowledge.

All *Satsangees* are *Gopals* – reminding each other of the Knowledge, coming together for Knowledge. That is *Gopal. Be a protector of this Knowledge.*

September 21, 1995
Bangalore Ashram, India

15. SILENCE

Prayer within breath
   Is silence
Love within Infinity
   Is silence
Wisdom without words
   Is silence
Compassion without aim
   Is silence
Action without doer
   Is silence
Smiling with all the Existence
   Is silence!

An Intimate Note To The Sincere Seeker

16. THE BIG MIND

You know there is a big mind and a small mind. Sometimes the Big Mind wins over the small mind, and sometimes it is the other way around.

When the small mind wins over, it is misery; when the Big Mind wins, it is joy. The small mind promises joy and leaves your hand empty. The Big Mind may bring a resistance in the beginning but later fills you with joy.

Jai means victory.

Guru means great.

Deva means the Divine who is fun-loving, playful, light.

Jai Guru Dev means victory to the Greatness in you, victory to the Big Mind in you that is both dignified and playful.

Usually one who is playful is not dignified, and one who is dignified is not playful. But the Divine in you – the Big Mind – is both together.

Jai Guru Dev need not be thought of as victory to the Master. Rather, it is victory to your own Self, your own Big Mind over the wailing small mind.

17. The Only Thing You Must Remember

The only thing you must remember is how fortunate you are. When you forget this, you become sad.

Sorrow indicates:

1) your attachment to negative qualities, and

2) your attachment to positive qualities.

Your negative qualities make you sad. And when you think you are so great, you start blaming others; this also makes you become sad.

The purpose of sorrow is to bring you back to the Self, which is all joy. But this realisation is possible only through Knowledge – awareness. Knowledge leads sorrow towards the Self. Without Knowledge, the sorrow does not get completed and instead multiplies. Knowledge completes sorrow.

Only with the power of Knowledge do you transcend sorrow.

In this Path you have everything. This beautiful Knowledge is complete with all flavours in it: wisdom, laughter, service, silence, singing, dancing, celebration, *yagnas*, complaints problems, complications, and chaos to add spice.

Life is so colourful!

18. FREEDOM AND DISCIPLINE

Freedom and discipline are opposites. And they are also complementary.

The purpose of defence is to protect freedom. But is there freedom in defence? Do soldiers have freedom? No, they are bound, not allowed to put the right foot down when told the left foot. Their steps are measured; they are unable even to walk with a natural rhythm. There is no freedom in defence, yet this is what protects the freedom of the country!

Freedom without discipline is like a country without a defence. Discipline protects freedom. They both go hand in hand. Understand this and move ahead in life. You have certain restrictions that allow you your freedom. You can focus either on freedom or discipline, and be happy or unhappy.

Fences have a definite place and purpose. If you build a fence all over the entire property, then where will you put your home? Yet a well placed fence protects the property. Love puts you on track. Fear also puts you back on track, as is the case with religions that have put fear as the main motivating force.

Nature itself induces fear in a child at a certain age. A child has no fear when very young; he gets 100% love and attention from the mother. But as he grows more independent, nature brings in an iota of fear; he learns to become cautious. With increasing freedom, the child learns to walk more carefully.

There is a state of absolute freedom, unlimited bliss, the freedom *Advaita** talks about. But the *Advaita* Knowledge has been totally misused according to people's fancies and conveniences. We need to be very practical. There must be freedom in the mind, love in the heart, and discipline in action. Fear of losing freedom brings discipline and defence. And the purpose of defence is to eliminate fear.

On this Path, Knowledge is your freedom - and also your defence.

**the non-dual philosophy of the Upanishads expounded in detail by Adi Shankara*

19. DISCIPLESHIP ENDS

Knowledge has an end. Knowledge completes.

So also does discipleship, for the disciple is aimed at acquiring Knowledge. Once you cross the water, however nice the boat is, you get out.

After twelve years, the disciple completes his studies. The master does a ceremony called *Samavarta*. He asks the disciple to now behave at par with him and allow the Divine – the *Brahman* – to manifest; he thus ends the discipleship.

Sakha is a beloved companion in life and death. A *Sakha* only wants the beloved, he longs only for the beloved. He doesn't care about Knowledge or liberation. His love is infinite, and infinity can never be full. His love is complete in its eternal incompleteness. There is no end on the path of love...

Arjuna was a *Sakha* to *Krishna*, and although *Krishna* was a perfect Master, he was a *Sakha*, too.

What are you:
*   a shishya (disciple),*
*   or a Sakha (beloved companion)?*

20. *SAKHA:* YOUR RELIABLE SENSE

There are three Sanskrit words: *sukha,* joy; *duhkha,* sorrow; and *Sakha,* companion. These have one thing in common: *kha,* which means senses.

The Self experiences the world through the senses. When the senses are with the Self, that is *sukha* (joy), because the Self is the source of all joy or pleasure. When the senses are turned away from the Self – in the mud, lost in an object – that is *duhkha* (misery). Mud, misery, mind – they are all connected.

Sukha is the nature of Self. And all sense objects are a diving board to take you back to the Self. You close your eyes in a pleasant experience: when you smell a flower, when you taste or touch something nice. *Sukha* is that which takes you to the Self.

Duhkha is that which takes you away from the Self. Sorrow means that you have been caught in an object that has pulled you off your Self.

Sakha is the companion who is there for you in all experiences of *sukha* and *duhkha.* Knowledge is your companion, and the Master is the embodiment of Knowledge. If you are stuck in an object, his wisdom pulls you out and leads you back to your Self.

Sakha (sa-kha) also means He is the senses. *Sakha* is one who has become your senses. It means you get Knowledge through him; he is your sixth sense. As you trust your mind, so you trust him. Usually a friend is an object of your senses, but a *Sakha* has become your senses.

Sakha means, "He is my senses, I see the world through his wisdom."

Your head will be in the mud in a few years; in the meantime, don't put mud in your head while you are still alive! See through the eyes of the Master and you will see the whole world as divine.

✍ *News Flash:*

Gurudev spoke at the United Nations 50th Anniversary Celebration on October 22. Here are a few quotes:

"Spiritual education is needed to uncover the knowledge that we are, first, part of the Divine, and second, we are human beings.

"In this age, even when technology has advanced so far, we have cared very little for the emotional and spiritual needs of people. Neither at home nor in school have we been taught how to release negative emotions. Either we regret the past and worry about the future or we get stuck in negativity."

"A stress-free mind and disease-free body are the birthrights of every human being. Only true spiritual knowledge can help us to handle our mind and bring us back to the present moment."

"Breathing techniques, meditation, and yoga can be used as powerful tools to release tensions and negative emotions, enabling one to live more fully in the present moment."

21. SCEPTICISM

Ignorance is being a sceptic and not knowing it.

If you think you are a sceptic, you are no longer a sceptic! You already have a clue of something beyond. So, in reality, you can never know when you are a sceptic!

A sceptic is stuck in a paradigm that closes off all other possibilities. But this creation contains all possibilities. As you understand how paradigms shift, scepticism drops.

A real scientist can never afford to be a sceptic because scepticism will not probe into unknown areas of existence. Scepticism is an "I know it all" attitude, and this attitude is unscientific. Scepticism is dispelled by Knowledge.

Do not recognize someone's scepticism and try to argue. Arguments only strengthen scepticism. Fear of losing one's freedom brings more resistance and causes more scepticism.

Deep inside every human being there is faith and love – Scepticism is only a thin layer. If you hold in your mind *This person is a sceptic*, you only empower his or her scepticism.

Your silence and the smile from your heart will dispel any scepticism. There is nothing better than silence to break it. Silence means a quality of consciousness, not just keeping your lips tight.

Scepticism comes only in people who walk with boundaries. Children have no scepticism. They live in their fantasy worlds, worlds of many possibilities. Their worlds are of innocence, joy, beauty, and love.

22. SHAUCHA AND ASHAUCHA

When you are miserable, what has happened?

You have gone away from the Self. This is called *ashaucha*. It means you have become unclean.

In India when someone dies, the close relatives are said to be *ashaucha* for ten days because they are very sad. They are impure because they have moved away from the Self. After ten days of being with that experience and reading the *Gita*, being with the Knowledge and pulling themselves back into the Self, then they are called *shaucha*. They have purged out the impurities that came during those events.

This happens again and again in life. You become *ashaucha* and you have to get back to *shaucha*. Go deeper into yourself, then real *shaucha* happens.

Shaucha's benefits are clarity of intellect, a pleasing mind, focused awareness, a say over the senses – and thus eligibility to realise the Self.

Shaucha is being disinterested in the habitual tendencies of your own senses. You have the understanding- *Oh yes, here is this old familiar tendency coming up again. Come on, I have had this experience enough and still the body craves for it again.*

By being disinterested for a moment in one's own body and senses – just an idea, a sort of distaste – you will find that the situation changes.

Why do people love each other so much, have such an intimate relationship, and then fight? *Ashaucha* has happened.

If you don't get a distaste for the tendency of the senses, then distaste for the object of the senses is bound to come; you will blame the person or object.

Your attraction or craving is only as long as you think someone is "other." When you think they are part of you, the attraction dies out. That is why a husband or wife is not attracted to the partner but to someone else – because the partner has already become a part of them.

When you realise everyone is part of your Self, you enjoy the whole world without a sense of craving.

> *When ashaucha happens, come back to shaucha quickly. Suppose you get drowned in any worldly event. Just remember: "I have become ashaucha; that is why I am suffering in misery. "Then come back to shaucha. Your practices, meditation, Sudarshan Kriya, service, and Satsang will all help you.*

23. BOREDOM AND SADHANA

What is boredom?

Just a repetition without interest or love. That causes a monotonous state of mind and overshadows the Self.

Spiritual practices (*Sadhana*) are again a repetition whose purpose is to destroy the boredom and reunite you with the Self. A practice itself creates boredom, but as you continue, you penetrate the boredom and destroy it once and for all. Whether the practice gives you joy or boredom, it must be continued. Only your practices, your *Sadhana*, can overcome the mind.

The Self is love and love is always repetitive. Love letters are simply repetitive and yet there is no boredom there.

If you are so bored with yourself, how much more boring are you to others?

Root out the boredom in you through deep and continued meditation. Wake up and walk upwards.

24. WHO ARE YOU: BRAHMA, VISHNU, SHIVA - OR GURU?

There are three forces: *Brahma Shakti, Vishnu Shakti,* and *Shiva Shakti.* You may have one of these dominant.

Brahma Shakti is the force to create something new. *Vishnu Shakti* is the ability to maintain.

Shiva Shakti infuses new life or destroys the old and brings transformation.

Some of you have *Brahma Shakti.* You may create something well, but you may not be able to maintain it. For example, you may make friends fast, but your friendships do not last long.

Some of you cannot create but you are good at maintaining – for example, those who have long-lasting friendships but who have difficulty making new friends. Here *Vishnu Shakti* is dominant. Some of you have more *Shiva Shakti.* You can bring in new life or transformation, or you can destroy the whole setup.

With *Guru Shakti,* all these three *shaktis* have blossomed fully. So identify which *shakti* you have more of and aspire for *Guru Shakti.*

> Guru makes a group,
> but a group cannot make a Guru.

25. How to Maintain Intimacy

What breaks intimacy?

- Ego or taking a position

- Desire

- Taking intimacy for granted

- Finding imperfection in oneself or others

- Expectations

- Insensitivity or over-sensitivity

- Lack of *vivek* or *vairagya* (discretion or dispassion)

- Judgments

- Grumbling or lack of gratitude

How can you maintain intimacy?

Intimacy is dissolving into infinity, which brings you to the moment. You go beyond the events.

Look beyond the events, dissolve into infinity, and be in the moment.

This is the way to maintain intimacy.

✍ *If you attend Satsang, you don't get much; but if you don't, you lose a lot. Just to maintain where you are, what you are, you need to attend weekly Satsang.*

Now, take an exercise: Every day do individual Satsang and skilfully talk ten minutes of Knowledge with someone – anyone. You are so used to talking gossip. Now, for two weeks, share the Knowledge – especially to those not coming to weekly Satsang.

Say, "Everything is temporary, everything is changing." Speak some Knowledge on the changing nature of the world.

26. ALL ARE SEARCHING FOR SWEETS; THE ONE WHO FINDS THEM GIVES THEM AWAY

Gurudev was on the porch with a group of people.

He sent Kashi to get the sweets from inside the *kutir*,* but Kashi returned saying he could not find them. He went again and again, three times, and still he could not find them. Then Gurudev himself went in. He came out with the sweets and gave them to everyone.

This is exactly what happens in life. Many want sweetness in life. Some are searching hard, but only one finds. And when that one finds, he gives to everyone.

Everyone is "blissed in", and some are "blissed out", too!

---

* *a cottage or bungalow*

27. OVERCOMING EVENTS

All the problems that you face in life are because you attach over importance to events. The events grow bigger while you remain smaller.

Say, for example, you are riding a motorbike on a busy street and in front of you another vehicle is emitting exhaust fumes. You have three options:

1.   You can complain, somehow bear with it,

       and still follow the vehicle.

2.   You can slow down or wait for some time to

       allow the vehicle to move far away from you.

3.   You can use your skill, overtake the vehicle,

       and forget about it.

As in the first case, most of you stick on the events and are miserable, like inhaling fumes throughout your journey.

In the second case, you don't get permanent relief, because another bigger vehicle might come in front of you. Running away from events is not the permanent solution.

Wise people use their skill to surmount the event. If the vehicle is in perfect condition, the skill is effective.

Conditioning the vehicle is *Sadhana* – practice. And skill is the grace of the Guru.

> *The mistakes you have made in the past have made you humble; you need not make mistakes in the future to become humble.*

28. THE WASHING MACHINE

Our body is like a washing machine. Our mind is like cloth. Love is like pure water. Knowledge is detergent. Each lifetime is one wash cycle.

The mind comes into the body to get cleansed and pure. But if you put in mud instead of detergent, your clothes become dirtier than before. You will have to go on putting your clothes in the washing machine to get them cleaned. And the process repeats again and again.

Similarly, you will have many more births until you stop repeating the mistakes that you have made.

29. DIVINE IS ALL CELEBRATION

A poor man celebrates the new year once a year. A rich man celebrates each day. But the richest man celebrates every moment.

How rich are you? Do you celebrate once a year? Once a month? Every day? If you celebrate every moment, you are the Lord of Creation.

Review the year while you celebrate. This is your homework. What did you do? What did you achieve? How useful were you this past year?

Sit for an hour and think about every week, one minute per week, and see the year's growth in less than an hour. With a flower, on New Year's Day, offer the whole year to the Divine.

✍ Spreading the Fragrance

During Satsang, Gurudev opened a small, nicely-wrapped present - a tiny bottle of jasmine perfume. He twisted off the cap and sniffed the lovely fragrance. He poured a small amount on some paper and waved it in the air, wafting the scent to all corners of the hall. Everyone could then enjoy it.

Gurudev explained that it is not enough simply to have the fragrance. We have to know how to spread it. Flowers have fragrance, but it is the wind that spreads it. In the same way, each one of us is wonderful within – we are beautiful, caring, and loving. But we need to know how to spread the fragrance.

Satsang is that wind that spreads this fragrance to everyone.

30. New Year's Celebration

New year's was a grand celebration... like every day! And everyone was unusually crazy... like every day! Gurudev was fantastically charming... like every day!

And a basket full of chocolates was on the couch... like every day! They were in the shape of bees today. And they started flying from the Guru's hand.

> *JUST BE*
> *Joy is dissolving... losing your identity.*
> *Rest is dissolving... losing your identity.*
> *Love is dissolving... losing your identity.*
> *The message for 1996 is... JUST BE !*
> *Relax and just be.*
> *That doesn't mean be lazy... no !*
> *Be very busy... and just be;*
> *The events come and go, they perish like flowers.*
> *But every event and every person contains some honey.*
> *Like a bee, just take the honey out of every event and*
> *every moment - and move on.*
> *Be like a busy bee and be in the Being.*

Question: What is the nectar of life?

Gurudev: Infinity... Divinity.

31. WRAPPING PAPER

All sensory pleasures in the world are like wrapping paper; the true bliss is the Presence inside.

Divine love is the present, yet we hold on to the paper and believe we have already enjoyed the gift. It's like putting a chocolate in your mouth with the foil wrapping still on. A little chocolate may seep through, but the foil makes sores in the mouth.

Unwrap the present. The whole world is there for you to enjoy. The wise know how to enjoy the gift inside, while the ignorant get stuck to the paper.

✍ *Wally told Gurudev: I have some property for you to consider as an ashram in the U.S.*

Gurudev: I want every home to be an ashram.

How many of you consider your home to be an ashram? If not, what keeps your home from being an ashram? What are the impediments? What do you think are the qualities of an ashram?

32. Is Guru Satisfied or Unsatisfied?

A student's job is to satisfy the master. But how can you satisfy someone who is already satisfied?

> *If Guru is satisfied, your growth is stunted.*
> *If Guru is unsatisfied, he's away from the Self.*
> *If Guru is satisfied, what can inspire you to grow?*
> *If he's unsatisfied, he cannot be a Guru.*
> *If he's satisfied, he cannot be a Guru.*

So what is the answer?

✍ News Flash:

The Master arrived for the first time in the Croatian capital of Zagreb on January 15. As soon as we landed, we drove straight to one of the largest concert halls in Zagreb. Gurudev first met with a group of over a hundred professionals, including doctors and members of the press. A few hours later, the hall filled to capacity for his evening lecture. The national television station filmed the talk. Before addressing the large crowd, Gurudev went out to the lobby to greet over a hundred people who were unable to enter. His exquisite talk saturated the atmosphere with a soft feeling of grace and peace. Many waited outside for over two hours to get a glimpse of Gurudev.

The next evening Gurudev gave his very first talk in Ljubljana Slovenia. Hundreds crowded into the World Trade Centre and soon overloaded Gurudev with flowers. He continued to talk for an hour and a half because the enthusiastic crowd would not let him finish. Immense gratitude and celebration charged the air. The Art of Living groups in Croatia and Slovenia did such an excellent job.

Gurudev now flies to New York for a television interview and then it's on to the Advanced Course in Hawaii !

33. ADVICE FROM HAWAII

What type of time do you give the divine?

Usually you give the time that is leftover, when you have nothing else to do, when no guests are coming, there are no parties to go to, no nice movies to watch, no weddings to attend. Such time you give. Yet this is not quality time.

Give quality time to the Divine. You will be rewarded. If your prayers are not answered, it is because you have never given quality time. Give *Satsang* and meditation your highest priority.

> *Give prime time to the Divine.*
> *You will be rewarded.*

✍ **News Splash:**

Here in Hawaii we're enjoying a fun-filled course this week, for you know God Loves Fun. The first copies arrived of the long awaited book, Gurudev Sri Sri Ravi Shankar: The Way of Grace, and David and Gary presented them to Gurudev.

Satsang is open to the public each evening. The huge waves of the Hawaiian shores cannot compete with the waves of bliss at Satsang. Gurudev brought out deep Knowledge from the most mundane questions. We will bring out these tapes for you soon.

✍ **Lu Riddle:** *What is most freely given yet not taken?*

1. *Compliments? (...No.)*
2. *Blame? (...No, people take blame.)*
3. *Money? (...No, money is readily taken, not freely given.)*
4. *Happiness? (...Nobody can give happiness.)*
5. *??*

Clue: It hangs in space like an orphan. No one owns it. Like an overripe papaya in Hawaii, it rots. The answer to this riddle lies in the beginning. ALOHA!

*Available to the reader through the Divine Shops

34. THE MOST BEAUTIFUL SPOT IN THE UNIVERSE

There is a place you can come where everything is beautiful.

Tourists travel from place to place looking for beauty. With photos and souvenirs they try to take the beauty back home with them. They only get tired and tanned.

Yet the most beautiful spot anywhere is right here. When you come here, you find that everything is so beautiful wherever you are.

Where is this place?
Don't look here and there; come within you.
When you are here, then any place becomes beautiful.
Then wherever you go, you add beauty there.

If you are unhappy, even the moon irritates you, sweet things nauseate, music disturbs. When you are calm and centred inside, noise is musical, clouds are magical, rain is liquid love.

Book yourself on a trip to this most beautiful place in the universe. Then you'll find that every day is a vacation and a celebration.

✍ *News Splash from the surf:*

A lady driving along the coast of Kaua'i just started singing our bhajans which she had never heard before. Later, she found herself at our Satsang.

A Hawaiian Princess, Owana, wondered why she felt compelled to drive in circles around a hotel in Honolulu. She later discovered from a devotee that Gurudev was staying in that hotel. The next night she was singing her deeply felt native Hawaiian songs at Gurudev's feet.

On Sunday, a woman named Mary spent the day at an ancient temple site (heiau) where she prayed to meet her spiritual teacher and be shown the way Home. The next day she met Gurudev and became instantly devoted.

P.S. The answer to last week's riddle is "advice," which hangs like an orphan in space; the giver keeps on giving, with no one to take...

35. INDEBTEDNESS OR ABUNDANCE?

Question: God is all-abundant, totally full, and we are all connected to God. Then why are we in debt, except for some? Why do they have, and we don't have?

Gurudev: Is it only money you lack? When you say you are indebted, that means you have received something! Otherwise how can you be indebted? Those who have received should feel indebted. Be thankful for having received. The more abundance you have, the more indebted you will feel. And when you feel indebted and grateful, more abundance comes to you.

> *Feel indebted. Feel grateful.*
> *Then abundance grows.*

Abundance and indebtedness coexist.

Someone in the group: *An abundance of indebtedness!*

Gurudev: You think you are indebted, but you really are not.

Yet it is better to feel totally indebted, because every bit of what you have doesn't belong to you anyway, including your own body. When you are infinitely indebted for your body, for Knowledge, for things you have received, and for your own life, then you bask in the abundance of the Creator.

Someone in the group: *I feel very indebted. Thank you!*

✍ *News Flash :*

Physicians of Apple Valley, California, organised memorable meetings and Satsangs. Gurudev appeared on CNN News and in the local media and newspapers for several days before the much awaited event. Local TV made announcements every hour.

From there to electrifying Satsangs in packed halls in Los Angeles. Divya and the drummers got everyone on their feet.

A funny thing happened at the Los Angeles airport. When Gurudev went through the metal detector, the alarm went off. He took off his shawl which contained a gold brocade and again tried to pass through. Again the alarm went off! Of course, he wasn't wearing a belt or any such thing. Someone suggested that it could be his mala (beads). With an amused smile, he removed it, yet off went the alarm again! Now there was not much left for Gurudev to take off. The guard was perplexed. Politely, he asked Gurudev to step aside for a metal check with a hand-held device. After a couple of tries, they found him "clean" and let him pass. With everyone applauding, Gurudev came out giggling.

Lloyd and his students organised 700 people to welcome the Master at the University of Northeast Missouri.

In Fort Lauderdale, the church filled with decorations and devotion, Knowledge and grace. The hurricane of sattva* has moved on to Miami.

*purity, righteousness

36. ABIDING IN THE SELF

Abiding in the self, you become the valentine for the whole world. Spirit is the valentine of matter and matter is the valentine of the spirit. They are made for each other. They uphold each other. If you hold onto matter and do not respect the spirit, then matter is not pleased. If you honour the spirit, then you will care for the world, and when you care for the world, it will take care of you.

I am the valentine of the whole world and I reside in every heart. If you are my valentine, you will see me everywhere.

Have the same love for everyone, with different flavours. You cannot behave the same way with everyone, but you can love all of them. Love transcends behaviour and etiquette.

✍ News Flash:

Just a week before Gurudev's arrival, Raj woke up in the middle of the night in Loughborough. He thought that a light was coming from the clock. He looked at Gurudev's picture and saw light coming from it. This light grew and filled the room. He made sure that there was no outside light left on. The divine light stayed on for about ten minutes.

Upholland, Lancashire held an Advanced Course in Gurudev's presence.

Gurudev gave a talk on "Ayurveda and the Art of Living" at the Liverpool Medical Institution. The hall was packed – standing room only. Though Gurudev gave a brilliant talk, he thought it was mundane!

Gurudev's entourage moved with luggage and cars at its own speed and proceeded to Stourbridge in the Midlands for an event organised by Stourbridge Earth Mysteries. His talk was simply great! We moved on to London and arrived at 3 o'clock in the morning for "The U.K. Tired of Living Teachers Meeting" with baggage, blankets, pillows, plastic bags, pots and pans, and the usual divine chaos!!

37. KNOWLEDGE AND FAITH

In science you have knowledge first, then faith follows. In spirituality, faith comes first, then Knowledge follows.

For example, the knowledge of pesticides and chemical plant fertilizers came through science, and people had faith in them; all over the world they have been used. Then another knowledge came that these were not good and the faith shifted to organic farming. The same with antibiotics.

A particular knowledge brought faith, yet when the knowledge changed, then the faith also changed. The knowledge and faith of science is from an isolated "happening" instead of from a fully blossomed Knowledge of life.

In spirituality, faith is first and Knowledge comes later. Like *Sudarshan Kriya, pranayama, yoga asanas* and meditation – first you have faith and then Knowledge follows. For example, if you do *pranayama* faithfully, then you get the Knowledge of *prana*; if you do your meditation faithfully, the Knowledge of consciousness follows. Even an illiterate person, through faith, attains deep Knowledge.

Science considers even human beings as matter; spirituality considers even earth as mother, even rivers and mountains as living beings.

Science regards life as matter,
Spirituality regards even matter as life.

✍ *News Flash:*

Gurudev celebrated Shivaratri at the German Academy. Devotees put their hearts and souls into making the place so beautiful. The puja and Satsang transported everyone to another plane, and as usual, laughter filled the corridors of the new Academy. The big hall is already too small, to the surprise of everyone. Our own spring water replaced Pepsi and Coke!

The night before we left, Lakshmi called Gurudev from Norway. Gurudev told her we would arrive at the airport at exactly 12:15 PM. It kept Lakshmi wondering and confused because she expected to greet us almost an hour earlier.

The next day, the giggling gang made their way to the airport but had left some luggage behind at the hotel. The flight was conveniently delayed – very unusual for SAS airlines. We retrieved the missing luggage and we all arrived in Norway – at 12:15 on the dot!

38. RESPECT

Why do you respect someone?

Because of their good qualities, right? Like honesty, wisdom, love, talents, behaviours. But all these change in time. And when they change, you lose respect. You only respect greatness.

I have tremendous respect for each and everyone. Not for their greatness or wisdom or talent, but for their very person. I respect everyone totally. So I can never lose respect for anybody, howsoever they may be.

One doesn't need to be great in order to be respected.

Respecting life itself makes you great.

Don't look for respect from others; that makes you weak.

Have respect for your Self and no one can take away your self-respect.

✍ **News Flash:** *From Norway:*

Plastered with big posters of Gurudev, Ingrid's van caught the attention of traffic. Posters were all over Oslo; Sheila made a poster crusade.

Vinod and Ingrid turned a reluctant ambassador into an enthusiastic devotee who stayed up all night reading the book **Gurudev Sri Sri Ravi Shankar: The Way of Grace.**

Adventure time: We all went to a ski simulator and sledded three kilometers downhill. Everyone tumbled down into the snow, our hands and feet frozen. It was -10°C and everyone was wearing heavy winter clothes, but there was Gurudev, sledding with only sandals and shawl. He didn't get a speck of snow on himself

Then on to Copenhagen – the capital of Denmark: It was a media event; people from TV, radio, and the newspaper queued into the hotel and the TV crew followed us to packed and lively public talks.

From Stockholm, Sweden: A TV crew came into the meditation hall to interview Gurudev. They asked him what he thought about the New Age and if Art of Living was part of the New Age. With a vivid smile, Gurudev replied, "Age is always new."

One of Sweden's most respected TV journalists for a major channel featured Gurudev and the Dalai Lama.

Evening talks bubbled with humour, brilliant questions, and laughter. All the "hard nuts" started popping like popcorn. As usual, the best talks are never recorded.

The Master arrived on February 28 in Bangalore minus his luggage. He mentioned that he came into the world the same way – with no baggage!

39. DESIRE AND JOY

All desires are for happiness. That is the goal of every desire, isn't it? Yet how often does your desire lead you to the goal?

Have you thought about the nature of desire? It simply means joy tomorrow and not now, doesn't it?

Joy is never tomorrow. It is always now.

When you are joyful, how can you have desires? And how can you be joyful right now when you have desires?

Desire appears to lead you to happiness. In fact it cannot.

And that is why it is *maya**.

What do you say?

✍ *News Flash:*

Participants from all corners of India attended an Advanced Course from March 1-5. The Ashram bustled with activity. Despite a large number of young devotees, the course was unusually silent – which broke with the boisterous celebration of Holi, the Festival of Colours.

We held Satsang in the open air with the sound of drums and the beat of our hearts, the radiant full moon soaking us in bright colours, Gurudev's wisdom, our laughter – and our tears.

*illusion .

40. Faith and Love

God does not wish you to have more faith because it will mean more work for Him. Then you will start to control Him and He will have to run behind you.

God is the servant of faithful servants; He does not want too many servants telling Him what He should be doing!

Love is the highest strength, yet it makes you absolutely weak. So God – the Enlightened One – Nature – does not want you to have more faith or love. With too much faith and love, you make God weak.

So, it is better for God that you have less faith. Things can go on as they are. Why transform? Be happy.

> *Meditation is seeing God in yourself.*
> *Love is seeing God in the person next to you.*
> *Knowledge is seeing God everywhere.*
>
> *Expression of love is service.*
> *Expression of joy is your smile.*
> *Expression of peace is meditation.*
> *Expressing God is conscious action.*

News Flash:

Everything was meticulously planned and organised before Gurudev arrived in Delhi. Then at the airport, a spontaneous Satsang developed as airport personnel and other passengers also joined in. The well-organised plans went haywire and the usual divine chaos followed. Everything was settled in a flash but the organisers were left holding their plans on paper!

At Saritha Vihar Satsang, the sweets and flowers made a carpet in the large hall that matched the fragrance of joy and celebration.

The next day at Karol Bagh, the authorities had more than one reason to raise their eyebrows – traffic jams on the roads, a stampede in the hall, and people forgetting their families in their eagerness to follow the "Gurumobile."

Then on to Rishikesh and the Teachers Refresher Course.

Rishikesh: The lush green Himalayas; the holy Ganges roars, gurgles, sometimes murmurs; peacocks call in the early morning; temple bells chime at sunrise; the breeze carries the chant of Vedic hymns at all times; we take dips in the cold waters, shedding shawls and sweaters on our way in, leaving most reluctantly; we sit with the Master in the evening and watch the sunset; we share electrifying Satsangs; Gurudev gives discourses on the Bhagavad Gita; we are transported into a timeless space...

41. Questions & Dealing with Desire

A boy asked a question, and before Gurudev could answer, he was ready with another question.

To this Gurudev said,

"If you hold on to the question, how will you receive the answer?"

Give away the question to me and then you will find that you are already in the answer.

Desires arise on their own... don't they? Do they ask you before they come? When they come, what do you do with them? And if you don't want to have any desire, then that itself is another desire.

Now here is a clue for you:

If you want to get on a plane or go to a movie, then you have to buy a ticket. This ticket needs to be given at the door. If you hold onto the ticket, how will you go in?

If you want to be admitted to a college, you must fill out an application form and then you must submit it; you cannot hold onto it.

On the journey of life, you have to keep submitting your desires and not hold onto them. And as you keep submitting them, fewer desires come up.

Unfortunate are those who keep on desiring and yet their desires are not fulfilled;

A little more fortunate are those whose desires get fulfilled over a long period of time;

More fortunate are those whose desires get fulfilled as soon as they arise;

The most fortunate are those who have no desires because there is fulfilment before a desire can arise.

Gurudev is still in Rishikesh, where 350 people arrived from all over India for the Advanced Course – a hundred more than expected. The volunteers ran around arranging more rooms at the ashrams. During Satsang the hall spilled over with participants whose faces radiated ecstasy in the Master's presence.

Today is Gudi Padwa and Ugadi – the new year celebrated in many parts of India. All 350 devotees went for a dip in the holy Ganges at 4:30 AM with Gurudev oblivious to the icy temperature of the water.

Swami Pragyanandji, the renowned 75-year old saint of Rishikesh, had a vision in which he saw Gurudev as Brahma, Vishnu, and Mahesh (Shiva). He then performed a puja to Gurudev.

42. BLAME AND MISERY

When a worldly man is miserable, he blames the people around him, the system, and the world in general.

When a seeker is miserable, he blames not only the world – he also blames the Path, the Knowledge, and himself.

It is better not to be a seeker so that you blame less. But then, a seeker (sadhak) also enjoys everything much more. There is more love in life and more pain. When there is more joy, the contrast is greater.

> *A certain level of maturity is needed to see things as they are and not to blame the Path, the Self, or the world.*

Do you see what I am saying?

If one jumps across this chasm of blame and misery, then there is no fall. It is like a quantum leap.

The Divine does not test you. Testing is part of ignorance. Who is it that will put something to a test? Only one who does not know something. God knows your capacity, so why should He have to test you?

Then, why is there misery? It is for titiksha, forbearance in you. And forbearance can be increased by prayerful surrender – and by things that vigorously challenge your patience! (Laughter)

✍ *News Flash:*

The grand finale to the Rishikesh course: a picnic to Neelkant Hills and holy Haridwar, followed by a wild Satsang in New Delhi. Gurudev is now back at the Ashram for a quiet three days before his Australian tour.

News from the U.K.: Gurudev had given a rose to a lady on February 13. She called to say that the flower is still amazingly fresh and fragrant after six weeks! This miracle inspired an otherwise unwilling lady to take the Healing Breath Workshop.

Important exercise: Find out what has been with you forever. Belma says she asked herself this question twenty years ago and she knows all the answers... and that there is only one answer...

43. ATTACHMENTS

Attachments cause feverish breath and feverish breath takes away peace of mind. Then you are in pieces and you fall prey to misery.

Before you get scattered too much, gather yourself and rid your breath of feverishness through surrender and *Sadhana* (spiritual practices). Unfortunately, most people do not notice what is happening until it is too late.

When someone is drowning in the ocean of attachments, surrender is the life jacket they can put on and wait for the rescue team. Without fighting the attachments, observe the feverish breath and go to the cool place of silence within.

Your first step is to direct your attachment to the Knowledge, to the Divine.

Your non-attachment to the mundane is your charm.
Your attachment to the Divine is your beauty.

✍ **News Flash:**
Thursday was Rama's birthday, so Gurudev gave a stunning talk on Rama. At the Madras Satsang, many dignitaries, including the former President of India and his family, came to receive the Master's blessings. Brilliant questions and answers created a moving Satsang.

Singapore snatched a Satsang on the way to Australia.

Perth packed them in and Sydney was swirling. Two religious fundamentalists verbally attacked Gurudev as soon as he entered the hall, shocking the audience. Unshaken, Gurudev delivered a powerful and compassionate discourse.

✍ *Gurudev was sitting in the airport in Perth, Western Australia, when he asked Joy what she does.*

"I'm an interior decorator," she said.
"Oh, we do the same job," he replied.

44. VIVEK

If you say that you have no one in this world, then you are disowning me. And if you disown me, then I cannot do anything for you.

Vivek means discrimination – the knowledge that everything is changing. Time and again you have to reawaken to this – that the world, people, your body, your emotions, are all constantly changing.

When you experience sorrow, understand that *vivek* has been overshadowed.

Question: What am I here for?

Gurudev: Find out what you are not here for:

1. *You are not here to blame;*
2. *You are not here to cry;*
3. *You are not here to sleep;*
4. *You are not here to show off;*
5. *You are not here to fight;*
6. *You are not here to be miserable;*
7. *You are not here to be angry;*
8. *You are not here to worry.*

When you follow fun, misery follows you...

When you follow Knowledge, fun follows you.

✍ **News Flash:**

In Melbourne, Australia, Gurudev activated the fire alarm, and at the airport he activated the metal detector. After a beautiful Advanced Course, Gurudev is now in joyful Jakarta, where Kim and her entourage greeted the Master with great fanfare at the airport. He later blessed the land for a new ashram, an initiative taken by our dear Kim's husband, Mr. Tolani. Jakarta is vibrating with four Satsangs a day and flooding with tears of joy and devotion.

45. WORDS

We attach meaning to words, and we distort them, too. For example, the word *brainwashing*. Your brain, like your body, needs washing sometimes. You don't want to walk around with a dirty brain, a dirty mind. What is wrong with the word *brainwashing*? It indicates a clean brain, a clean mind. But it is used in a derogatory manner.

And the word *disillusioned*. It is good when you become disillusioned. You are out of the illusion and have come to reality. And *purana* - it means *that which is new in the town, the most modern*. But today it conveys the sense of being very old.

Meanings of words change in the course of time. The word *enthused* comes from the Greek which means *God is with us*. Then *enthused* came to mean *crazy*, and today the whole meaning of the word has changed again.

Don't be stuck with words. Your worries are words. Your ideas are words. Wisdom is beyond words. It is your very Being, the essence of all words. See and relate beyond words. Then there is no lie in your life.

If you manipulate words, it is a lie;
If you play on words, it is a joke;
If you rely on words, it is ignorance;
If you transcend words, it is wisdom.

✎ News Flash:

Gurudev received a royal welcome at the resort with traditional Balinese dance and garlands. Press and TV crews invaded the hotel and splashed the news throughout Indonesia. Gurudev put all the press people into silent meditation and they came out with big smiles. Now they are arranging courses.

A thousand stars reflected over the Indian Ocean and the cliffside pool. The silence generated from our course was so profound that the hotel staff themselves spontaneously started observing silence, communicating with us only through gestures and notes. Mr. and Mrs. Tolani and their team did an outstanding job.

We enjoyed a sumptuous farewell dinner outside by the lotus pools, followed by a Balinese dance drama from the Ramayana. Drops began to fall from the heavens during our lively Satsang; by evening's end we were singing and dancing in the rain with the Master.

46. KARMA

Strange are the ways of *karma*. The more you understand, the more amazed you become.

Karma brings people together and separates them. It causes some to be weak and some to be strong. It makes some rich and some poor. All the struggle in the world, whatever there may be, is the bondage of *karma*. Its ways cut across all logic and reasoning. This understanding lifts you up and keeps you from getting stuck to events or personalities, which in turn helps you in your journey to the Self.

Question: So a thief can say it is my *karma* to steal?

Gurudev: Yes, and then the police have the *karma* to catch him, too! *(Laughter)*

Only human life has the ability to be free from *karma*. And only a few thousands aim to be free from it. *Karma* cannot be eliminated by performing actions...

Only Grace can burn the bonds of karma.

✍ *News Flash:*

A Bali sunset watched us as we swam under a rainbow in a cliffside pool overlooking the Indonesian Ocean.

We visited many temples on the coast. The local people honoured Gurudev by taking him into an ancient Shiva temple that does not allow tourists.

Huge crowds welcomed Gurudev in Singapore. Scores of people had to be turned away from a public utility auditorium. Chinese musicians, Indian dancers, and many dignitaries were present, including ministers and officials of Singapore and Malaysia. Gurudev gave four wonderful Satsangs a day in devotees' homes, with delightfully delicious food everywhere. Many Art of Living courses are now in progress, including those for the corporate sector. The tour's highlight was a living room Satsang when Gurudev surprised us with a rapid-fire and awakening talk on the Upanishads that left everyone spellbound and speechless.

After a lightning Satsang in Chennai, Gurudev is back at the Ashram for a series of celebrations.

47. SANYAS & YOUR ASSOCIATIONS

What is *Sanyas?*

*I am nothing and I want nothing, or
I am everything and I have everything.*

Sanyas is being colourless or multicoloured.

Your associations or company can either elevate you or push you down. Company causes first an attraction and then later delusion. This keeps your mind swinging between the two extremes of love and hatred. With the power of Knowledge and *Satsang,* you can rise above this dilemma.

✍ *News Flash:*

Late news: Gurudev took over fifty people to see the night safari in Singapore, the only night safari in the world. The guide kept saying that our group was unusually lucky because every animal in the forest came near the tram "to take darshan* !" The local people were so surprised.

✍ *In India, eight prominent saints honoured Gurudev in a private meeting at one of their ashrams. Each saint has hundreds of thousands of devotees and they each run their own schools, hospitals, and ashrams. Four of them, who were just introduced to Gurudev, followed us for a brief tour of our Bangalore Ashram, where the skies opened and grace poured down in buckets this week. While Gurudev and the saints were all on the top of the hill at Sumeru Mantap, lightning and thunder surrounded us. Everyone got drenched and ran to Gurudev's kutir. Immediately these very popular and formal sanyasis began to shed their orange garments. But what to give them to wear? Soon they were all wearing Gurudev's white dhotis and being fed by his hand, looking more like a group of joyful children happy to be home again. Somehow in their new clothes they began to relax and smile and laugh, and soon they were radiating the Master's grace from deep inside. All of us were awed to see how these formal heads of institutions were transformed. As they left, they humbly asked for Gurudev's blessings and invited him to their ashrams. They said, "Mother Nature gave us all a bath before we entered your temple, Gurudev."*

The first Advanced Course has started at the Ashram.

*blessings that flow to you from seeing the Master or from the Master's glimpse towards you.

48. ILLUSION

Illusion means error of perception, and knowing illusion as illusion is Knowledge.

Our experience of the world is based on perception that is erroneous, so our experience of the world is an illusion. And each experience leaves a hangover that clouds the intellect.

The experiencer is the only reality. Look for the seer, the experiencer, in between experiences.

> Wake up this moment. Shake your head of all past experiences and look at the pure Being that I am and that you are.

Question: How do you distinguish the experience and the experiencer?

Gurudev: Are you all really here? Are you listening? Now close your eyes and see who is listening, who is questioning, who is sitting, and who wants what? Who is confused? You may not get any answer but that is fine. Never mind.

✍ **News Flash:**

A Chinese movie maker tried his level best to sign up Gurudev for his latest blockbuster. Gurudev said, "I don't know acting," and the movie maker said, "Just be natural, accept the situation as it is, take responsibility, be 100%." The movie is about a wise man who brought Buddhism to China. The movie maker said that through this mega-performance, the Art of Living would reach the whole of China. Gurudev winked at his devotees and said, "Should I change my profession?"

The first Advanced Course ended and the second has begun. The Ashram is bustling with people. Every inch of space is occupied – three times the holding capacity of the Ashram and yet no complaints. No chaos! So smooth! Only laughter and new songs have filled Sumeru Mantap.

✍ **Gurudev's 40th birthday is May 13, 1996**

Let us keep the Master specially in our awareness this day. If we prepare a meal let it be a meal worthy to serve him. If we go to a movie let it be a movie we would take him to see. When we speak of others, let us speak only the kind words we would say in his presence. Let us celebrate together the fullness of his grace on this special day.

49. SELF

Self is not the mind – body complex. This is an erroneous notion. Neither the body nor the mind is the Self.

All the *yoga asanas* you do are for the body. All the meditation you do is for the mind.

The purpose for this body to exist is to make you aware of how beautiful you are – and to make it possible to live all the values you cherish and create a world of divinity around you.

> *Whether calm or disturbed,*
> *your mind remains mind.*
> *Whether sick or well,*
> *your body remains body.*
> *Self is all-encompassing.*
> *Service without attitude*
> *Love without reason*
> *Knowledge without intellect*
> *Life beyond time and events*
> *IS WHAT YOU ARE.*

✍ **News Flash:**

Tents were pitched to house a thousand devotees who came from all over for Gurudev's 40th birthday celebration. Sacred Vedic chants enlivened the morning air; in the evening everyone danced with candles in their hands, which made Sumeru Mantap look like a festive cake.

The third Advanced Course has begun.

50. ENLIGHTENMENT

Enlightenment is beyond seasons like the evergreen coconut tree.

Sometimes the question comes up: "What's the use of all these courses if someone's behaviour has not changed?"

Yet the Knowledge acquired by a human being cannot be measured or judged by external behaviour. Someone may behave as though they have absorbed all the Knowledge, but internally they have not. The reverse is also true. Someone who seems not to have changed at all may have absorbed quite a lot.

Ordinary people just look at the behaviour; the intelligent one looks beyond behaviour and is amazed by the play of consciousness (*Brahman*).

Behaviour affects relationships;
Attitude affects behaviour;
Knowledge or ignorance affects attitude;
Grace brings forth Knowledge.

Inside, you are like a tree – barren in some seasons and at other times blossomed.

Enlightenment is beyond seasons – like an evergreen coconut tree that yields its fruit throughout the year.

✍ *News Flash:*

The third Advanced Course (in Tamil) melted not only the heart but also a gallstone of a participant! Many more healings were reported; minds opened, blocked arteries opened also. The rains held off for almost an hour as an intense Satsang was underway in Sumeru Mantap.

Gurudev is presiding over a large "Conference for Awakening the Society," organised by several spiritual heads of state, before he takes off for Paris.

51. SAMADHI

A single cell becomes the whole body. Somewhere it is fingernails, somewhere it is nose and tongue, but all is a manifestation of a single cell. In the same way, the entire universe is made up of a single substance.

Feeling that everything is made up of one thing – this heals the body and mind and balances the *doshas**. This becomes *savitarka-samadhi* (equanimity with logical awareness).

Awareness during deep sleep is *jada-samadhi* (equanimity with inertia). Sleep is the main factor in healing. Medicines will not help without sleep and rest. And *jada-samadhi* is many times more restful than ordinary sleep.

Samadhi with ecstasy has no logic. This is *nirvitarka-samadhi* (equanimity with bliss).

> *Nirvitarka-samadhi is even beyond the experience of bliss– undefinable, beyond words.*

✍ **News Flash:**

The Advanced Course was held at the Hotel Leonardo da Vinci, just on the outskirts of Paris. The manager of the hotel expressed that his place was never filled with so much love and light. The Satsang, sightseeing, the feast on the boat, Paris at night – these made the entire day a rendezvous with the Divine.

The next morning five cars and a minivan set out for Holland without any proper address. Miraculously, everybody reached the lecture hall in time. Some fumed that they had not been given any address or telephone number. They all cooled down in one minute when Gurudev smiled and said, "Have trust and fun. If you lose your smile for small things, then what is the use of being with me? It is a double waste of time – yours and mine."

The celebration continued past midnight and this Weekly Knowledge was born.

**The three major constitutional types – vata, pitta, and kapha – that make up one's individual body/mind complex, as revealed by the ancient natural health science of Ayurveda*

52. WHAT YOU KNOW

What shall we talk about today?

What is the point in talking about something of which you know nothing? There is no point in talking about what you already know... and no point in talking about what you don't know! *(Laughter)*

Stefano: What about something you think you know but don't know?

Gurudev: We can talk about something you think you know but you don't know, or something you think you don't know but you know. *(Laughter)*

> *There is no end to learning, but there is an end to unlearning. That is when you become totally hollow and empty.*

✍ *Riddle: What is something precious that you lose somewhere and find somewhere else? (Answer next week)*

✍ *News Flash:*

On the way back from Holland to the German Academy, we had a picnic on the bank of the river Rhine near beautiful Boppard. The Academy was full to capacity with Teacher Training Phases 1 and 2 and the Advanced Course all in full swing.

Our spring water has a mind of its own. It flows for some people and stops for others. Whenever Kirpal goes with Gurudev's jug, the water joyfully rushes forth!

June 13, 1996
St. Louis, Missouri

Today marks the end of the first year of the Weekly Knowledge. The year started in Big Sur and is ending in St. Louis; it began in KNOWLEDGE and is concluding in SEVA (selfless service for others). The Weekly Knowledge now goes to over 300 Satsang groups, touching 7,000 people every week around the world.

53. SEVA IS SAVIOUR

The way to expand from individual to universal consciousness is to share others' sorrow and joy. As you grow with time, your consciousness should also grow. When you expand in Knowledge over time, depression is not possible. Your innermost source is joy.

The way to overcome personal misery is to share universal misery! The way to expand personal joy is to share universal joy. Instead of thinking 'What about me?', 'What can I gain from this world?', think 'What can I do for the world?' When everyone comes from the point of contributing to society, you will have a Divine society. We have to educate ourselves and culture our individual consciousness to expand with time in the Knowledge... from What about me? to What can I contribute?

If you are not having good experiences in meditation, then do more *Seva* – you will gain merit and your meditation will go deeper. When you bring some relief or freedom to someone through *Seva*, good vibrations and blessings come to you.

Seva brings merit;
Merit allows you to go deeper in meditation;
Meditation brings back your smile.

✍ Answer to last week's riddle:

That something which is precious to you is your smile – your joy. You lose it in the world and find it in the Self, in Satsang. If you can't find it here, forget about it! You can't find it anywhere.

✍News Flash:

After a quick two-day stopover in Boston with overflowing crowds at Interface and Harvard's Kennedy School of Government and with lively late night Satsangs, Gurudev arrived in Pittsburgh to a packed schedule of household Satsangs, temple visits, two lectures, and a celebration to inaugurate our new Centre, complete with cake flying in all directions!

Linda had this extra joy of having Gurudev throw slices of cake all over her immaculate living room. She managed to maintain only a slightly strained smile, knowing that her Master spattered her furniture with love; to point out her overattachment to order. Had anyone else done this, they would have been in big trouble.

54. When We are Joyful

When we are joyful, we don't look for perfection. If you are looking for perfection, then you are not at the source of joy.

Perfection hides; imperfection shows off.

The world appears imperfect on the surface, but underneath, all is perfect. The wise will not dwell on the surface but will probe into the depth. Things are not blurred; your vision is blurred. Infinite actions exist in the wholeness of consciousness, and yet the consciousness remains perfect and untouched. As *Satsang*ees, realise this now and be at Home.

Joy is the realisation that there is no vacation from wisdom.

✍ **News Flash from B.B.C. (Beautiful British Columbia):**

"The Art of Living circus has come to town," exclaimed the Chicago organisers as a gaggle of giggling devotees gathered from the Midwest. People were seen driving in circles, skipping sleep and of course, laughing with Gurudev, our "sit-down" comedian.

We rushed on to Portland (Dean says we have all become "Rushins" instead of Americans, Indians and Canadians). At the Old Church, there was not even standing space. The sight of the Master put a smile on every face.

In Vancouver, the aboriginal people warmly hosted Gurudev at the University of British Columbia. The sky, the sea, the snow capped mountains, the tall trees and the waterfalls all seemed to whisper the Knowledge.

Sudarshana left the room for five minutes and returned asking, "What did I miss?" Marcy said, "Enlightenment!"

✍ *Healing Experience:* *There were many reported healings recently. In St. Louis, a man presented a dozen red roses to Gurudev while tears of gratitude rolled down everyone's cheeks. His wife retells the story:*

My husband Mike has never been one to complain about physical aches and pains in all our twenty-four years of marriage. He will go to work no matter how ill he is. I've seen him endure pulled muscles, fever, flu, chronic arthritis and an abscessed tooth without taking pain medication. So when he began complaining about his shoulder, I knew it was serious.

A trip to our family doctor resulted in an appointment with a neurologist. The MRI showed damage to nerves and muscles; the diagnosis after X rays was a torn rotator cuff. Surgery was scheduled for June 13 at 10:00 am.

We received a flyer in the mail about a lecture and meditation with Gurudev Ravi Shankar, scheduled for June 12. We thought it would be a good way to spend the evening just before the surgery.

Many of the things we heard during the talk sounded familiar. Gurudev's voice even sounded familiar! We felt a real need to speak to Gurudev, and despite a line that seemed to be 300 people long, we took our place. Mike is usually not too patient, and since he was in pain, I still can't explain why we stood there to meet someone we would probably never see again.

And what do you say to a holy man you know nothing about? "Nice to meet you?" "How are you?" With so many people, would he even care about two more?

After saying hello, I found myself asking him for my husband's safety during the next day's surgery. Embarrassed by making such a request to a complete stranger, I returned to my seat.

Gurudev turned to someone behind him and asked for a rose. He handed it to Mike and said to keep the rose by his side during the night and "all will be well".

On the way home, we discussed the whole evening and decided that the rose was a "sweet gesture" and that Gurudev was a "nice man". How our perception would grow over the next few days!

The next day Mike checked into the hospital. Our doctor said the routine surgery would take about an hour. Twenty minutes later, I looked up and saw him motioning for me. He had such an odd look on his face; I asked if he had just killed Mike, since not enough time had elapsed to complete the procedure. He shook his head and said, "I can't explain what happened. When we cut into Mike's shoulder, there was no tear. I checked the MRI twice. It's on the MRI but he doesn't have it now. My assistant is closing now."

The next morning it dawned on us that the holy man had healed Mike's shoulder! We called Martina Boudreau at the Art of Living Centre in St. Louis, where Gurudev was staying. We got directions and off we went.

Arriving at Martina's, kind people helped me to get Mike settled in a chair while we waited for Gurudev, whose presence I felt even before he entered the room. Thankfully, Mike was able to tell his story, as I was too overwhelmed to speak.

Gurudev asked only two questions of my husband: "All is well?" and, after Mike's story, "What is an MRI?"

Someone explained an MRI and Gurudev's response was, "Oh, there is a machine that makes a picture of what I can see?"

–Cathy Champion

55. Judgments and Good Company

Though you have heard "don't judge," judgment comes unavoidably in day-to-day life. By the actions and behaviours of people, you either approve or disapprove.

But always remember that everything is changing, and do not hold on to the judgment. Otherwise your judgment gets solidified like a rock. It brings misery for you and for others.

If judgments are lighter, like air, like a breeze, they bring in fragrance, then move away. Or they could bring a foul smell, then move away. But they should not stay forever.

Judgments are so subtle that you are not even aware of their existence. Judging or labelling someone as judgmental is also a judgment. Only in the state of Being, when you are full of love and compassion, can you ever be free from all judgments.

Yet the world cannot move without judgments. Until you judge something as good or bad, you cannot do any action. If you see rotten apples in the market, you say, "They are no good" because you will buy only good ones. If someone lies to you ten times, you think next time he speaks it also could be a lie. A judgment happens automatically.

> See the possibility that people and things can change at any time and don't hold on to judgments.

You need to judge your company. Your company can pull you up or pull you down. The company that drags you down towards doubt, dejection, blame, complaints, anger, delusion and desires is bad company. The company that pulls you up towards joy, enthusiasm, service, love, trust and Knowledge is good company.

When someone complains, first you listen, then you nod, then you sympathize, then you complain.

Denise: I confess, you are absolutely right.

Robert: Join the party!

Gurudev: Your company can create hell for you in heaven – or heaven for you in hell. Judge for yourself...!

The Circus goes to Ottawa: Enthusiastic Susannah and party organised a hall at the palatial Chateau Laurier, next to the Parliament buildings: chandeliers, gold-framed mirrors, plush carpets, an elegant and regal setting. There sat Gurudev on a beautifully decorated seat – next to a huge pile of super-sized bananas. In the darshan line he handed out over 300 bananas, one by one – like a banana vendor. Bananas were everywhere.

Gurudev said, "Let's all close our eyes and meditate," while everyone sat peeling their bananas. Denise got stuck with her banana peel; she didn't know what to do with it. She and everyone else meditated – peel in hand – like some sort of religious ceremony.

Thanks to Janice, the Ayurvedic Course was a great success. The celebration continues in Montreal...

✍ Koan (riddle)

You better straighten out and become we. We are always one and you could be two.

56. GOD IS A THOROUGH BUSINESSMAN

The divine has given you all the small pleasures in the world but has kept the bliss to Himself*. To get the highest bliss you have to go to Him and Him alone.

Don't be too smart with the Divine and try to fool Him. Most of your prayers and rituals are just attempts to trick the Divine. You try to give the least and get the maximum out of the Divine, and He knows. He's an astute businessman; He will trick you even more. If you sweep something under the carpet, He will sweep something under the floor.

> Be sincere; do not try to outsmart the Divine.
> Once you get the bliss, then everything else is joyful.
> Without the bliss, any joy in the world will not stay.

✍ *News Flash:*

We emerged from silence to celebrate the fifth anniversary of the Montreal Ashram. The lake scene was a fairy tale setting: full moon rising above the trees, fireworks crackling across the sky, the sweet flute melodies around the bonfire. Gurudev took us spinning on a candlelit raft while everyone sang. In all the fun and excitement, we forgot to serve the anniversary cake.

After a talk in Montreal, Denise drove off with Gurudev with all the car doors open. Ramola ran from behind and jumped in. In the fever to get into the Guru's car, someone left luggage, another left her purse, another left shoes – they all left their minds.

Gurudev and Phillip have just left for Toronto and then will go to Colorado. On July 14, an Interfaith Prayer and Meditation Conference will be sponsored by the Art of Living in Washington, D.C. Ten swamis from India have been invited.

Thomas called Gurudev to tell him about a forest fire raging at Lake Tahoe that had burned many million - dollar homes. It had come up to his property, burned his tool shed, but stopped short of his front door. Neither his home – where many Satsangs have been held – nor his garden were damaged.

*or Herself

57. Surrender and Responsibility

Some people say, "surrender and let god do everything." Others say, "It's my responsibility." Devotees often say, "Let Thy Will be done,"– then take it easy getting to the goal!

We have to make this clear: Surrender is saying, "Let Thy Will be done," and "Thy Will" is for you to take responsibility for the whole world!

This may appear contradictory, but I tell you surrender and responsibility go hand in hand. The more you surrender, the more responsive you become.

One who is irresponsible cannot surrender. Why is someone irresponsible? He is lazy or fearful or both. If you are lazy or fearful, you cannot be surrendered in love.

Total responsibility is total surrender. It's a little hard to chew, but this is the truth.

Suppose you are surrendered to the Knowledge. That means you are committed to sharing it with others, and you take responsibility to see that it flourishes. Responsibility is the dynamic expression of life in the present moment.

When you take responsibility and you find blocks, remember surrender.

When you get shaken, remember that the basis of responsibility is surrender. This releases you from the weight of doership and gives you strength to move ahead. Surrendering and taking responsibility without doership is the skill of the wise.

Total irresponsibility is impossible for you.

Limited responsibility tires you and makes you weak.

Unlimited responsibility empowers you and brings you joy.

Set a time-bound goal and give a direction to your life force.

✍ *News Flash:*

The fireworks arrived with Gurudev on July Fourth at Colorado's largest Advanced Course and Healing Breath Workshop ever. We dressed the hall with red, white and blue balloons and ribbons in celebration of independence – for the United States and for our spirits. As we watched the explosions spread across the horizon, Gurudev said, "That looks just like your minds."

Gurudev took a hike in the mountains and met an enthusiastic crowd in Colorado Springs before flying on to California for Satsang with 150 people at Anu and N.J.'s Apple Valley home.

The Art of Living entourage then moved to northern California for nonstop talks and Satsangs on Gurudev's summer tour.

58. RESPECT EVERYBODY AS YOU RESPECT ME

Respect everybody as you respect me, but don't expect from everyone what you expect from me.

You usually do it the other way: You don't respect everybody as you respect me, but you expect them to give you joy and behave ideally. When they don't live up to your expectations, you get frustrated and you blame or curse them. By cursing, you lose your spiritual energy. When you can bless, your energy goes up.

The world is full of differences; arguments are inevitable. With forbearance, patience and wisdom, skilfully make your way up.

Fools will make you wiser. The number of fools around you indicates the strength of your centeredness. Don't try to get rid of them! If you lose your centre, you will have no patience to put up with them. When you are established in the Self, you find that even fools come up with wisdom; they are your own reflection, there is no "other".

Fools offer you frustration and wisdom and make your life juicy.

Question: How can you stop thinking that others are fools?

Gurudev: You don't have to. You can see all the people in the whole world as fools. The advantage is that you don't get attached to fools *(Laughter)*. Otherwise, if you think people are sane, you will want to join them.

You can think *Everybody is a fool* and be cool.

✍ *News Flash from Washington, D.C.:*

Susannah opened the Interfaith Prayer and Meditation Conference with her beautiful Hallelujah bhajan and everyone joined in. Children sang traditional devotional songs and delegates from many faiths lit candles, offered deeply felt prayers, sang sweet hymns, and led us in meditation. Represented faiths included the African Methodist Episcopal Church, Baha'i, Buddhism, Church of Christ, Presbyterian, Islam, Sufism, the Unity Church, Freemasons, Hinduism and Sikh, among others. Nine visiting swamis from the Adichunchuna Giri order in Karnataka, India have been traveling with us. In a dramatic entrance they approached the stage in their saffron robes and gave their blessings to Gurudev. Master of ceremonies John Osborne stayed so centred that nobody even noticed the last-minute program changes.

59. Doing versus Happening

See the whole past as a "happening" and the present as a "doing."

If you see the past as a "doing," then ego and regret come along. And when you see the present as a "happening," then laziness and unawareness set in.

If you apply the "doing" for the future, it brings tension and worry.

If you apply the "happening" for the future, it might bring some confidence and also lethargy.

Let the "happening" be for the past. Let the "doing" be for the present. And the future is a mix of both.

The wise will see "doing" in "happening" and "happening" in "doing" simultaneously. Only someone who is 100% in "doing" can recognize the "happening." Are you confused now? *(Laughter)*

One who does a lot of work will never say he did a lot. When someone says he did "a lot" of work, that means he could do even more; he has not done enough. Work does not tire you as much as the sense of doership does. Be 100 percent in "doing" without the sense of doership.

All the talents you have are for others. If you have a good voice, it is for others. If you are a good cook, it is for others. If you write a good book, it is for others – you don't sit and read your own book! If you are a good carpenter, it is for others. If you are a good surgeon, it is for others – you cannot do your own surgery. If you are a school teacher, it is for others. All your work and talents are useful for others.

Make use of your talents, or they will not be given to you again.

✍ **News Flash:**

Metamorphosis: The German Academy is transformed overnight! Dedicated volunteers are working tirelessly to prepare the accommodations for the upcoming assembly. The enthusiasm for Seva has gone beyond limits. Gurudev has to walk around in the middle of the night telling people to go to bed. Even the postman has been polishing the letter box outside without knowing why.

Guru Purnima is moving into the German Academy.

July 31, 1996 - Guru Purnima Day
German Academy, Bad Antogast, Germany
Today is a gift from God—that is why it is called "Present!"

60. DON'T BE GRATEFUL!

Warning! Watch out! This week's knowledge contains explosives! It can explode your head or your heart. If it explodes your heart – nothing is left! If it explodes your head – everything is attained!

Gurudev: How many of you are grateful here?

(Everybody raises their hand.)

If you are grateful, you don't belong to me!

(Everyone is shocked.)

When someone gives you something, you are grateful – that means you feel separate from them. You do not feel grateful to yourself. Gratefulness means you do not feel part of the Master.

Meike: You don't feel grateful to your own hand that feeds you.

Angelika: Small children don't feel grateful as long as they feel oneness. They take everything for granted.

Gurudev: When you go beyond gratefulness, then union happens. Neither "I" nor "you" remains. You are part of the Master. You are one Being with a thousand heads and a thousand arms but with one heart.

Gratefulness is inevitable. You have got to be grateful on the Path, but you have to transcend gratefulness. Better stop being grateful. *(Laughter)*

When you are grateful, then you become the centre of attention – you feel more important. When you are grateful to God for having received something beautiful, eyesight for example, who is important – you or God?

You! Your gratitude indicates ego.

Richard: So you are not grateful?

Gurudev: I am simply great and I am full! *(Laughter)* Don't be grateful; just be great – and be full. This Knowledge could be dangerous without devotion!

When you are part of the Master, you have every right to be happy. You have every right to Knowledge, happiness, and the whole universe!

Balder: Could you compare our relationship to friends with our relationship to the Master?

Gurudev: *Your friends tie you to the world, to matter. The Master ties you to the Divine, to the spirit.*

✍ *News Flash:*

Guru Purnima was celebrated all around the world. At the German Academy, the Seva Warriors had worked such magic on the whole building that people who had been there earlier could not believe their eyes. After Satsang we took a "moon walk" on the mountain; everyone was full.

61. FAITH, DEVOTION AND MEDITATION

Faith is the subject of head;
Devotion is the subject of heart;
And meditation connects both.

A mature intellect is devoted. A mature heart is full of Knowledge. And meditation matures your intellect as well as your heart.

John: Yet people with good intellect seem to have less faith.

Gurudev: Head puts more faith in matter and heart puts faith more in the abstract. It's next to impossible that an intellectual person has total lack of faith or total lack of devotion. It's only a question of maturity and balance.

✍ **News Flash:**

During Gurudev's visit to Washington, D.C., Dr. Ganesh Prabhu, a leading cardiovascular surgeon, formerly of Johns Hopkins Hospital, wanted to evaluate the effects of Sudarshan Kriya on Gurudev's heart rate. He hooked Gurudev up to a halter monitor and together they did Sudarshan Kriya. During the rest afterwards, Gurudev's heart rate dropped to just two beats per minute and stopped completely twice.

Even more "impossible" was when Dr. Prabhu unhooked the monitor from Gurudev. Naturally, the monitor should have ceased recording. However, Dr. Prabhu was astonished that the monitor continued to record a heartbeat of 50 per minute for the next twelve hours. The monitor stopped recording only when Gurudev arrived at the L.A. airport and was greeted with a whole new group of devotees. Dr. Prabhu called Gurudev excitedly and asked, "What happened, what happened?" Never in his career had he seen anything like this.

Gurudev later commented that a Master can slow down or stop his respiration and heartbeat at will. The chairperson at a prominent medical university said that two heartbeats per minute is medically impossible. But we guarantee Gurudev is really alive!

Gurudev arrived in Los Angeles for the long-awaited Summer Celebration with 350 course participants and Ann McFadden at the helm of sixty people on Seva teams. Nine swamis who were our guests began an intensive sightseeing campaign, dragging Wally and John through Disneyland, Universal Studios, and Sea World starting at 8:00 in the morning.

After a grand Satsang in San Diego with the swamis, Gurudev spoke at a memorable Prayer Conference at the renowned Agape Centre in Santa Monica. Each speaker talked eloquently that evening about unity. Afterwards, Gurudev rose, paused for several moments, and declared, "Unity is impossible." The audience held its breath. He went on to say that in order for there to be unity, there has to be two, yet there is only One in the whole universe. People began breathing normally again.

The next day, Gurudev gave a beautiful lawn talk at the Unity Church in Tustin. "All of your life becomes a meditation," he described. "Whether you look at the trees or the flowers or talk with people, you are in meditation." He encouraged people to stay steadfast with their daily meditation practices. After the talk, we all looked up and saw a big puffy heart in the clear blue sky.

62. Infinite Patience and Smart Shopping

Suppose you go to god to get a boon. When your intention is to get a boon, then you are in a hurry.

Another person knows he already owns God; he is not in a hurry for anything. Infinite patience comes up in him.

Question: What do you mean by "owning God"?

Realizing that the Divinity and His entire creation already belong to you. Usually you shop in a hurry at the supermarket and rush back home. But when the whole store is already in your home, you're not in a rush to shop; you're at ease.

Your hurry to get something throws you off balance and makes you small. Have an "eternal wait"–infinite patience. Realise that God belongs to you. Through this awareness or through practices you will reach infinite patience.

Question: To develop patience, do we observe the impatience?

Just observe the thoughts and feelings and don't regret them.

When you know you are part of the divine plan, you stop demanding. You know everything is being done for you. You are taken care of.

Usually we hurry the mind and are slow in our action. Impatience means hurry in the mind; lethargy means slowness in action. It is better the other way around:

Patience in the mind and dynamism in action is the right formula.

✍ **News Flash:**

Thousands came to the Santa Monica Civic Auditorium to hear the Master's wisdom, experience profound silence in guided meditations, and celebrate with singing and dancing.

Beginning Monday, August 5, Gurudev gave talks each evening on the following topics, which were made available on tape to people immediately as they left the hall* :

- *The Ancient New Age*
- *The Cosmic Connection: Planet, Stars and Life*
- *The Ultimate Relationship*
- *Jesus: Embodiment of Love*
- *Buddha: Manifestation of Silence*
- *Krishna: Absolute Joy*
- *Death and Beyond*

It was a big week. Newspapers published articles, television shows ran interviews, and hundreds attended Healing Breath Workshops and Advanced Courses.

No one was concerned about the Blackout of '96, which affected six states between Canada and Mexico. Gurudev promised us the power would come back on in time for the talk that evening and it did!

*Available to the reader through the Divine Shops

63. Surrender, Shame and Shyness

In surrender, the head bends and meets the heart. A head that does not bend has no value. The head that is stiff will have to bend sometime, either in surrender or in shame. And the head that bends in surrender will never have to bend in shame.

Shame accompanies arrogance. Shame is inflicted by society and is acquired.

Shyness accompanies love. See how children are endowed with shyness; it is natural to them.

> *Shame brings guilt;*
> *Shyness adds to your beauty.*
> *Retain your shyness and surrender your shame.*

✍ *News Flash:*

Parag and Parul were surprised when food brought for Gurudev and four others fed forty people, and still there was extra.

The Advanced Teacher Training in Pacific Palisades left the teachers with renewed wisdom and fire. In the evenings, people crowded into Verna's home to see Gurudev. The slamming of car doors after midnight kept waking up the entire Bayliss neighbourhood. The last night, Gurudev took everyone to the beach instead.

En route to England, Gurudev gave a premier Satsang in Princeton, New Jersey. Rajshree's family hosted a Satsang in Yonkers.

Gurudev gave four television interviews on this tour, including shows for the Discovery Channel and Korean TV. Before boarding the plane to the U.K., he took forty people to the amusement park for water rides and fun on the roller coaster.

64. Special... or Ordinary?

Are you special... or ordinary?

What makes you special on the Path?

(Everyone is silent)

You are special because your perception, observation, and expression have advanced.

What makes you ordinary is... that you are special! *(Laughter)* Everyone thinks that he or she is special in some way!

Hasn't your perception improved? You see the cause behind every cause – the Divine – and you see the Great Plan behind every small plan. You don't see an intention behind others' mistakes, and you are not a "doubting Thomas."

Kiran: Who was "doubting Thomas"?

Shirley: Thomas doubted Jesus.

Bhanu: But I think he also got enlightened!

Stefano: Yes, but he was not sure! *(Laughter)*

And before getting onto the Path, you never observed your emotions. Now you observe all your emotions, positive or negative, love or hatred, anger or compassion, pain or pleasure. Your observation has improved.

And your expression has improved. Though everyone in their core has all good qualities, those who are unfortunate and stressed have not found an expression for them. Yet you express these great qualities.

And sooooo... you are extra... ordinary!

✍ **News Flash:**

The hot media topic of the week on the Guernsey Islands was Gurudev's long-awaited visit.

Jean and Renwick invited parliamentarians and health care professionals for a lively meeting with Gurudev.

We all got to laughing about how Gurudev can talk fluently on any subject put before him. We reminded ourselves of a public Satsang from a previous tour. Gurudev had asked the audience for topics on which to speak, and one gentleman suggested "used cars." Gurudev spoke nonstop about used cars the entire evening and compared them to our body and mind.

Gurudev arrived in Norway for a residential week-long Healing Breath Workshop with 150 people, historic for Scandinavia.

65. Whether You Win or Lose

After *Satsang*, a group of about 150 people sat with Gurudev and playfully argued with him, telling him how mean he is that he doesn't spend much time with them and yet he has stolen their hearts. *Gurudev* kept "winning" over their protests by twisting their arguments; everybody laughed and had a great time.

Gurudev: Whether you win or lose an argument with me, you are still laughing. Why?

Because you have a total sense of belonging. With a sense of belonging, real play happens; winning or losing is irrelevant.

Normally, what happens to you when you lose an argument? You get sad and upset, hurt and angry. But whether you lose or win an argument with me, you are still happy. How come?

- There is the sense of belonging;
- Your love stands out above everything else (like perfection, comfort, desires, etc.);
- You put the "Being" before the happening;
- Your confidence is in the ultimate good.

Can you have this same attitude with everyone?

Krishna's life was full of conflicts, yet he kept smiling and dancing. May you dance through all the conflicts and contribute to this planet.

✍ **News Flash:**

Bombay was in a hot mood for a wild Satsang in cool weather. Then on to Surat, which was hectic. Thousands gathered to get a glimpse of Gurudev. The next morning in Baroda, Gurudev addressed a rapt audience of 700 senior executives.

The assembly hall of the palace of Baroda was a royal setting for the evening Satsang. Kartik set up closed-circuit TVs so the overflowing crowd did not feel lost.

Even a curious cat could not squeeze into the jam-packed Satsang in Ahmedabad as Gurudev rose to address thousands who desired his darshan and Knowledge.

Today is Krishna's birthday and all planes are leading to Bangalore.

66. THE WELL-BAKED POT

If you pour water into a half-baked pot, the pot becomes ruined and the water is also wasted. If the pot is well baked and strong, it will hold up whether you put water into the pot or put the pot into water.

During *Satsang* that evening, a devotee presented a beautiful handcrafted pot to Gurudev. Another devotee gave a bouquet of roses. Placing the bouquet into the pot, *Gurudev* said,

"If the pot is well-baked, then it will hold the flowers."

Then a gift of sweets was given to Gurudev, who added, "When you flower, the sweets come to you."

Then came another box of sweets – *Sandesh* brand – and *Gurudev* concluded,

"This is today's *sandesh*." (*Sandesh* is the Hindi word for message.)

✍ News Flash:

Gurudev addressed an international congress of Catholic priests. At the end of Gurudev's talk they followed him with smiles. Arun said, "The winter in the hall was transformed into spring."

Two residential Advanced Courses, one Healing Breath Workshop, one Sahaj Samadhi Meditation Course, and a Teacher Training Course are all running simultaneously at the Bangalore Ashram with over 350 participants. We need more rooms!

67. THE FALL THAT RISES

You see only the fall of the water. You don't see how the ocean becomes a cloud; it is a secret. But the cloud becoming the ocean is obvious.

In the world, only a few can notice your inner growth and height, but your outer expressions are apparent.

Never brood that people don't understand you. They can see only your expressions!

✍ *News Flash:*

On the Ganesha festival day, Gurudev gave a most revealing talk on Ganesha, the elephant-headed deity - its name, form, symbolisms, qualities, and many secrets.

Gurudev was invited to inaugurate the Shiva temple and the Satsang hall at Adichunchuna Giri Mutt Blind School. Several buses and cars with 125 teacher trainees accompanied Gurudev.

After the ceremonies, we enjoyed an exquisite evening walk under pink and golden skies, leading to a magnificent waterfall.

Dinesh: *"We should have come here without you, Gurudev; now we are looking only at you."*

Gurudev: *"Hmmm... look at the water. The waterfall is beautiful. If a rock falls, it shatters, but when water falls, it generates power and beauty. Being somebody is like being a stone; being nobody is like being the water; being everybody is like water vapour."*

68. WHICH IS MORE EXPENSIVE: YOUR SMILE OR YOUR ANGER?

Mahesh: Do you ever get angry?

Gurudev: I can, but it's very expensive.

Usually, you give your anger freely and your smile rarely, as though a smile is costly. In ignorance, anger is cheaper and a smile is costly. In Knowledge, a smile is free – like the sunshine, air, and water – and anger is extremely expensive, like a diamond. Conclusion:

Make your smile cheaper and anger expensive.

✍ **News Flash:**

After a busy course schedule at the Bangalore Ashram, Gurudev addressed a large group of professionals and industrialists in Rajkot. Later, a spirited Satsang with 3,000 devotees set a joyous example of life celebrated in all its fullness.

Gurudev has now left for an Advanced Course of nearly 700 participants in Koijavaran, Baroda.

✍ *Although the Weekly Knowledge was prepared on time last week (#67), there was a delay in sending it. This brought an interesting fax from Susannah Rowley (an attorney) and the, Ottawa Satsang group on September 21:*

Thank you for this week's very eloquent Knowledge Fax. We continue to ponder its meaning. We rely on clues that you have given previously. You have said, "I am always talking to you. You only have to look for a sign."

We recognize that many people will say, "There was no Knowledge Fax this week." Of course, they are mistaken. Some people will say, "The Guru finally missed a deadline. Of course, he is just human, like everyone else. He probably ran out of things to say, got tired. Maybe there was no computer nearby. Maybe he called in sick." Some people, asleep, may not have noticed.

Knowing that the Guru is communicating even when he says nothing at all, we seek the deeper meaning of the week's Knowledge sheet (or nonsheet!). Let us simply say we seek the deeper meaning of this week's sandesh.

Option 1: It is all changing. Everything is changing. Nothing stays for all time. Life is teaching us, at every moment, the art of letting go. Even Knowledge Faxes will not be here forever. Letting go. Ultimately we must let go of even the Knowledge as an object, as something "out there."

Option 2: I am the Knowledge. Live the Knowledge, become the Knowledge – that is what we must aspire to. The Knowledge Fax is not just a piece of paper, a bit of amusement each week that titillates the intellect and that we promptly forget and then go about our mundane lives.

Sub-Option 2.1: Enough Knowledge has been given; digest that. We must assimilate what has already been given and make it a part of us. There is a rhythm in all things. The cycle of the year goes around again; the cycle of the Knowledge as well. Let us remember and relearn the Knowledge given in the previous cycle.

Option 3: Grace and Gratitude. "To those who have, more will be given. To those who have not, even what little they have will be taken away." How much gratitude have we had for the Knowledge that has been given each week? How much have we valued the Knowledge Faxes? How much awareness, how much attention have we put on them? Have they become just another routine, something else to take for granted? Wherever we put our attention, that will increase. Have we put enough attention on the Knowledge sheets each week?

Option 4: Silence. Truth is beyond words. Therefore, whatever we speak is false. Only in silence can we know the Truth. Only in silence can we be the Truth. Meditate; be silent; know thy Self.

Option 5: The Unbaked Pot. When you pour water into an unbaked pot, the water is wasted, and so is the pot. Before you put water into a pot, you should bake the pot. The Guru is now baking all the pots. When they are baked, then he will be able to fill them with the water of Knowledge. But for now, why waste all that good water?

Objection: But how can the pots be baked without the Fire of Knowledge? This is a very good point. I suppose there are other fires. The fire of criticism and humiliation; the fire of hunger; the fire of lust; the fire of longing; the physical fire of heat. You should ask the Guru to speak on the five fires.

Option 6: The Answer to Last Week's Non-riddle. Look for the meaning hidden in all the events. And a non-event is also an event. There was a "sandesh" contained within the box of Sandesh sweets given to the Guru last week. Similarly, what is the meaning hidden in this week's non-fax? "Let those who have ears hear." Hear the silence; this is what we must do.

Option 7: Just Testing. The Guru is testing our level of dismay at not receiving a fax this week. It seems that the level of dismay was appropriately high, as it now appears a fax has indeed been sent, albeit belatedly. (I just called Bill Hayden. Poor Bill. Apparently a good proportion of the people on the continent also called him.) So what to read into this? Possibility: The Guru is softhearted; he cannot bear our disappointment. Or: The Guru is disappointed; we did not receive the silent fax he sent, so he was obliged to send a fax containing words. Or: The Guru is pleased; our collective dismay at not receiving a fax this week proved to him that we do deeply value the Knowledge given each week and we are extremely grateful. Or???

69. THE PERFECT BALANCE

People who are free regret that they don't have discipline. They keep promising they will become disciplined.

People who are disciplined look for the end; discipline is not an end in itself, it is a means.

Look at people who have no discipline; they are miserable. Freedom without discipline is absolute misery. And discipline without freedom is suffocating. Orderliness is monotonous and chaos is stressful. We have to make our discipline free and our freedom disciplined.

People who have company all the time look for the comforts of solitude. People who are in solitude feel so lonely and want company. People in a cold place want a warm place. People in a warm place love something cool. This is the dilemma of life.

Everyone is looking for perfect balance.

Perfect balance is like a razor's edge.
It can be found only in the Self.

✍ News Flash:

The big Advanced Course at the ashram of Kripalu Maharaj (the founder of Kripalu Yoga) at Kayavaran, India, brought a celebration. There was one teacher to care for each 25 people, so no one felt lost in the big group. Many people shared their miraculous stories.

The moonlight Satsangs and Christmas lights transformed the ashram into Brindavan*. On the last evening, Gurudev received 400 garlands from devotees. Each garland that hung around his neck, when removed, took a few strands of hair with it.

This course started in bliss and ended up in chaos, including an impatient airplane that left Gurudev behind!

✍ Riddle:

There is no road to this town and there are no steps to this house. How do you get in? Figure it out!

---

*the ancient city in India where Krishna lived, in those days a lush garden paradise.

October 9, 1996
Mumbai, India

70. The Nine Nights of Navaratri

Navaratri means nine nights and the new night. Creation happens in darkness, in the womb of the mother and underneath the soil. Nine months in the womb are like nine long nights where the spirit takes human form.

Night provides rejuvenation and rest. People come home from work at night and celebrate, rejoice, and pray. At night, the entire creation goes to sleep, including the Ashram night watchman.

These nine nights of *Navaratri* are precious; they are enriched with subtle energy. Sixty-four impulses of the Divine Mother govern the subtle creation and are responsible for restoring all earthly and spiritual benefits. These impulses are contained within one's awakened consciousness. The nine nights of *Navaratri* are celebrated to rekindle those divine impulses and to renew the inner depth of our lives.

> *Cleanse your body and cleanse your soul.*
> *Cleanse your body with water;*
> *Cleanse your soul with Knowledge, pranayam,*
> *Sudarshan Kriya, and meditation.*

✍ *News Flash:*

The German Academy hosted an intense Teacher Training Course. Then Gurudev went on to Minsk and Belarus, where people had come from as far as Siberia to meet the Master for the first time. One family had spent seven months' salary and another family had sold their house in order to come. Many recounted miracles that had happened to them. Over 1,000 people filled the stadium.

Russian television covered Gurudev's arrival in Mumbai, and there was a grand reception. The waterfall of flowers surrounding Gurudev's seat seemed to reach out for his darshan.

October 16, 1996
Bangalore Ashram, India

71. CELEBRATING THE SILENCE

One who has given you everything has also given you freedom. Honour the freedom and make good use of all things given to you.

> *Your sankalpas (intentions) and desires separate you from God.*
> *Offer them all to the Divine. Then you are divine... you are God...you are free, lacking nothing.*

Your mind does not belong to you. Don't blame it. Let the Big Self embrace it.

Effort is the key in the relative; effortlessness is the key to the Absolute.

✑ *News Flash:*

Silence.

72. Sincerity and Blessings

Question: Many ask for blessings, but only a few will receive. Why?

Gurudev: The giver is always giving but the taker is not there – the sincerity is missing. One who gives blessings gives freely, but the one who receives has to be sincere. The qualification to receive blessings is sincerity. And everyone is free to be sincere at any time.

Question: Why do people choose to be sincere only sometimes?

Gurudev: Because of the illusion that they are going to miss some mundane pleasure. Hankering after pleasure makes them insincere. When you are sincere, you simply enjoy pleasure without craving for it.

Poor people fight for food. Rich people share their food. Richer are those people who share power. Richer still are those who share fame. Richest are those who share themselves. The richness of a person is indicated by his ability to share and not by what he hoards.

Sincerity is being in touch with your depth.

✍ *News Flash:*

The silence here came alive with Vedic chanting. The whole Ashram vibrated with divine energy; the renowned pundits, who have performed many yagyas* before, felt the difference here. As the activities of the pundits increased, the devotees became more serene and still. As the celebration became louder and more colourful, the silence became deeper and more profound. Each passing day Gurudev grew more radiant. Those who walked by his kutir experienced various fragrances that changed every few minutes.

---

*Vedic procedures that purify and uplift individual consciousness and the surroundings

73. IN THE SOLITUDE OF THE SELF

Buddha is not on the peak, rather the peak is beneath Buddha. One who goes up to the peak comes down, but the peak seeks the one who is stationed higher, in the inner space.

Shiva is called *Chandrashekhara*, which means the mind that is in *Shiva* (transcendence) and is always above the peak.

People run after parties and celebrations, but for the one who does not run after them, parties and celebrations follow him wherever he goes.

> *If you run after parties, loneliness comes to you;*
> *If you are in the solitude of the Self, parties surround you.*

✍ *News Flash:*

On the final day of Navaratri, many people, including children, sat transfixed in one place for nine hours to witness the yagya.

The silence came aloud with the chanting of the pundits accompanied by Indian clarinet and drums. Even the puja vessels started to vibrate.

Gurudev made a stop in Mumbai (Bombay) for a "last-minute notice" Satsang with hundreds of people and wild singing.

Satsangs and celebration moved on to Hong Kong, where two lectures were held in the artful Hong Kong Science Museum.

November 6, 1996
Kyoto, Japan

74. SEE THE DIVINE

If you can't see the divine in me, then open your eyes! If you can see the Divine in me, then you are a part of me; you cannot be away from me. If you feel a part of me, you will see the Divine in yourself. And when you see the Divine in yourself, you'll see the Divine in everyone.

✍ *News Flash:*

On invitation of the United Nations, Art of Living teachers departed for Armenia to conduct a course for conflict resolution among the warring factions.

Sandy and party arrived in Japan for a wacky and awakening Satsang in Kobe, then proceeded to Tokyo, where Tom, Chieko, Hydei, and Nobuko had organised a talk.

The Za-Zen Master of the Tofukuji Temple in Kyoto invited Gurudev to his monastery for an engaging dialogue. He was moved by Gurudev's presence.

Gurudev chaired the International Conference of the Great Religions of Asia at Ryukoku University in Kyoto. Speakers included spiritual leaders from around the world, but listeners felt stuffy and sleepy.

The press reporters were curious about the changing fragrances in Gurudev's presence; for us, it was Gurudev as usual.

75. ANNIHILATE CONFLICT

When you are in a harmonious environment, your mind picks up any excuse to be in conflict. Often small things are enough to create a big turmoil. Have you noticed this?

When your survival is at stake, you don't complain that nobody loves you. But when you are safe and secure, you start demanding attention. Many people create conflict in order to get attention.

Ask yourself this question: Do you seek harmony in every situation, or do you seek to widen the differences and prove your righteousness?

> *The seed of negativity and the tendency for conflict in you can be annihilated only by Sadhana*.*

✐ News Flash:

At the Bangalore Ashram, some people wanted white bread to be served at breakfast. Some were opposed to this, and it caused a big conflict. (It was the only reason they could find to quarrel!) One phone call from Gurudev set everyone in astonishment.

A smiling crowd met Gurudev at the airport with a diplomatic reception and piles of flowers everywhere. Gurudev addressed a group of medical professionals in the afternoon and religious leaders at an interfaith conference that evening. An Advanced Course followed at a hilltop retreat centre. We were happy to see a lady in her mid-thirties who now had no difficulty walking; she had been in a wheelchair and unable to walk for several years until she met Gurudev on a previous Advanced Course.

On the last day of the course, Gurudev and Sharmila cooked for 20 volunteers who had stayed back to clean. At dinner, 60 hungry people showed up and there was food enough for everyone.

Amid tears and laughter, the party moved on to Kuala Lumpur. The honourable Minister for Works attended the official launching of the Malaysian Art of Living Society. Several prominent leaders came to receive blessings from the Master. One of them asked, "What is the limit of want?" Gurudev replied, "Unhappiness". It was a colourful evening of dinner and Satsang.

---

*spiritual practices

76. DESIRE AND PRAYERFULNESS

For your prayer to be answered, the desire has to be intense. The greater the intensity of desire and the later it gets fulfilled, the greater will be the gratitude.

For desire to become intense, time and need are required. Intense desire leads you to devotion.

When a desire is fulfilled, it loses its charm and significance in the overwhelming feeling of gratitude.

The son of a farmer in India had a lifelong desire to go to England, and he prayed deeply for it. When the news of his trip finally materialized, he was filled with such immense gratitude that he no longer cared whether he went or not.

Often people think they are unfortunate if their desires don't get fulfilled quickly. An intense desire can either frustrate you or make you prayerful. In prayerfulness, there is gratitude and devotion. Any intense experience makes you whole.

Your consciousness is like corn:
With the heat of Knowledge,
consciousness pops up
and becomes white and fluffy.

✍ *News Flash:*

Gurudev and his entourage moved from Kuala Lumpur to Bangkok. Once again the metal detector mysteriously beeped as Gurudev passed through it.

The Master gave a fiery Satsang to a multiethnic audience. Teachers will be busy for the whole next month!

Kolkata, the City of Joy, was overjoyed with Gurudev's arrival. Banners flew all over the city and people stampeded the magnificent Birla Sabhaghar city auditorium. Everyone and everything fell into the pervading bliss. Later, the garden of Bharti and S.B. Ganguly danced with lights, melodious birds, Bengali sweets, and smiling faces everywhere.

The moon lit the night for our next Satsang on the bank of the Nalban Park Salt Lake. The superb teamwork in Calcutta ensured that all our activities here flowed effortlessly.

77. FAITH AND HAPPINESS

It is only through merit that you can have faith. When you lack faith, happiness is neither in the inner nor the outer world.

Happiness springs from faith. Happiness is forgetting the body consciousness; pain or sorrow is holding on to body consciousness. When you are happy, you don't feel the body, and when you are miserable, you have aches and pains.

Question: Then why in meditation is the attention taken to various parts of the body?

Gurudev: For an arrow to go forward, you have to pull it back. In the same way, when you take the attention to various parts of the body, it frees you from body consciousness.

✍ *News Flash:*

From Gurudev's first whirlwind tour in the Punjab:

Joginder Singh, an 86-year old man who had been colour blind for the last ten years, regained his sense of hue. Now his gray world has again become a colour movie.

Mr. Sunil Gulati, Director of the Government Department of Health, had lost mobility of his neck due to an accident in 1984. The Master casually put his hand on Mr. Gulati's neck, who found the next day, to his surprise, he had regained total mobility.

Another man disappointed his surgeon because he was healed on the fourth day of the course.

During the Whole Life Fair, Nityanand found a new style of introducing people to the course: Two gentlemen came to our booth and asked, "What is this?" Nityanand replied with a mechanical rhythm, "Neither I know nor you – just sign up!" The gentlemen, who were tired of listening to the lengthy explanations from all the other booths, jumped up and said, "This is the real thing!" They both signed up for the course.

78. How to Deal with Rude Behaviour

What do you do when someone behaves very rudely towards you?

- Get upset
- React rudely back
- Get frustrated
- Run away and avoid the person or situation
- Blame the person
- Preach to the person

None of these will in any way strengthen you. Then what are the options? See rude behaviour in this light:

- It indicates the intensity of their commitment
- It indicates their stress and insensitivity
- It projects the upbringing of the person
- It shows a behavioural pattern
- It shows lack of Knowledge

- It shows lack of observation of the mind and its sensations
- It shows you behaviour to avoid

- It is an opportunity for you to welcome and absorb the rudeness
- It strengthens your mind
- It reveals the love that you are as unconditional

The next time when someone is rude to you, just give back a broad smile. If you can digest their rudeness, nothing whatsoever can shake you.

Gurudev came from Delhi for an overnight stay at the Bangalore Ashram and left the next morning for the state of Kerala. Enthusiastic devotees in Cochin renovated their homes for the occasion. Thousands appreciated the elaborate Satsang arrangements in colourful Trichur. The balikas (young girls) in traditional attire carried lights and flowers; the Kerala-style decorated elephants and umbrellas presented a spectacular welcome. Many people shared healing experiences.

The whole troop moved to Trivandrum, the town of infinity, where the king of Kerala received Gurudev at the Senate Hall with a packed audience of 4,000. Colourful umbrellas, elephants, traditional horns and drums, Vedic chants that filled the air people were enraptured for three-and-a-half hours. The next morning, newspapers overflowed with stories of the Art of Living Satsang.

December 12, 1996
Bangalore Ashram, India

79. PLEASURE

The mind that seeks pleasure cannot be centred. When you are centred, all pleasures come to you anyway, but they cannot charm you any longer because you are the source of the charm.

The mind that seeks pleasure can never achieve the highest.

And if you enjoy drowning in your suffering, you cannot be centred; you are far away from the Path.

If you are after pleasure, forget about *Satsang*. Why are you wasting your time? This is the Art of Leaving.

You either seek pleasure or come to me.

Susannah: What should we do when people talk negatively?

Gurudev: From your side, give license to everybody to talk about anything, about anybody, anywhere, at any time.

Exercise: Talk maximum negativity about everybody this whole week. This is a challenge.

✍ **News Flash:**

Murli had a severe allergy. He could not talk, and he could hardly eat or drink. His tongue was swollen. It was an alarming condition. Then Gurudev arrived. He told Murli to take some medicine and tapped him on the throat. Murli was cured in the next few minutes. It was as if nothing had happened (though he did not listen to the Master and he forgot to take the medicine).

People who came to the Advanced Course to be in silence were blasted by loud raucous music from the local village. Participants had come all the way from Germany for Bangalore's sunny winter weather and instead got dreary clouds, chilling wind, and rain. Frequent power cuts ensured that people took cold water baths in the morning. Gurudev's voice went hoarse and he needed a tap on his own throat!

80. The Five Aspects of the Universe

You have five aspects to yourself:

1) *asti* (is – ness), 2) *bhati* (knowledge, expression), 3) *preeti* (love), 4) *nama* (name), and 5) *rupa* (form).

Matter has two aspects: *nama* and *rupa* (name and form). Consciousness has three aspects: *asti* (is-ness), *bhati* (it knows and expresses), and *preeti* (it is loving). This is the secret of the whole universe. *Maya* (ignorance or delusion) is not being aware of the three aspects of consciousness and getting caught up in the names and forms of matter.

Question: Why are we imperfect?

Gurudev: So that we can grow to perfection. Life is a movement from imperfection to perfection. A seed contains the tree, but to become a tree it must cease to be a seed. In life you can either see imperfection at every step, or you can see a movement from one perfection to another perfection.

Wherever you put your attention, that will grow. If you put your attention on the lack of something, the lack will increase.

✍ *News Flash:*

At 9:00 AM sharp on December 12, Gurudev suddenly assumed the role of a Seva Commander and chased everyone out of the dining hall into their Seva activities! The new regime lasted only half a day, but it uplifted the energy of the Ashram.

December 25, 1996 – Christmas Day
Lake Lucerne, Switzerland

81. Self-Reliance and Surrender

Self-reliance needs enormous courage. When there is nobody else or you want to depend on yourself for everything, you need a lot of courage.

Surrender needs less courage. A person who cannot surrender cannot be self – reliant either.

If you don't have enough courage to surrender, then it is not possible to be self – reliant; you simply fool yourself. If you don't have a hundred dollars, you cannot have a thousand dollars. Even a little fear is detrimental to self – reliance.

Self – reliance contains surrender. Fifty dollars contains ten dollars.

Often people think that surrender is a way to escape from their responsibilities, then they end up blaming the Divine for all their problems. In fact, true surrender is taking total responsibility for everything.

Susannah: How can we do that?

Gurudev: You take responsibility and you pray for help.

Surrender eventually leads you to self-reliance because there is nothing other than the Big Self.

✍ *News Flash:*

From Bangalore, 45 devotees travelled with Gurudev to Madras, where a Satsang of 3,500 people served as a farewell party on the eve of his departure from India. A choir composed of 70 school girls serenaded the Master with heartfelt bhajans in a gigantic marble hall.

India's bougainvillaea, coconut palms, and warm December weather have shifted to Switzerland's mist-shrouded Alpine peaks, snow-laced trees, and the swans on Lake Lucerne. Course participants have gone into silence this morning to celebrate Christmas in a deep and authentic way.

Gurudev's message for Christmas:

Be a fountain of love.

82. New Year's Celebration

The year 1997 is fortunate because you are living at this time. You are not living for yourself, but for the world. Whatever the world needs or wants, you are there. So this year is fortunate that you are on the earth during this time.

Usually people make a wish for the New Year. This year, make no wish. Let the New Year celebrate you. If it wants to bring you nicer things, let it.

Usually you are lost in celebration. But when you let time celebrate you, you are a witness amidst celebration.

Let time celebrate your presence.
You keep smiling as ever.

✍ News Flash:

According to the Vedic calendar, 19,558,085,097 solar years have passed since the beginning of this earth. The NASA scientists will one day authenticate this. There are 20,000 years in Kali Yuga, which began with the death of Krishna 5,097 years ago.

Here in Switzerland the snow is celebrating our presence.

83. PADMANABHA: THE LOTUS NAVEL

Different organs of our body are governed by different *devas*. The solar plexus is connected with the sun, that's why it is called solar plexus. When the first rays of the sun fall on the solar plexus, it is very good for your body. This is why it is good to do *Surya Namaskar* (sun salutation *yoga asana*) in the early morning.

The solar plexus has a profound impact on the central nervous system, optic nerves, stomach, and what we usually call our "gut feeling." It is the second brain in your body. Usually the solar plexus is slightly bigger than an almond. With the practice of *yoga asanas*, meditation, and *Sudarshan Kriya*, the solar plexus can become as large as an apricot. Then it performs better and balances the bodily functions.

When the solar plexus contracts, one feels horrible, sad, depressed; all the negative feelings come.
When the solar plexus expands, the intuitive mind awakens; the mind becomes clear and focused.

Krishna was called *Padmanabha*, meaning whose navel is the size of a lotus flower. If you become *Padmanabha*, you become absolutely creative. *Brahma*, the Creator, is said to be born out of a blossomed solar plexus.

These days, the solar plexus remains small, but the tummy keeps getting bigger.

✍ *News Flash:*

Hans-Peter went to pick up someone in a rented car and suddenly realised he was in a rented body, too.

Lake Lucerne was covered in fog during the entire course – a misty magical winter wonderland. At the end of our two-week stay, Gurudev mentioned that he would take us up the mountain and the sky would clear for us. The next afternoon, course participants trekked with Gurudev up the Rigi via cable tram and train, unmindful of our coughs and sneezes imported from 20 different nations. Arriving at the mountain top, we found ourselves engulfed in a dense fog. We could not even see the snowy Alps that surrounded us. "You said the sky would clear, Gurudev," complained several devotees. "Wait, wait," replied the Master. Not a half a minute later, someone shouted, "Look!" and pointed straight up. A patch of clear blue sky had just appeared directly above our heads, and over the next several minutes – to the "Dos" and "Ahs" of the group – it grew larger before our eyes.

The Teacher Refresher Course at the German Academy is now in full swing. The atmosphere is joyous and fully charged up.

84. BHAKTI

Bhakti (devotional love) contains four letters: *bha, ka,* ta, and *i* (pronounced *ee*). *Bha* means fulfilment and nourishment; *ka* is a means of knowing; ta means redeeming, saving, salvation (*tarana*); *i* (*ee*) is energy, *shakti*.

Bhakti nourishes you. *Bhakti* is the right Knowledge, the means of knowing. When *bhakti* is there, doubts don't come. *Bhakti* saves you. *Bhakti* gives you the most energy.

Bhakti contains the seed of all these qualities. All the emotional upheavals one goes through are because one doesn't know *bhakti*.

A river has two banks that allow water to flow in a particular direction. In a flood, water is scattered all over. When your emotions get flooded everywhere, your mind is in a mess. When all your intense feelings flow in one direction, that is most powerful; that is *bhakti*.

A sign of intelligence is bhakti and surrender.

✍ **News Flash:**

Gurudev escaped for a day from the German Academy to meet with the World Health Organisation in Geneva. Afterwards he completed the European Teacher Refresher week, meeting with groups from each country before taking off to Trinidad. The Trinidad Minister of Social Development greeted Gurudev at the airport and later the President and Prime Minister received him. Throngs of people came each evening to hear the Master.

85. ACCEPT THE WORLD AT ITS WORST

Suppose the worst of the world is given to you.

What would you do with it?

You should not complain if you get the worst. If you have received the worst, then things can only get better. And you are here to make it better.

Jim: When things are at their very worst, there is only time and space. *(Laughter)*

Patty: When you see life as suffering, then you go within.

Paula: It is like running out of breath and you have to inhale.

> *What happens when you have to do something all by yourself – and no one comes to help? Here are three options:*
>
> 1. *Be frustrated and complain.*
>
> 2. *Thank others for not helping so that you can take all the credit.*
>
> 3. *Be grateful, pray deeply, and know that you will get all the energy needed to do it alone. There is only one Doer.*

✍ **News Flash:**

Gurudev's party made a lightning visit to Dominica, where the Cabinet Minister for Education and Social Welfare had organised a program, then whisked off to the Caribbean island of St. Lucia. A diplomatic reception on the island of Curacao (near Venezuela) preceded a premiere public Satsang with empty seats for nobody. Martine and Dr. Chu presented Gurudev to a large Satsang in Panama; ditto for Marjorie in Costa Rica. Manu (from Hong Kong) is organizing courses all over Central and South America.

One day Gurudev walked along the beach with some devotees and noticed a huge desalination plant (converts saltwater to fresh water) costing millions of dollars. A coconut tree grew nearby. Gurudev pointed out that the tree is a natural desalination "plant"; it takes saltwater from the earth and makes fresh water inside the coconut. The Master's Knowledge is like the coconut tree – transforming the salty mud of the world into the fresh waters of bliss.

This trip gave a huge boost to our activities here. Gurudev and his teachings are now becoming known throughout the Caribbean and Central America.

86. INDIGESTION OF KNOWLEDGE

Knowledge must be properly digested and assimilated. Indigestion of the Knowledge leads to development of a subtle ego which has no cure. Subtle ego gives rise to habits that are not life-supporting.

Indigestion of Knowledge leads to:

- Subtle ego
- Being adamant
- Tendency to preach
- Using Knowledge for one's own small ends
- Familiarity without depth or understanding – flakiness
- Disinterest, taking for granted, lack of awareness
- "Heart" burn

Your inability to break a habit can cause a pinch; when you are deeply pained, that will rid you of the habit. When you feel pained by your shortcomings, you are a *sadhak* (seeker). Pain takes you out of addiction.

When you are in love with the Divine, you can digest the Knowledge. Love is the appetizer, *Seva* is exercise; without love and *Seva*, Knowledge becomes indigestible.

So everyone list the loving Seva you have done for the world.

Marielle: If love is the appetizer, what is the main course?

Gurudev: Knowledge.

Daniel : What is the dessert?

Gurudev: Myself!! *(Laughter)*

P.S. Next week everyone write a Knowledge note with your own news flash and send it to your national centre with your name on it.

✍ *News Flash:*

Reverend Michael Beckwith, founder of the Agape Church in Santa Monica, honoured Gurudev in a speech to his congregation. Divya inspired everyone with her joyous bhajans. On Monday, Gurudev attracted crowds at the Miramar Sheraton Hotel. A lady in her fifties who had lost mobility in her arm from an accident found the following day that she could easily move her arm.

87. UNKNOWN KNOWLEDGE

Do you recall this from last week's knowledge?

P.S. Next week everyone write a Knowledge note with your own news flash and send it to your national centre with your name on it.

It seems that *Gurudev* was serious. He was asking last night about the missing Knowledge and said that he was looking forward to reading other people's Knowledge this week rather than sending out one as usual. He said that people read the Knowledge and then forget it, so he wants people to write their own this time.

✍ *News Flash:*

Gurudev is in Philadelphia today, New Jersey tomorrow, and Florida on Sunday for a week-long silence course.

✍ *Devotees respond !*

Here are a few samples of Knowledge notes that people sent after Gurudev's (second) request:

February 10, 1997
Flint, Michigan

THE LITTLE MONSTER IN MY HEAD

There is the problem of this ego. It is the little monster who lives in my head, crouched behind my good senses, waiting for the opportunity to cause trouble. It always wants to be right. It doesn't matter if it is right or not; it will rationalize, it will justify, it will risk friends, family, and peace of mind – just to win, to be "better."

Now, knowing this, I have the advantage. When this ego tries to convince me it is okay to manipulate others, or behave like a spoiled child, or be angry at someone for doing the same thing I do, I can look at the situation and say, "Hmmm, here is this little ego playing its games again." But only if I choose to do so.

The key is that I do have a choice. This ego would like me to think otherwise – that life is a competition to be won or lost. It would like me to react to its endless tricks instead of laughing at its antics. It would like me to perpetuate its games. But when I use the Knowledge, I observe and absolve rather than react and retaliate; then I sail through the situations I encounter, unaffected and unafraid.

"Right" and "wrong" are concepts in the mind. What is important is the love in my heart. With this Knowledge, I am free.

– Dawne Ferguson

✍ **News Flash:**

We sometimes feel isolated here in Flint, but the Art of Living is alive and well. The Satsang e-mail list is a valuable connection. We look forward to the day when we will welcome the Master to Michigan and introduce him at last to friends, family, and others, that they may experience his grace.

THE DIVINE MIRROR

We cannot see the mirror while looking at the objects it reflects. We lose ourselves in the objects. Like this, we get caught up in the world until we become aware of the Divine that reflects this world.

A kitten plays with its image in the mirror because it believes there is another cat to play with. We also get caught in the game of life because we believe there is somebody else to play with. Becoming aware of the Divine mirror frees us from this misconception: there is no two.

– Philippe Gaudrat

✍ *News Flash:*

Gurudev had a wonderful idea at the German Academy: he will tour France this spring, giving Satsangs and public talks here and there. He will also lead an Advanced Course outside Paris. Everybody is really excited by this.

February 5, 1997
Tokyo, Japan

HOPELESS

Are you feeling hopeless? Destroyed and wiped out by life? By something you did or you can't stop doing? By something that was done to you?

What's the use? Utter despair. You cannot go on living and you cannot die. You are really a mess. Are you feeling this way?

This is hopeless.

It's a beautiful place. No, I am not making fun. Once your mind has shut down, even for a little while, there are no more excuses, no more rationalizations, no more fantasies, no more arguments, no more complaints, no more running, no more trying to understand or to be understood – just the pain... you... and the tears. Hopeless.

And now your mind is quiet. Now you can feel some peace. Now you can look at that pain and accept it totally, without judgment. You can surrender.

Then you can walk right inside that pain and find a huge surprise: You can feel the love inside. You find that at the very centre of what you've been trying to lose is what you've been looking for. And even with the pain, help is already there.

Hopeless is a wonderful place.

– Tommie Schmitz

✍ News Flash:

Wally Zeman arrived to teach in Osaka-Kobe and Tokyo .

Things are moving so quickly in Japan!

BREATH: DOORWAY TO SILENCE

When you're racing through your day and tension builds, have you ever noticed that it won't subside – even if you tell yourself to relax – without first taking a deep breath in and out?

The breath gives us access to the healing powers within our body. In an instant, we can find our inner resting place through the breath.

– Robin Mastro

✍ *News Flash:*

Last Friday evening we taught ujjayi breathing to the Seattle Antioch University Egypt Expedition Team, which departs in April. They loved it!

Our group is strong and happy, and thanks to two great tabla players, our bhajans are rockin' and rollin'!

UNENDING WEALTH

When Craig was playing his sitar, he was struck by the fact that the "drone" (continuous tone) of a raga seems to go on forever. This note, sa, is that root note which underpins all the beautiful melodies. *Dhana* means wealth. So *Sadhana* means that wealth that goes on forever!

We cannot take any worldly treasures with us when we die, but the wealth from *Sadhana* stays with us always!

– Craig and Jenny Pruess

News Flash:

A course participant who had been hospitalized for two months with chronic fatigue syndrome is now so grateful that he has found "The Art of Healing"! His sense of humour returned after just one weekend workshop.

February 11, 1997
Ahmedabad, India

WHY ARE YOU STILL FRUSTRATED?

It's like this:

You've got a cup, and you drink of it... love, joy, peace, contentment. After the Art of Living course, your cup, as they say, runneth over. And for some time you are fine, everything is hunky-dory and pip-pip. Then a bit of anger or frustration creeps in.

Why?

Well... are you doing *Seva*??? Your cup is too small for you now! You want – you need – more. Doing *Sadhana* and *Satsang* fills the cup, but *Seva* gets you a new bigger cup. A few hours of *Seva* can push your consciousness into *samadhi*.

Do *Seva*. Get a bigger cup. Do *Sadhana* and *Satsang* and fill it up. Then drink and enjoy... (hic!) Get it!!??!

– *Bawa*

✍ *News Flash:*

My days in Mumbai were jam-packed. About 200 people joined for the Maha-Kriya, the first in Mumbai.

THE PERFECT PLAN

Your life is perfect. It is a perfect plan; it is a spontaneous miracle; it is both every moment.

The creation is perfect. How do birds know to migrate? How do maple leaves know to turn crimson and fall to the ground? Winter comes and you think you will never feel the sun again, but then you see the first green shoots of spring bursting through the snow. How does the flower survive? It is a miracle.

The human body is a perfectly planned machine. How could our network of bones, veins, muscles, and organs ever have been created? You look into the eyes of a newborn and you are speechless.

You have only to open your eyes for three seconds to observe the unfathomable Intelligence at play.

And what about you and your life? Do you think this perfect Creator stops with you? We spend endless hours trying to figure out why this and why that. Do you ever wonder why trees give out oxygen? We don't question that part of the plan. But when it comes to our own lives, we question constantly.

The mind tries to figure out that which cannot be understood. Trust in the plan of creation. Nature, who has brilliantly designed the creation down to the very atom, will spend no less attention on the details of your life. Your situation, your challenges, are all perfect. Relax, trust, and let go.

– Pamela Poole'

✍ News Flash:

A wild and wonderful party at Barbara's shook the entire house as we sang into the wee hours on Saturday night. There was a ton of good food and too many desserts, which we gobbled up as we exchanged Valentine's gifts.

Guru is not who you think he is!

We see the Guru through our own eyes. Often we see him as a separate individual like everyone else. He just happens to be totally happy and serene.

This is because of our own egoistic perspective.

From the Guru's viewpoint, everyone is one continuum of Self. He does not see a separation. You are as precious to him as he is to himself. He does not see a person or devotee becoming free, but his own Self waking up to himself, like when your arm or leg falls asleep and then regains its sense again.

The Roller Coaster

Living life fully is like a roller coaster ride. There is whirling, spinning, fast-paced perceptions, and adventure! If you are tense and holding on tight, resisting each turn, you will feel exhausted and sick at the end. But if you can relax and have faith that the builder of the ride made it for your fun and safety, then you feel thrilled, energized, and joyful!

– Jeff Houk

✍ *News Flash:*

My job feels more like a dance than work...

NOTE FROM A DEVOTEE

Someone has called your Guru a devil. What do you do?

1. Get into an argument.

2. Say nothing, and silently wish the person health and happiness.

3. Say nothing, but wish you had.

4. Envision your life without your Guru and allow the tears of love to speak for you.

    – Kevin Hop.

✒ *News Flash:*

At a recent course, Gurudev turned the participants into bees. Everyone spent the day collecting honey.

WHERE IS HE?

To those dying of hunger,
   God comes in the form of food.
To the helpless newborn child,
   God comes as mother.
To the sincere seeker of Truth,
   God comes as Guru.

– Joe Hardy

✍ News Flash:

I was praying to Gurudev and gently "telling him off."

Six hours later and from six thousand miles away, Gurudev phoned me to say, "I heard your prayer and I am answering your call – come to me..."

FAITH OF THE FAITHFUL

It takes a special faith to walk the spiritual Path. It is rare in this world. Without it, sooner or later people will fall away.

What is this faith?

Just this: A firm "knowing" that nothing in the material world will ever finally satisfy you, that what you seek is within.

Without this faith, you will not make time for your spiritual practices. You will always be too busy chasing some glitter in the world.

Jesus said, "The kingdom of God is within you." Yet we still pursue the objects. We forget that things do not create joy in us.

A worldly attraction is like a mirage in the desert – it always evaporates once you reach it. Fleeting, unable to be possessed, it only hints of the heaven residing deep within us at all times.

It's so easy to find an excuse to fall away from our practices: "I don't have time to breathe, I don't have time to meditate, I must work, I must go to the store, I must do this, I must do that..." Excuses mean we have more faith in the world and less in the spirit. Faith in the world causes unfaithfulness in our *Sadhana*. We soon exhaust our joy and become tired.

After you bake in the desert long enough, you will eventually want to soak in the bliss of your Being. Again walk the Path in earnest – while maintaining your worldly duties. Gracefully balancing both, you become faithful to your Self.

– David Burge

✍ *News Flash:*

People in our tropical Satsang started out a year ago with breathing and meditation; today they are surfing the big waves of gratitude and devotion. Our fun times revolve continually around the Master, his teachings, and his growing Presence in our lives.

THE MUSIC OF LIFE

God is the unseen conductor. The Master is the one hooking us up to the melody until we can play it again on our own. Once we catch hold of the rhythm, the Master skilfully steps back to let the music flow.

– Andrew Behla

✍ *News Flash:*

Gurudev just finished an Advance Course at Camp Shalom in Malibu. The participants were treated to sunshine and silence in a tranquil canyon with streams and a waterfall. Love flowed from every corner of the camp as our bhajans ignited into ecstasy.

This morning Gurudev flies to New York to light another fire.

Gossip

Gossip is like the spider web:
 sticky
 dangerous
 almost invisible
 and spreading out in all directions.
 It catches all flying things
 from the common bug
 to the most beautiful of butterflies
 and in its clutches it slowly devours them.

Knowledge is like the wind:
 subtle
 transparent
 yet powerful and strong.
 It tears the web of gossip to shreds
 freeing all living things
 and lifting them to the heavens.

– Scott Hague

✍ News Flash:

Gurudev declares a moratorium on gossip! "Now is the time to take a vow, for the next six months, until Guru Purnima, to be without gossip. From now on, when you are about to gossip about someone, the object of your gossip must be present in the room. Or, if you are about to spread a rumour or slanderous thing about someone, you must change it into a compliment. The resulting wave of good will, support, and enthusiasm will lift people to the heavens."

NONVIOLENCE AND GRATITUDE FOR CATS

Even we cats can practice *ahimsa* (nonviolence). Do not feel that the Knowledge need not apply simply because you are not a human.

Take chipmunks for instance. When you find a nest of baby chipmunks, it is natural to want to play with those funny little creatures. They move so fast, running around. This is a lot of fun. Playing is okay. But remember: they are also little darlings. Sometimes you want to put them in your mouth. It's fine to carry them around, but do not bite into them. This is very important.

When you watch the other animals outside the window, like squirrels eating nuts your human has left, or birds in the feeder, remember how lucky you are to have a human who feeds you and takes care of you and goes to work to pay the rent for you so you don't have to live outside in the freezing cold winter. We cats also can be grateful.

A cat who cultivates the qualities of gratitude and nonviolence is a very special animal. Such a cat may be allowed to attend *Satsang* and even meet the Master.

– Mrs. Darling, the Cat

✍ *News Flash:*

Once I found a nest of baby chipmunks, and every day I would take one, carry it away, and play with it. I played with them until they were really very tired. Exhausted. Then I would carry them to Susannah, who would put them in a cage and bring them to the Wildlife Rehabilitation Centre. They told Susannah that they had never seen a chipmunk brought in by a cat owner that didn't have a wound, but these chipmunks were absolutely untouched.

(Well, except for one; I accidentally did make a tiny mark on the leg.)

Once I brought a bird inside. I wanted to play with it. It is so tantalizing and interesting, the way it moves so quickly. But I didn't hurt it. After a while I just ignored it. When Susannah got home from work, she found it upstairs sitting on the bathroom floor. She opened the window and it flew away.

So you see, it is really possible for a cat to practice ahimsa. I am a model cat; I have mastered ahimsa.

The next thing I will tackle is pride.

88. BE LOVED

When Knowledge is lodged in you as wisdom, it will never leave you. Wisdom lodges in your heart.

Make the Divine your Valentine, your sweet Beloved. This is the last thing – and the first thing – to do.

Keep your heart in a safe place; it is too delicate. Events and small things make strong impressions on it. To keep your heart safe and your mind sane, you cannot find a better place than the Divine. The passing time and events will not be able to touch you; they will not create a scar.

A precious stone needs a setting around it – gold or silver – to hold it; Wisdom and Knowledge are the setting that will hold your heart in the Divine.

Make the Divine your Valentine.
Just be...and know that you are loved.
That is Beloved.

✍ *News Flash:*

From Los Angeles, Gurudev and the entourage visited New Jersey, New York, Philadelphia, and Houston for Satsangs and packed talks. Credit goes to all the organisers of these events. Then it was on to Fort Lauderdale where Knowledge notes continue to pour in from all corners, and each of them is simply astounding.

P.S. How many of you work hard? Wait 'til next week for the answer.

89. Seva Blessings

When you do *Seva*, don't think you are doing a favour for somebody. Your *Seva* has rewarded you immediately. Your reward is for sure and is always more than your doing.

Your expectation of reward turns *Seva* into labour. If you think you have done a lot, you will do very little. Just see that you have done little; then you will do more.

Seva means that even when you don't see an immediate reward, there is no complaint; labour means that even after an immediate reward, there are complaints.

Be grateful for any opportunity to do Seva.

✍ *News Flash:*

Like the professional translator in Costa Rica who got spaced out and could not translate, our air hostesses lost their minds, found their hearts, and become instant gopis*.

*women devotees, a reference to the milkmaids who, absorbed in love for Krishna, sang and danced in ecstasy; the masculine form of gopi is gopa.

90. SHARE YOUR JOY

When you share your misery, it doesn't reduce. When you don't share your joy, it reduces.

> *Share your problems only with the Divine, not with Tom, Dick, or Harry – that just increases the problem.*

Share your joy with everybody.

Darren: How do you help people who share misery with you?

Gurudev: I have a thousand and one ways. Often it happens that when they share their problem with me, it is immediately resolved. Other times it requires some patience. Just know that all will be taken care of.

Mary: How can we help people who share their misery with us?

Gurudev: Listen to others – yet don't listen. Because if your mind gets stuck there as well, then not only are they miserable, you also get miserable. Be caring and share with them the Knowledge.

✍ ***News Flash:***

The full moon greeted the Master as he arrived on Hawaii's island of Maui for the first time. He gave an intimate Satsang to a handful of people, then on to David and Gary's ashram home on the Garden Island of Kaua'i.

That evening at Satsang, Gurudev was quiet for a full 45 minutes. While many people soaked themselves in this sublime silence, others got fidgety. Several people left. One woman walked out and went to a phone booth in Hanalei. "He just sat there and didn't say a thing!" she complained to her friend. Meanwhile, a man from Maui stood at the next phone stall, desperately hoping to locate someone on the mainland for better directions to the home. He had just met Gurudev at the Maui Satsang and had become enraptured with him; now he had flown to Kaua'i to attend our Satsang, but he was lost. When he heard this woman on the adjacent phone fuming about the silent saint, he immediately hung up his phone and blurted, "Where IS he?? I must see him!!" which must have startled this woman. She did give him the directions and ten minutes later he arrived at our Satsang.

On the following two evenings, Gurudev was more talkative; the house vibrated with sublime wisdom, people asked questions and received answers, and songs echoed down the lush valley.

Gurudev had come to rest, but didn't rest, yet he was not restless. He outlined a new course for teenagers called "ART Excel" (All Round-Training for Excellence). The Governor of Hawaii and the mayor of Honolulu each wrote letters to Gurudev that expressed their appreciation for his work in Hawaii. A final talk at a hotel in Honolulu rounded out Gurudev's "Hawaiian vacation."

91. ANGELS

Infinity has diverse qualities, and specific qualities assume names. They are called angels.

Angels are simply rays of your Big Self. They are like your extended arms. They are there to serve you when you are centred. Like roots and stems and leaves that come out of a sprouted seed, all the angels in your life manifest when you are centred.

Like all the colours that are present in white sunlight, all the angels are present in your higher Self. Bliss is their breath, dispassion is their abode.

Angels rejoice in your company, but you have nothing to gain from them. They only come around those who have nothing to gain from them.

The bestower of dispassion is *Shiva*, that Consciousness that is bliss, innocence, and omnipresence. *Krishna* is the outer manifestation of *Shiva*. The inner silence of *Krishna* is *Shiva*.

✍ *News Flash:*

Meticulous devotees in Jakarta had spent extensive hours on elaborate reception plans at the airport. Gurudev played a trick, with John's help, and arrived one day early, foiling their plans!

In Jakarta, packed Satsangs and packed tummies delighted all especially Gurudev. The new ashram under construction, funded entirely by donations from devotees, is expected to be ready for occupancy in July. The celebrations continue in Singapore.

92. The Eleventh Commandment

Being in a crowd when you are alone is ignorance. Enlightenment is being alone in a crowd; a feeling of oneness in a crowd – this is a sign of wisdom.

Some know how to celebrate only when they are in a crowd; some can rejoice only alone in silence. I tell you to do both.

Knowledge of life brings confidence, and Knowledge of death makes you fearless and centred.

> Celebrate while you are alone and
> Celebrate when you are with people.
> Celebrate the silence and
> Celebrate the noise.
> Celebrate life and
> Celebrate death.

> This is the Eleventh Commandment!

✎ *News Flash:*

The energy at the Ashram peaked on Shivaratri; Gurudev's dance left everyone spellbound.

At an Ahmedabad sports stadium, 8,000 people joined together into one big delirious Satsang with Gurudev.

The next day, one of our Art of Living teachers passed away. Gurudev embraced the family members and in minutes lifted the gloom. This experience brought a depth and dispassion to the entire group; they celebrated by singing "Jai Jai Radha Ramana Hari Bol." The bereaved family will join Gurudev in Rishikesh.

In Delhi, the spiritually saturated capital of India, billboards were seen at every major intersection. The thrilling Satsang and meditation captivated thousands.

93. A Friend is an Enemy, an Enemy is a Friend

In the company of your friends, you lose your centeredness. It is your enemy that puts you back into your Self. Your friend sympathizes with you and makes you believe in matter. Your enemy makes you feel helpless and takes you to the spirit.

So your enemy is your friend, and your friend is your enemy!

> *Krishna said to Arjuna: One who is unfriendly everywhere - his consciousness is stable and his awareness is established...!*

✍ *News Flash:*

On the day Gurudev arrived, the residents of Rishikesh revived with the first rain in several months. Teachers from all over India have congregated for their annual refresher program. Gurudev is taking a short respite to go through the mountains of mail!

In Urugalli, Karnataka, our doctors conducted a free medical camp; 2,500 villagers were diagnosed and given medicines.

From four die-hard devotees from buoyant Baroda, rapidly recovering from a traffic accident: "Thanks to Gurudev's grace and the loving Seva of Baroda Satsangees, we are all strong and rejoicing. There is life on earth and life after death. For one brief moment, we were blessed with the vision of both. Now we are truly celebrating this life – its pain, humour, chaos, and joy, in total gratitude and surrender to the Divine."

March 26, 1997
Rishikesh, India

94. SIMPLE OR COMPLEX?

Life is utterly simple and yet most complex. You have to simultaneously attend to both facets. When life appears most complex, turn to simplicity; simplicity brings peace. When you are peaceful, attend to the complexity; that will make you more skilful.

If you are only with simplicity, it makes you lazy and dull; growth is not there. Being only with complexity makes you angry and frustrated; then there is no life at all. The intelligent ones skilfully balance these two and rejoice in both.

When you recognize both the simplicity and the complexity of life, you'll be skilfully peaceful!

> *White is the pure simplicity.*
> *Colours are the complexity of life.*
> *When your heart is pure,*
> *your life becomes so colourful.*

Vikram: Gurudev, you are all white and yet so colourful...

Pramila: Like our Knowledge, which is profound yet so simple!

✍ *News Flash:*

Almost every teacher in India reported inspiring and miraculous experiences, either personally or from their students. Holi, the Festival of Colours during the full moon, incited a colour rampage which ended with a mass dip in the Ganges at sunset. Six hundred people have gathered for the first Advanced Course.

95. EXPAND YOUR VICES

If you cannot get rid of vices, increase them! Give them a bigger dimension and a different direction:

- Anger: What is the point of getting angry about small events? Be angry about the Infinite, about *Brahman*.

- Pride, ego: If you cannot get rid of pride, take pride in owning the Divine.

- Greed: Be greedy for *Satsang*.

- Cravings: Crave for truth.

- Aversion: Be averse to aversions.

- Jealousy: Be jealous about *Seva*.

- Intoxication: Get intoxicated with the Divine.

- Attachment: Attach yourself to the Master.

Joy is love for what is.
Sorrow is love for what is not.

✍ **News Flash:**

The teacher trainees are being baked at different temperatures in the Divine Oven! Rishikesh is resonating with Art of Living bhajans, and the second Advanced Course is starting with 600 people. Tuesday night after Satsang, people wandered around the Ashram and marveled at the changing fragrances: rose, gardenia, jasmine, and sandalwood.

96. THE PRIMAL INSTINCT

Fear is an impression of the past reflecting about the future of the present. When people deny fear, they become egocentric; when they recognize and accept fear, they go beyond it... and become free.

Total lack of fear is possible only in utter chaos or utmost orderliness. Neither a fool nor a saint has fear. But everywhere in between there is fear.

Fear is a primal instinct, essential to preserve orderliness in the world. Fear of death preserves life. Fear of wrong keeps the right. Fear of sickness brings hygiene. Fear of misery keeps you righteous. A pinch of fear is necessary to keep things moving smoothly. A child has a pinch of fear so it is careful and alert while walking.

Fear is love standing upside down. Everything that can be interpreted with love can also be interpreted with fear. For example, a child clinging to its mother can be interpreted in both ways – as out of love or out of fear.

The primal instinct of fear can be totally transformed through awareness of Divine Love.

> *Do not try to eliminate fear! Just meditate and know that you are*
> *nobody ... or that you belong to Someone special...*

✍ *News Flash:*

Once again on the banks of the Ganges, the sublime Knowledge of the Ashtavakra Gita* and the Narada Bhakti Sutras* flowed in Hindi from the Source.

At 0430 hours, the entire course went for a dip in the Ganges and welcomed the New Year's sun. The second Advanced Course ended with a flamboyant celebration that continued way past midnight.

On April third at 2230 hours, seven devotees got enlightened. Their names will be revealed after some time...

*Available to the reader through the Divine Shops.

97. SATSANG IS SHELTER

Why do people need homes? Can they live without shelter like animals in the forest? Even intelligent animals make their homes.

Man needs protection from the changing elements of nature, so he builds a shelter for physical comforts. In the same way, for spiritual and mental comfort, *Satsang* is the shelter.

One who does not come to *Satsang* is like a wild animal. *Satsang* makes one civilized. *Satsang* is your shelter from the harsh and changing influences on your life.

Satsang is the nest in which you can rest.

If you are a taker of happiness, you get misery.

If you are a giver of happiness, you get joy and love.

✍ News Flash:

As the month-long stay in Rishikesh came to an end, many saints of the region came to greet Gurudev and bless the Art of Living family. They wished we could stay longer.

A very serious sadhu who had built himself a stone hut kept saying to Gurudev, "Why do you always have so many people with you? Why don't you come here alone and stay here with me?" He sang such beautiful bhajans about dispassion, yet by the time Gurudev was leaving he was regretting he was not one who was following in the crowd.

Enthusiastic devotees in Delhi had a farewell Satsang as the party boarded the flight to Kolkata.

98. THREE KINDS OF LOVE

There are three kinds of love: That which comes out of charm, that which comes out of familiarity, and Divine Love. Do you see what I'm saying?

Love that comes out of charm does not last long. Out of unfamiliarity you are attracted, then once you become familiar, you quickly lose the attraction and boredom sets in, like in most marriages. This type of love diminishes and brings fear, uncertainty, insecurity, and sadness.

Love that comes out of familiarity grows. You feel more comfortable, for example, with an old familiar friend rather than with a new person. But this love has no thrill, no enthusiasm, no fire to it.

Divine Love supersedes both these. Divine Love is ever new. The closer you come, the more charm and depth is there. Divine Love has comfort, enthusiasm, and familiarity. There is never boredom, and everyone keeps on their toes.

> *Worldly love can be like an ocean, yet an ocean has a bottom. Divine Love is like the sky – limitless, infinite. From the bottom of the ocean, soar into the vast sky.*

Anything more about Divine Love?

Listen to the *Bhakti Sutras**.

✍ *News Flash:*

During a visit to Adichunchuna Giri Ashram, Gurudev mentioned to the head swami that he must return soon to the Bangalore Ashram, as his devotees were waiting for him.

"No, let them wait," replied the swami. "Waiting for the Guru is tapas (penance). Waiting for the world is tapa (torture)."

In the northeastern region of Guwahati, the generally conservative and closed society crowd turned jubilant and wild. An elaborate banquet for 1,500 devotees followed the Satsang. Then 180 devotees filled four buses and twelve cars for a trip to Shillong, the Meghalayan capital which is also called "the Scotland of the East." En route, we stopped for a picnic on the banks of a large lake and took rides on a speedboat. All the Satsangees of Shillong behaved like an old bunch though

*Available to the reader through the Divine Shops.

they were meeting Gurudev for the first time. On Gurudev's return, Kolkata had a mega-Satsang in the Science City Auditorium. Gurudev is now back in Bangalore.

Gurudev's name is recorded in the Sukha Nadi (a 5,000-year old palm leaf scripture), where it says that Lord Krishna's spirit resides in him. The deity from the Mother Divine temple, located 300 kilometers from our Ashram, wrote that Mother Divine is extremely happy about the work of our Ashram, that the spirits of both Lord Krishna and Mother Divine reside in Gurudev, and that all of Gurudev's devotees are in the most right Path and are peaceful, calm, and settled.

99. WHAT ENHANCES YOUR BEAUTY?

When you are not complaining and you are responsible, courageous, confident, hollow and empty, then you are inexplicably beautiful.

The worldly mind is a complaining mind; the Divine mind is a dancing mind. Complaining without indicating a solution is irresponsibility. A person who does not take action to correct something has no right to complain. And when a person can act and correct, he will not complain. If the solutions are not workable, finding alternative solutions is courage.

Complaining is a sign of weakness, the nature of utter ignorance when one does not know the Self. Complaints take away the Beauty that is inborn in you – and this shows up more on one who walks the Path.

For external beauty, you put on things; for real Beauty, you have to drop all things (including your complaints).

For external beauty, you have make-up;
For real Beauty, realise you are already "made up"!

✍ *News Flash:*

Public Satsangs were thronged by thousands and broadcast live. An ART Excel course for children is in full swing.

Homes for the homeless and sanitation facilities for the surrounding village are the latest Seva projects initiated by Gurudev. Already 15 houses are coming up fast. A number of people asked Gurudev why he would sanction new houses for villagers when the Ashram itself is already burdened with a need for more rooms. "The more rooms we have, the more people will come," he replied. "It is a never ending shortage. If we say we will do Seva only after our own needs are met, it will never happen." So we took that project and made the whole village happy.

In Singapore, those who tell others to live in the present were busy planning! But the plans were again toppled when Gurudev did not arrive as scheduled.

This week's Knowledge ended with a cooooooooool splash from Gurudev's water bottle.

100. DROP YOUR SELF-IMAGE

Kashiap: How can we make everyone happy?

Gurudev: Become me.

Rama: How do we become you?

What stands between you and me is your self-image. Your self-image restricts you from being me. Your self-image, whether good or bad, causes misery.

When you think good about yourself, in a subtle manner you think bad about others. Then feelings like anger, jealousy, and hatred follow.

When you think bad about yourself, you feel low, and again you start getting angry and hating everyone.

When you think good about yourself,
you are in trouble.

When you think bad about yourself,
you are in greater trouble!

So drop your self-image.

✍ *News Flash:*

The Malaysian Advanced Course ended on Sunday and the celebration moved on for the first time to the island country of Mauritius, off the east coast of Africa. Although preparations for Gurudev's visit were ongoing for weeks, all the jigsaw pieces fell into place at the last moment. Three grand Satsangs were held with filled halls. The Prime Minister and many Cabinet Ministers also came for the Master's blessing.

It took 200 top police officers and the Commissioner of Police to capture Gurudev for a talk at the Police Headquarters. The officers (in uniform) were mesmerized. They ended up singing bhajans and afterwards came up to hug Gurudev. Many promised to join the Art of Living Satsang group. One police officer remarked to Sharda that Gurudev is a "stress breaker," but for Sharda and others, he is rather a "heartbreaker."

✍ *Remember that May 13 is Gurudev's birthday! We would like to see how many children our local communities can support between May 13 and the Advanced Course at Lake Tahoe this July. Contact Carla Riechman, our Dollar-a-Day coordinator, at (301) 588-6422 or laughter@his.com to learn more about this wonderful program and how you can be a part of this birthday present to Gurudev.*

101. THE WORLD BELONGS TO YOU

Pleasure or pain is an intense sensation in this 4-6 foot body. When we are not caught up in them, we can truly say, "I belong to you." All cravings, aversions, desires, and doubts fall off – and in a moment the world belongs to you.

All your miseries surround the I, I, I. "I want this, I like that, I don't like this..."

> *Just let go. The sun rises and sets, the grass grows, the river flows, the moon shines, and I am here forever!*

How do you feel if someone praises you?

Answers: Shy, happy, great, embarrassed...

It does something to you, doesn't it? But it doesn't do anything to me! When you praise the moon, the mountains, Lake Lucerne, the Black Forest... it doesn't do anything to them. They remain the same. Just like that, I am part of nature. If you enjoy praising me, you may do so. In fact, you have no choice! *(Laughter)*

You can do with me whatever you like; I am there for you. I am your toy!

✍ *News Flash:*

In Mauritius, time stood still in Satish's house, where Gurudev stayed; all six clocks and all watches mysteriously stopped!

Gurudev moved on to South Africa, where he addressed vivacious crowds in Pretoria and Johannesburg, then on to Botswana, where he was received by the President at the State House. Later, Gurudev visited a government hospital and distributed gifts of food, clothes, and toys to the ailing children in the pediatric ward. The children loved it! Gurudev was like Santa Claus but with a black beard and trim tummy!

Gurudev distributed blankets and food to the aged and disabled of the entire village of Modipane. The people were overwhelmed and greeted the Master with joy and cheer.

Hardworking devotees in Botswana are organizing big Healing Breath Workshops and great Satsangs. The tired group went on an African safari and found two leopards, five elephants, a vulture with a broken wing, and two monkeys, but that day the only enthusiastic person was the guide!

The gang giggled on and on. Instead of sugar, Hema spooned hot pickle into her tea!

Ahmedabad devotees organised a blood donation camp and Bangalore devotees a mass feeding of the poor.

Here in Bad Antogast there was a five-storey birthday cake for Gurudev with marzipan swans. Instead of "How are you?" Gurudev greeted everyone with "How am I?"

102. DEDICATION AND COMMITMENT

Your car runs out of fuel and you have to refill it again and again.

In the same way, your dedication and commitment run out in the course of time and need constant renewal! You have to dedicate and rededicate, again and again.

Often people take their dedication for granted; then the mind starts to demand or complain. When your dedication is not full, it leads to grumbling and complaints.

Total dedication brings enormous enthusiasm, zeal, trust, and challenge – and does not leave any room for ego.

✍ News Flash:

Spring was in full bloom at our German Academy, and so were all our hearts.

The first silent seeds have been sown in Austria. A bus full of devotees drove eight to ten hours all the way from Croatia to Vienna to meet Gurudev for a couple of hours.

Today's full moon is dedicated to Buddha, and now is the time to rededicate yourself.

103. THE WAY OUT OF SORROW

If you are unhappy, you better check if one or all of these is lacking:

- *Tapas* (penance)

- *Vairagya* (dispassion)

- *Sharanagati* (surrender)

Tapas is agreeing with the moment, total acceptance of all pleasant or unpleasant situations.

Vairagya means *I want nothing and I am nothing. Sharanagati* is I am here for you, for your joy.

If you are grumbling, then these are lacking. When you accept the situation, when you take it as tapas, you cannot grumble; when you come from a state of dispassion (I don't want anything), you don't grumble; and if you are surrendered, you will have no complaints.

If you don't do it willingly, you will do it later in desperation. First you will say, "Nothing can be done." Then later in anger and desperation you will say, "I give up, I want nothing, I have no choice – to hell with it!"

> *All these three – penance, dispassion and surrender – they purify your mind and uplift you in joy.*

✍ News Flash:

On Buddha Purnima, Gurudev became so engrossed in singing a new bhajan that he did not go to his Innsbruck talk. The next day he surprised the unhappy organiser and made her happy.

A full house in Paris sent a wave of enthusiasm all over France. Three cars and a bus departed for ten major cities on Gurudev's "Tour de France."

Carla Riechman has received a lively response for Gurudev's birthday present of sponsored children at his beloved Ashram.

Gurudev has structured special ART Excel programs for children and teenagers, available for the first time during summer Advanced Courses.

June 3, 1997
En route on the Tour de France

104. THE DIVINE BEYOND TIME

An ignorant person either believes or disbelieves somebody. The wise one neither believes nor disbelieves. His faith rests on *kala* (time).

When the time is good, even a foe will behave like a friend. When the time is not good, even a friend will behave like a foe. The wise believe in *Mahakala* (the Grand Time or *Shiva*) – the Divine beyond time.

In the world of time, there is always room for improvement. Only Being is perfect all the time.

Take refuge in Being and become incorrigible.

✍ **News Flash:**

The discovery of the week is that Gurudev has a three-piece suit (Brahma, Vishnu, and Shiva) and only one suitcase!

The miracle of the week is that our angry, reluctant, and uncooperative bus driver for the Tour de France became friendly and very patient with the Art of Living circus. Now he believes that Gurudev is more successful than President Chirac. By the end of the tour he was serving us so intently that he forgot his own baggage. This tour gave a big boost to the Art of Living in France, and the Advanced Course has now begun at an exotic Zen temple.

Many other courses are happening all over the world, including those in South Africa, India, and a course for cancer patients in New York City.

105. Every Stone is Precious

A sculptor for a temple uses all types of stones.

Certain stones he uses for the foundations. These never appear outside.

From certain stones which are good to carve, the sculptor makes the walls and pillars of the temple.

From other stones he makes the steps.

Certain stones become the tower of the temple.

Only those stones which are extremely suitable for carving will become installed as the Deity.

When a stone becomes part of the temple, it no longer remains a stone. It becomes sculpture, art – it becomes the Living Deity.

In the same way, many people come to the Master. According to the degree of their surrender, they are installed by the Master.

All are essential.

If there were no steps, how could a person reach the temple?

If there were no foundation, how could the temple be there at all?

What can a tower do without pillars?

For a sculptor, each stone is precious and valuable.

106. Sensitivity and Strength

Those who are sensitive often feel weak. Those who feel strong are often insensitive.

Some people are sensitive to themselves but insensitive to others. They often feel that others are the "bad guys."

Those who are sensitive to others but not to themselves often end up feeling Halies.

Some conclude it's better not to be sensitive, because sensitivity brings pain. They shut off. But mind you, if you are not sensitive, you will lose all the finer things in life, too – intuition, beauty, and ecstasy of love.

Insensitive people usually do not recognize their weakness. And those who are sensitive do not recognize that their sensitivity is their strength.

This path and this Knowledge make you strong and sensitive.

Sensitivity is intuition. Sensitivity is compassion. Sensitivity is love. Sensitivity is the real strength: calmness, endurance, silence, non-reactiveness, confidence, faith – and a smile.

Be both sensitive and strong.

✍ *News Flash:*

From India: The children at the ashram school have the best test scores in the entire district, and the enrolment has doubled to four hundred and fifty.

Exercise:

In your own Satsang group, see how both sensitivity and strength have grown.

107. THE PERSONAL AND THE IMPERSONAL

When you love something, it becomes alive. With love, the whole creation becomes personal.

For children, everything is personal. Children make each toy come alive. Even a tree has a face, even the sun laughs, and even a stone attracts reverence when it becomes personal.

Susannah: Yes! In a temple even a stone is elevated to the level of spirit.

Gurudev: In love, you raise even objects to life. If you remove love, even people become objects.

Violence is removing love. How could a person kill another? Only when they see them as an object, not as a person.

Dean: The military trains soldiers to see people as objects.

Gurudev: People who see God as impersonal do not progress. The impersonal cannot attract your love or reverence.

Dean and Susannah: That's why we need a Guru!

Chan: When we personalize something, we make it real. So then, what is reality?

Gurudev: YOU are the Reality. You are not the thoughts, you are not the emotions – nor the actions. You are not even a person...!

The Weekly Knowledge books for the first two years are being released by David and Gary. In a debate about whether or not to include the News Flashes, the majority voted in favor.

Every day Gurudev continues to be inundated with letters that report amazing healing experiences.

Art of Living Teachers in North America are now observing two weeks of intense Sadhana.

Advanced Courses are happening in Poona, Slovenia, Botswana and Montreal.

People are enjoying a totally different side of Gurudev this week with his fiery talks that have made everyone sit up and take notice.

Exercise:

What you now see as impersonal, see as personal. And when you feel any negative emotion towards anybody, see that person as impersonal – pretend that you are a robot.

108. The Golden Veil

Craving comes from encouraging the thought of pleasure.

Georgia: That's why we spend so much time in our minds!

Whether you encourage a worldly thought or a Divine thought, they both bring you pleasure. Worldly thoughts lead you from pleasure down to indulgence, disappointment and dejection. Divine thoughts take you from pleasure up to bliss, intelligence, and progress in life.

A worldly thought brings pleasure as memory, yet the actual experience of that pleasure may not be as great as the memory. A Divine thought materializes as Reality.

Question: What is a Divine thought?

Gurudev: "I am not the body; I am bliss, *satchitananda*; I am unbounded space; I am love; I am peace; I am light."

Question: What is a worldly thought?

Gurudev: It is a thought about money, sex, food, power, status and self-image.

Truth is hidden by the golden veil of the mundane. Pierce through this glittering sheath and know you are the Sun.

> *In the world, everybody is after GOLD; some are after GOOD; only a few are after GOD.*
> *Transcend GOLD, transcend the GOOD, and reach GOD.*

✍ **News Flash:**

As Advanced Course participants move from the small mind to the Big Mind, the children move super-sized frogs from the small pond to the big lake. Both frogs and humans are happy in their spacious abodes. The ART Excel* course is a big hit with the young people.

Vasishta makes regular visits each noontime, as we read his ancient teachings in the Yogavasishta.

---

*All-Round Training for Excellence – Sri Sri's program for youths.

109. WITH WHOM ARE YOU AT EASE?

With whom do you feel really comfortable and at ease?

With someone who does not question your love, someone who takes for granted that you love them. Isn't it?

When someone doubts your love and you constantly have to prove it, this becomes a heavy load on your head. They start questioning you and demanding explanations for all your actions. To explain everything you do is a burden. Your nature is to shed the burden because you don't feel comfortable. When you question the reason behind someone's action, you are asking for justice for yourself. You create a distance when you ask for justice. Your whole intention is to come close, but instead you create a distance.

You are the Eternal Witness. You are as much a witness to your own actions as you are to someone else's. When someone asks you for an explanation for your actions, they are speaking from doership and imposing that doership on you. This brings you discomfort.

Neither demand an explanation, nor give an explanation.

If somebody is just there with you, like a part of you, they don't question you. They are like your arm. There is a closeness and unity that goes beyond all demands and questions.

✎ *News Flash:*

The big frogs have hopped back to the small pond!

Pitaji* has arrived in North America for the first time and we are enjoying his stories from the Puranas.

A well-known acupuncturist from China, Dr. Sha, came to take Gurudev's blessings.

The question basket is bringing forth extraordinarily deep and beautiful knowledge.

**Gurudev's father*

110. LET LOVE BE

Let love be. Don't give love a name. When you give love a name, it becomes a relationship, and relationship restricts love.

There is love between you and me. Just let it be. If you name love as brother, sister, mother, father, Guru, you are making it into a relationship. Relationship restricts love.

What is your relationship to yourself? Are you your wife, brother, husband, Guru?

Let love be. Don't give it a name.

✍ *News Flash:*

At the end of the Montreal Advanced Course, Gurudev went for a swim. From underneath a waterfall, he beckoned, "If the course didn't help you become silent, then come sit under the waterfall."

The party moved on to the Agape Church in California where there was joyous singing of "Hoya Heya."

The phone is ringing off the hook as people from all over the world prepare to gather at Lake Tahoe for Guru Purnima.

111. MAKE EVERYTHING PERSONAL AND UNIVERSAL

'Manatha Sri Jaganatha'

'Madguru Sri Jagadguru'

'Madathma Sarva Bhutatma'

'Tasmai Sri Gurave Namah'

My Lord, Lord of Creation'

'My Master, Master of the Universe'

'My soul, soul of all living beings'

'To him, my gloriously radiant Master, I bow down'

Often what is universal we do not consider as personal, and what is personal we do not consider as belonging to everyone. What is "mine" and what is "universal" are found completely opposite. This causes greed, fear, jealousy, and lack of contentment.

On this *Guru Purnima*, wake up and realise that the Lord of the universe is very personal to you. Your personal Master is the Lord of the whole world. The Master is your very Self, and your Self is the very life in every being.

> *Make the universal personal and you become richer, wiser, stronger.*
> *Make the personal universal and you will find freedom,*
> *compassion, love.*

✐ News Flash:

The Guru Purnima explosion of bliss is still going on for six hundred course participants at Lake Tahoe and for devotees around the world. Gurudev continues to thrill us with singing, laughter, knowledge, and new meditations. Everyone and everything is sky high here – altitude, attitude, consciousness, cake, and water balloons. Many centres around the world celebrated Guru Purnima by starting Seva projects in their areas.

112. ON RESPECT

Question: What do you do if people don't respect you?

Gurudev: Thank them. They have given you freedom.

(Laughter and amazement)

When people respect you, they often take away your freedom. They expect you to smile at them, recognize them, behave in a certain way with them.

When people don't respect you, you are not obliged to answer their questions and you can drop all formalities. You can naturally smile or frown – you can be complete.

When people love and respect you, you are obliged to return their courtesies because you don't want to hurt them. When they don't respect or love you, they will not be hurt by your expressions. They set you free.

You often gain respect at the cost of your freedom. Wisdom is to put the freedom first and not bother about respect.

Question: Won't freedom bring arrogance?

Gurudev: True freedom is not an "I don't care" attitude; it is not stiff. It is an inner lightness with a genuine smile. When someone is stiff and arrogant, they are not free. Love blossoms only in freedom.

When there is love, respect simply follows you.

✍ *News Flash:*

Midway through the ART Excel Course at Lake Tahoe, the teenagers staged a "rebellion" against their course teachers. All problems dissolved as everyone sat in Gurudev's presence.

The American tour ended with an outdoor Satsang at Emerald Bay overlooking Lake Tahoe.

Now on to the European summer celebrations...

113. SACRIFICE

Sacrifice is letting go of something you are holding onto – something you are attached to which gives you pleasure – for something bigger that would bring good.

Sacrifice brings strength in life. Life without sacrifice is stagnant. Sacrifice gives you a quantum leap to a higher pedestal.

Often people think sacrifice makes life dull and joyless. In fact, it is sacrifice that makes life worth living. The amount of sacrifice in your life brings out your magnanimity and helps you move out of misery.

A life without sacrifice is worth nothing. Zeal, enthusiasm, strength and joy are all connected to sacrifice.

Question: Some people say, "I have sacrificed so much," and complain.

Gurudev: That is good. The thought of sacrifice has given them strength – to complain! This saves them from blaming themselves, otherwise they would be more depressed.

Sacrifice never goes unrewarded. There can be no love, no wisdom, no true joy without sacrifice.

Sacrifice makes you sacred.

Become sacred!

✍ *News Flash:*
A team of three Art of Living teachers went to facilitate the peace process between Armenia and Azerbaidzhan in Karabakh, conducting three courses for Army officials and another series for civilians. An article in the Moscow Times reported that the factions had agreed to stop fighting only two weeks after our team started work there.

From the German Academy: Imagine translations in ten languages simultaneously! Yet the course participants all speak one language – silence.

114. WINDOW SHUTTERS

To the degree that you are awake, everything around you brings knowledge. If you are not awake, even the most precious knowledge does not make any sense.

(Suddenly there was much noise from outside and Kiran went to shut the window.)

Awareness depends upon your ability to open and shut your windows. When there is a storm, you need to shut your windows – otherwise you will get wet. When it is hot and suffocating inside, you need to open your windows.

Your senses are like windows. When you are awake, you have the ability to open and shut your windows at will; then you are free.

If your windows cannot be shut or opened at will, you are bound. Attending to this is *Sadhana*, or spiritual practice.

✍ *News Flash:*

In Copenhagen, Gurudev was featured on "Good Morning Denmark."

Extensive media coverage of Gurudev's visit to Stockholm brought far more people for the evening program than could be accommodated. Gurudev first greeted those who could not get in –the last shall be first!

115. Raksha Bandhan

Today's full moon is dedicated to the seers – the *rishis*. It is called the *Raksha Bandhan*.

Bandhan means bondage; *raksha* means protection – a bondage that protects you.

Your bondage to the Knowledge, to the Master, to the Truth, to the Self – all saves you.

A rope can be tied to protect you or to strangle you. The small mind with mundane things can strangle you. The Big Mind, the Knowledge, saves you.

> *Your bondage to the Master, to the Truth, to the ancient Knowledge of the rishis — is your saviour.*

Raksha bandhan is the bondage that saves you. You are saved by your bondage to the *Satsang*.

Bondage is essential in life. Only let the bondage be to the Divine – in a life free from bondage.

Question: Who is an atheist?
Gurudev: One who has a concept of God.

Question: What is peace?
Gurudev: Undivided mind.

✒ *News Flash:*

Oslo, Norway: In the same hall where the Nobel Peace Prize is awarded, Gurudev's evening meditation brought priceless peace.

Arhus, Denmark: The Advanced Course hall was hot and humid and the speaker system did not work, but everyone dissolved into profound knowledge.

TV stations interviewed Gurudev, and several newspapers carried articles in Scandinavia.

116. TRUTH ONCE FOUND

The intellect divides and synthesizes.

Some creatures in the world synthesize and some creatures divide. But a human being has both abilities.

Ants synthesize; they build an anthill and collect things together. A beaver synthesizes by bringing wood together to build a dam. Birds also synthesize (such as the weaver birds).

Monkeys cannot synthesize, they divide everything. Give them a garland and they will tear it to pieces and throw it all over the place! A monkey can only divide and analyse.

A human being both divides (analyses) and synthesizes. The intellect analyses the relative world to find the Truth. And Truth once found synthesizes everything into One.

When the intellect becomes quiet, it brings out intelligence. Usually people think that gathering information makes one intelligent. This is not so. It is *samadhi* that brings intelligence.

An unintelligent man, though he may have all the information, cannot be creative. An intelligent man, even without much information, can be creative.

A sign of intelligence is to see the One in many and find the many in One.

There is an old Sanskrit proverb:

The first sign of intelligence is not to start anything.

The second sign of intelligence is: if you have started something, you have to continue it to the end.

So, if you have annoyed somebody, don't stop it in the middle, take him to the edge! (Laughter)

✍ *News Flash:*

Bellund, Denmark: One-hundred-fifty Advanced Course participants enjoyed good silence, meditations, and lively Satsangs with interesting questions and answers, tears of gratitude, and lots of laughter.

Gurudev's "secret" excursion to the beach had 50 devotees trailing behind. A driver became so blissed out in Gurudev's presence that he drove the fun-train off the normal beach track into main road traffic – to the amazement of the onlooking citizens.

With less than two weeks of preparation, the Hamburg devotees had a full hall for Gurudev's talk.

This week also included an Advanced Course in Kolkata, big Satsangs in Durban, Krishna's birthday celebrations at the German Academy, and Teacher Training at the Bangalore Ashram.

117. A Big Dilemma

If you have complete faith, there are no questions. If you have no faith, there is no point in asking, because how will you have faith in the answer?

Harish: What about the questions we ask you with complete faith?

Gurudev: If you have faith in God, when you know somebody is taking care of you, then what is the need to ask any question? If you have taken the Karnataka Express to Bangalore, is there a need to ask at every station, "Where is the train going?"

And when you have someone who is looking after your desires, then why go to an astrologer?

Rajesh: What about blind faith?

Gurudev: Faith is faith... it cannot be blind. What you call blind is not faith – at least not yours!

Blindness and faith cannot meet. It is when you lose faith that you become blind.

✍ *News Flash:*

The swamis from Adichunchunagiri Math arrived at our German Academy with a grand Satsang on Friday night and a picnic to the nearby waterfall on Sunday.

Mumbai: Four thousand people filled a beautiful hall for a fabulous Satsang and meditation led by Gurudev. The sound system had the hiccups (!), but miraculously delivered crystal clear sound whenever Gurudev spoke.

This Weekly Knowledge was written on the way to a spontaneous Satsang of 600 people, after which Gurudev returned to Bangalore.

118. How to Get Centred

Shift your awareness from the experience to the experiencer. All experiences are on the circumference; they keep on changing. The unchanging experiencer is at the centre. Again and again, come back to the experiencer.

If you are frustrated, instead of spending all your time on the experience of frustration, ask, "Who is frustrated?"

If you are unhappy, ask, "Who is unhappy?"

If you think you know something, ask, "Who knows?"

(Laughter)

If you think you are enlightened, ask, "Who is it that is enlightened?"

If you think you are ignorant, ask, "Who is ignorant?"

If you think poor me, ask, "Who is poor me?"

If you think you are highly devoted, ask, "Who is it that is devoted?"

Shed all your faces and face the I. Then you have truly come to me!

✍ *News Flash:*

In Pune, the Chief Minister of Maharashtra conferred the Guru Mahatmya Award upon Gurudev for outstanding contribution to humanity.

119. THE FIVE INSIGHTS

Love is your nature.

When love finds an expression, you often get caught up in the object. Your sight is caught outside. To return back to your nature, you need insight.

Pain is the first insight. It takes you away from the object and turns you towards your body and mind.

Energy is the second insight. A bolt of energy brings you back to your Self.

Divine love is the third insight. A glimpse makes you so complete and overrules all relative pleasures.

Ecstasy is the fourth insight. An elevation of consciousness with partial awareness of physical reality is ecstasy.

Non-dual awareness is the fifth insight, the realisation that all is made up of One and only One.

> *When love glows, It is bliss.*
> *When love flows, It is compassion.*
> *When love blows, it is anger.*
> *When love ferments, it is jealousy.*
> *When love is all "no's," it is hatred.*
> *When love acts, it is perfection.*
> *When love knows, it is ME!*

✍ *News Flash:*

Satsang groups are launching service projects, including free medical aid, sanitation, and housing for the poor, and blood donation camps. Every Satsang group is asked to take up Seva projects, keeping aside personal likes and dislikes.

120. Five Signs of the Satguru*

In the presence of the *Satguru*:

1. Knowledge flourishes

2. Sorrow diminishes

3. Joy wells up without any reason

4. Lack diminishes; abundance dawns

5. All talents manifest

To the degree you feel connected to the Master, these qualities manifest in your life.

Sit with your eyes closed and feel your connection with the Master.

✍ *News Flash:*

Renowned saints from all over India are visiting the Ashram. A series of Advanced Courses ended in tears of joy, followed by a brief respite for the Ashram volunteers.

Gurudev was a guest of honour with 15,000 people at the Adichunchunagiri ashram.

Preparations have begun for Navaratri (Nine Nights of Mother Divine).

Exercises for this week:

1. Make a knowledge sheet.

2. Make a commitment for a Seva project. The more you give, the more strength will be given to you.

3. Sit with your eyes closed for one minute and surrender your name. How do you feel... ? Dissolving the name is awareness; dissolving the form is meditation. The world is name and form; bliss transcends name and form.

*Master of Truth, the One who leads you all the way to Enlightenment.

October 1, 1997
Bangalore Ashram, India

121. SIX SIGNS OF A SEEKER

1. An acknowledgement that one knows very little
Many people think they know – without knowing. They get stuck in their limited knowledge. They never learn. The first thing a seeker knows is that he knows very little.

2. A willingness to learn
Many people acknowledge that they do not know, but they are not ready to learn.

3. Non-judgmental and open-minded
Some people would like to learn, but their close-minded and judgmental attitudes do not allow them.

4. A total, one-pointed commitment to the Path
Some people are open-minded, but they lack commitment and one-pointedness. They keep shopping here and there and never progress on one path.

5. Always puts truth and service before pleasure
Sometimes even committed and one-pointed people stray from the path in pursuit of momentary pleasures.

6. Patience and perseverance
Some people are committed, one-pointed, and are not swayed by pleasures, but if they lack patience and perseverance, they become restless and dejected.

✍ *News Flash:*

The festival of Navaratri has begun. Yagyas are being conducted during these nine days for the peace, prosperity, health, and happiness of all devotees (present and future!). More about yagyas next week.

Swami Pragyanandji, the renowned saint, is at the Ashram giving discourses on the Shrimad Bhagavatam, as Gurudev is in silence.

122. YAGYAS

Yagyas are the ancient method of enriching the subtle and to purify individual and collective consciousness.

Yagyas have three aspects:

1. *Devi Puja*: Honouring the Divine in all forms.

2. *Sangatikarana*: Hastening the process of evolution by unifying all the elements and people in creation.

3. *Dana*: Sharing with others; giving freely what one has been blessed with.

✍ *News Flash:*

The depth of Gurudev's silence contrasted sharply with the noisy, boisterous celebration. Activities started early in the morning and finished late at night. The meditation hall became a feast for the senses with Vedic chanting, the beat of drums, loud clarinets, the visiting swamis, and the usual ecstatic bhajans. The Ashram was fully lit and so were the faces. The poor from seven villages received new clothes and gifts; for many it was their first gift of new garments in their life and there was such gratitude. While the rich fasted and prayed, the poor feasted in this genuine celebration.

123. GOD AS A CHILD

You have always thought of God as a father, up in the heavens somewhere. But can you see God as a child?

When you think of God as a father, you will want to demand and take from Him. But when you see God as a child, you have no demands.

God is the very core of your existence. You are pregnant with God. You have to take care of your pregnancy and deliver this Child into the world. Most people do not deliver. Whosoever delivers can also grant wishes.

God is your child who clings onto you like a baby until you grow old and die. This Child clings onto the devotee, crying for nourishment. *Sadhana, Satsang,* and *Seva* are the nourishment.

Belma: You cannot pray to a child; you can only pray to your father.
Gurudev: Why do you want to pray? What do you want to ask? A good father already knows what to give.

Belma: But what about surrender?
Gurudev: Your surrender to a child is more authentic because there is no demand.

> *Take care of your God! Atheists lurk around the corner! Doubts, disbelief, and ignorance are the atheists in your mind—so better take care!*

✍ News Flash:

Like a bolt of lightning, the climax of the Navaratri celebrations came at high voltage. Even the learned pundits were visibly moved. At the grand finale, the Ashram reverberated with enormous energy, leaving everyone spellbound.

Devotees accompanied Gurudev on a visit to a village an hour away where we are providing shelter and self-employment training to the neediest of the women.

An Advanced Course has begun at the Ashram. This weekend Gurudev will tour the south, where a Satsang will be held in his honour in Shimoga – the town where Gurudev conducted his first course fifteen years ago.

124. FEEL BLESSED

Break through all the barriers and feel you are blessed. This is the one and only step you have to take – the rest will all happen.

This deep sense of feeling I am blessed can help you overcome all obstacles in life. You receive courage and confidence and you will open up for grace to pour in.

Once you realise you are blessed, then:

- All complaints disappear

- All grumbling disappear

- All insecurities disappear

- A sense of feeling unloved disappears

- Wanting love disappears

If you don't realise you are blessed, then doership begins.

To make a difference in your life, feel you are blessed. Especially for those on this path of Knowledge, there is every reason for you to feel blessed.

Feel you are blessed.
This is the first step towards the Self.

✍ *News Flash:*

Thousands thronged two Satsangs in Coimbatore to glimpse Gurudev. What a treat to experience 1800 people doing pranayama and Kriya together!

On the way to Shimoga, Gurudev visited the Temple of Mother Divine and was received with full honour. The Master arrived at Shimoga for a touching reunion with longtime devotees and a grand Satsang. Saints from various ashrams greeted Gurudev and all the devotees with warmth and enthusiasm. The entire village came out dancing to receive the Master with a 20-foot electric chariot strung with thousands of lights. (Gurudev looked embarrassed!)

125. DIWALI

Time and space are infinite. Grains of sand are countless. Atoms in the universe are innumerable. So also are the stars, the galaxies.

The same is with life on this planet. There is neither a beginning nor an end, because all is spherical. A sphere has no beginning and no end, no goal or direction.

Truth has no direction, no goal. Truth itself is the goal, and Truth is infinite.

Feeling and experiencing infinity within this finite body, living timelessness within the time span of life, uncovering bliss within the misery – this is what you are here for.

When this wisdom dawns, it gives rise to celebration. However, in celebration you may lose your focus or awareness. The ancient *rishis* knew this, so to maintain awareness amidst the gaiety of celebration, they brought sacredness and *puja* to every event.

Today is *Diwali*, the Festival of Lights. The streets and buildings are lit up with colourful lights.

The four aspects of *Diwali* are:

1. Lights – Symbolizing the spreading of Knowledge.

2. Firecrackers – Watching the firecrackers gives a relief to the explosive tendencies inside. When the explosion happens outside, the explosion inside is diffused.

3. Gifts and sweets – Sharing gifts and distributing sweets dispels bitterness and renews friendships.

4. Abundance – Feeling a sense of abundance brings awareness and gratefulness for what one has.

> *Celebrate the Knowledge and feel the abundance. Those who have will be given more!*

✍ **News Flash:**

The Ashram hosted a Family Day for local course graduates while guests were introduced to the Knowledge. A Maha-Kriya for 2000 and lunch for 4000 had volunteers jumping and dancing by the end of the day.

After Satsang in Pune, crowds crushed onto the stage for darshan with Gurudev as volunteers barely managed the enthusiastic mob. Thousands of pairs of neatly packaged and numbered shoes left at the entryway were trampled by the stampede that followed. Many people lost their shoes but were too happy to care.

Next morning, despite a peak-season Diwali business day, 1,800 course graduates joined Gurudev for Satsang.

Sixty blind women began a week-long residence course at the Bangalore Ashram.

126. LOVE IS YOUR VERY EXISTENCE

Suppose someone shows you a lot of love. What do you do?

1.   You do not know how to respond.

2.   You feel obliged and bound.

3.   You shrink or shy away.

4.   You feel foolish and awkward.

5.   You try to reciprocate even though it is not genuine.

6.   You doubt the love expressed or your worthiness.

7.   You become afraid of losing respect, because respect maintains a distance and love does not allow distance.

8.   Your ego hardens and does not allow you to receive and reciprocate.

9.   Anything else_____(fill in the blank)

The ability to receive love comes with the ability to give love. The more you are centred and by experience, know that you are love, the more you will feel at home with any amount of love that is expressed in any manner. Deep inside, you will know:

> *Love is not an emotion!*
> *Love is your very existence!*

✍ *News Flash:*

Diwali celebrations continue with candlelight Satsangs in the Valley of the Saints. Advanced Course participants broke all boundaries of course structure as 200 people dropped in unannounced! Thanks to the volunteers, smiles prevailed on all 200 faces. Course participants also cleaned up tons of garbage from the banks of the Ganges.

Indian teachers and organisers have resolved to start the following Sri Sri Seva Projects, and all Satsang groups are invited to join:

1. Donate a minimum of 2% of personal income towards rural development and hygiene.

2. Contact supermarkets/stores and encourage them to use paper or cloth bags instead of plastic.

November 13, 1997
Jaipur, India

127. YOUR EXPRESSIONS OF LOVE

You feel a lot of love for someone and they do not take it. What do you do?

- Get frustrated

- Turn the love into hatred and wish for revenge

- Again and again remind them how much you love them and how little they love you

- Become fussy and cranky

- Throw tantrums

- Feel humiliated and try to protect your respect

- Resolve never to love again

- Feel hurt and mistreated

- Try to be aloof and indifferent

... and you have seen that none of these work! They only make it worse.

What is the way out of this? How can you maintain your lovingness?

- Have patience.

- Be centred and limit your expression of love. Sometimes over expression of love puts people off.

- Change your expression of love.

- Take it for granted that they love you and accept their style of expression. Like a mother with three kids – one child talks, one child does not talk, one child throws tantrums – her love for each child is constant regardless of their behaviour.

- Genuinely acknowledge their love for you. This will turn your demand into gratefulness, and the more you are grateful in life, the more love comes your way.

- Know that hurt is part of love and take responsibility for it.

- Realise that when you move away from your centre, you will feel miserable and that the nature of worldliness is misery.

✒ *News Flash:*

On the Rishikesh course, deafening joy chased the silence into the mountains.

In New Delhi, a packed audience welcomed Gurudev to Siri Fort, the country's most prestigious auditorium.

Devotees in the Pink City of Jaipur crowned Gurudev with a turban and celebrated his visit in warm, friendly, and colourful Rajasthani style.

128. EGO

When is there ego?

1. When you don't get attention.
2. When you seem to be losing attention.
3. When you get attention. (Laughter)

Ego causes heaviness, discomfort, fear, anxiety. Ego doesn't let love flow.

Ego is separateness, non-belongingness, wanting to prove and to possess.

Ego can be transcended by knowing the Truth, by inquiring "Who am I?"

Often you feel contempt or jealousy towards someone with ego. Instead you should have compassion.

Ego has a positive aspect: ego drives one to do work. A person can do a job out of joy, compassion, or out of ego. Most of the work in the society is for boosting the ego. In *Satsang*, work is done out of love.

> *When you wake up and see that there is nothing to be proved and nothing to possess, ego dissolves.*

✍ *News Flash:*

The Satsang tour continued on to Hyderabad, where despite a cyclone warning, swarms of people came to be blessed by the Master and were surprised to hear him speaking chaste Telugu. Many healing experiences were shared. Gurudev's talk to doctors on the next day was simply stunning and, as with all his best talks, it was not recorded!

Fireworks and exuberant devotees welcomed Gurudev back to Bangalore. An Advanced Course is in progress and preparations are on for a big public Satsang in Bangalore on the twenty third.

129. MEMORY

Memory makes you miserable or wise.

Memory of experiences and events in the ever-changing world – however good or bad – constrict the vastness of the Self. They bind you.

Memory of your nature – the non-changing Self – expands and elevates awareness. This liberates you. You are what you are because of your memory. If you are ignorant, it is because of your memory. If you are enlightened, it is because of your memory.

Forgetfulness of the Infinite is misery. Forgetfulness of the trivial is ecstasy.

Question: How do we get rid of unpleasant memories and limitations?

Gurudev:

- Know the impermanent nature of the world and events.
- Realise that past events do not exist in the present.
- Accept the past and drop it.
- Be dispassionate and centred.
- Memory of the Self is gained in the company and service of the Enlightened.
- So Hum ! Increase *prana.*
- So what?!!
- And If none of this works – then go to the moon!!!

✍ *News Flash:*

Gurudev was the chief guest of a congregation of the Lions Clubs of Karnataka, attended by many dignitaries, where a number of service projects were initiated.

A massive rally was organised for environmental awareness in Bangalore, followed by a huge Satsang where Gurudev had everyone mesmerized as usual.

Gurudev escaped for a short trip to Delhi, leaving people at the Ashram surprised.

Baba Avtar Hari Maharaj, a renowned saint from Hardwar, is visiting the Ashram.

December 3, 1997
Calicut, India

130. INTELLECT

The intellect harbours inhibitions, likes and dislikes, approvals and disapprovals. The intellect also harbours wisdom, which brings forth intuition.

Question: Is intuition beyond intellect?

Gurudev: Yes, but it shines through the intellect.

Question: Are emotions and intellect contradictory?

Gurudev: They can be contradictory.

Question: When there is a conflict, which is better?

Gurudev: In conflict, there is no better conflict!

The pure intellect is not caught up in the emotional turbulence of the mind. The pure intellect rises beyond conflicts.

Usually the intellect gets coloured by emotions and becomes impure, like muddy water. Then it is unable to reflect the Self. A pure intellect, still and serene, reflects the Self.

Question: Is intellect affected by *karma*?

Gurudev: Karma does not afflict the pure intellect. Liberation purifies the intellect. The Sanskrit word for intellect is *buddhi*; one who is liberated is a *buddha*.

✍ *News Flash:*

Sri Avtar Hari blessed the Ashram and stayed with Gurudev for three days.

People from Russia, Poland, China, and other countries went on a trip to Kerala with Gurudev. Six thousand people gathered at the first stop at Thiruvananthapuram, the state capital.

At Cochin, the open ground by the seaside was fabulously decorated. Caparisoned elephants in traditional style, angels, flowers, and lamps accorded a warm welcome. The grounds packed in ten thousand people – imagine how much time it took for the darshan line!

In Thrissur, the cultural capital of Kerala, five thousand gathered for a grand Satsang at an indoor stadium. The teamwork at Thrissur was a unique example for all; this time around, the volunteers felt no pressure – they did less and accomplished more.

With not space even for an ant to crawl at the biggest auditorium in Calicut, many had to be content watching the Satsang on the closed circuit television outside.

Many healing experiences were reported during the Satsangs.

Gurudev is back at the Bangalore Ashram for another fortnight.

131. TIME AND MIND

When you are happy, the mind expands; then time appears too short.
When you are unhappy, the mind contracts; then time appears too long.

When the mind has equanimity, you transcend time.

To escape from time, many resort to alcohol, sleep, etc., but when the mind is dull or unconscious, it is unable to experience the Self.

Samadhi (no-mindedness, timelessness) is the real peace. A few moments of *samadhi* gives the mind a lot of energy. This is the greatest healer.

A thought is nothing but a ripple in this moment of time. This moment also has a mind of its own – a Big Mind which has infinite organizing power.

Before you fall into slumber and as soon as you wake up from sleep, in the moments of twilight of consciousness, experience this timelessness beyond mind!

✍ *News Flash:*

In Apple Valley, California, 80 homeless children received gifts at a special Christmas party.

In the slums in Mumbai, India, Satsangs and Seva projects have begun.

A blood donation camp was organised in Surat.

Some people in the surrounding villages of the Ashram were given free housing.

At Satsang, someone suggested that we have some deer, peacocks, swans, and doves at the Ashram. Gurudev promptly answered, "You are all dear to me! You are peacocks because you dance! Like swans you have vivek – the power of discrimination – and like doves you carry the message of peace to the world!"

132. FACES OF INFINITY

You have many faces, only you don't face them. When you come face to face with your faces, then conflicts, confusion, and chaos arise in you.

From time to time, in different phases, different faces appear. As you come close to your Being, all faces melt and leave you as the Space that you are.

At the gross level, you identify yourself as somebody.

As you move to more subtle levels, you may identify yourself as some energy, or an incarnation of some angel, saint, or prophet.

When you go beyond even this identity, you are whole, holy, the *Brahman – Purna Brahman Narayana.*

✍ News Flash:

The Ashram bid farewell to the Russians, but Southeast Asians, Southern Africans, Malaysians, and a LOT of Indians from all directions occupy every available space.

Amidst the hectic activity at the Ashram, there is deep silence and serenity. The Advanced Course, TTC, Sahaj Samadhi, Basic Course, and ART Excel are all in full swing.

133. CELEBRATION AND THE CHRISTMAS TREE

Human life is a combination of body (matter) and spirit (vibration). Isn't it?

Joy is forgetting that you are matter and becoming an intense vibration.

Carnal instincts also make you feel intense vibrations momentarily, and that's how they give a glimpse of joy. But the thing is, this joy is short-lived and it makes you dense later on.

Pleasure that comes from *Satsang* is of a higher nature. Mantras and singing create vibrations in the spirit. That's why when you sing, the ecstasy stays for a long time.

Pleasure from the gross is short-lived, tiring and binding. Pleasure in the subtle is long lasting, energizing, refreshing, and freeing.

When you know you are electricity (vibration/energy), then craving, greed, lust, and anger disappear. Then you become a true celebration.

Message for Christmas:

You are the Christmas tree that points upwards with branches on all sides. At the time of year when other trees are barren, you are green with many gifts to offer.

You bear gifts and lights — not for yourself, but for others. Remember that all the gifts you are carrying in your life are for others. Anyone who comes to you, offer them your gifts.

There were lots of presents around Gurudev's couch. John asked, "Are you going to open the gifts?" Gurudev winked, pointed at the people and replied, "I am always opening the gifts."

Your life is a gift. And you have come to unwrap this gift. In the process of unwrapping, remember to also save the wrapping papers. Your whole environment, situations, circumstances, and body are the wrapping papers.

Often when we unwrap, we tear the wrapping papers. At times we are in such a hurry that we even destroy the gifts. With patience and endurance, open your gifts – and save the wrappers!

✍ News Flash:

As hectic activities continued in the Bangalore Ashram, Gurudev moved on to Chennai for a huge Satsang. Then he went to Delhi where he met with the Vice President of India. An unscheduled Satsang of 1,200 devotees gathered just by word of mouth! That same night Gurudev left for Germany.

Every corridor and corner of the German Academy wears a festive look. Smiles from people of 18 countries are the moving decorations. The Seva team transformed the Academy into a warm and cozy home.

Many of the nicely wrapped gift boxes of various sizes given to Gurudev were found to be hollow and empty!

134. A Wise Person is Happy Even in Bad Times

People who serve will have good times even in bad times.

When there is famine or war, Red Cross people will be fine because they are serving. The more relief they can bring to others, the happier they feel. On the other hand, selfish people who just want to enjoy for themselves will be miserable even in good times.

In good times, people often lose their happiness over some small thing. Hosts often do not enjoy their parties because some little thing is missing, they forgot to invite somebody, somebody did not come, or some little thing went wrong. A wise person is happy even in bad times. A stupid person is unhappy even in good times.

YOU make the time good or bad. People usually blame the bad time and then wait for a good time. But even if an astrologer says you are in a hopeless time, you can make it good!

> *Like weather, time has its own impact on you. Your Satsangs and Sadhana are your shield, your protection!*

Realise that you are more than time and that you can move through time with your timeless connection to the Divine. Don't feel shy to speak about human and spiritual values. The time has come now to call the whole world!

The ALL is calling,

The ball is rolling!

Time is milling,

The soul is willing...

A new New Year's greeting: BE EVER NEW, HAPPY YOU!

✍ *News Flash:*

The first Advanced Course has finished in Germany and the second one has begun. Reports of service activities have come from various parts of the world.

January 7, 1998
Milano, Italy

135. You are Pure Electricity

Desires for sensory pleasure are electric in nature; they get neutralized as they move toward the objects of the senses.

If by your skill you could move desires within you – toward the centre of your existence – another dimension of everlasting pleasure, thrill, bliss, and undying love will all be yours.

Lust, greed, and jealousy are powerful because they are nothing but energy – and you are the source of it, pure electricity. Dedication and devotion keep your electricity pure and move you upward. When you realise you yourself are the electricity of pleasure, your cravings subside and serenity dawns. Also, remembering that you will die makes you alive now, free from cravings and aversions.

The wise ones are always careful not to get their minds entangled and dizzy.

✍ *News Flash:*

People from 22 countries took part in the Advanced Course in Germany thanks to the simultaneous translation system. Gurudev spoke on spiritual dimensions the entire week.

After a fantastic talk at a packed Milano auditorium, everyone held a baccara rose in their hand as they went out with a smile.

Gurudev is off to Slovenia and Croatia for a two-day visit. Amma* turns 70 this week; her birthday will be celebrated in Bangalore on the twelfth with a distribution of blankets and food to the poor.

*Gurudev's mother

136. POLITICS

Don't let politics sway you away from the Path. If you are afraid of politics, you cannot be successful in the spiritual realm.

You have to cross the barricade of politics. It is the test of your strength, your commitment, and your focus. You cannot avoid politics, but whether or not to harbour politics in your mind is your choice.

There were politics among the twelve apostles and also around Buddha. *Krishna* was in politics from head to toe. And you say you don't want politics? The greater your aversion, the more you harbour in your consciousness.

When you recognize politics in any group or *Satsang*, that is a blessing, an opportunity for you to be centred and go inward. You will not blame the group, run away from people, or chicken out, and you will enhance your skill to act while being unattached.

Advantages of politics:

- Brings up diversity in people

- Lets you see different viewpoints, ways, and tendencies

- Enhances your skill to communicate and act

- Brings centeredness and dispassion

- Shakes you up and makes you apply the Knowledge

- Enhances your capacity to accept and tolerate

- Makes you realise that this whole life is a game

The strong will smile through politics while the weak will lament.

Cross the threshold of politics and come to the Divine.

✍ News Flash:

Gurudev arrived in time to address the inter-religious conference organised by the parliamentarians of Croatia, followed by Satsang at the beautiful Sheraton Hotel, filled to capacity. Gurudev met with many dignitaries, and TV people from Croatia filmed a documentary.

In Trinidad, the Prime Minister and two other cabinet ministers met with Gurudev, expressing their gratitude for our work, and offering their wholehearted support. One of the ministers recalled Gurudev's comment last year that the Prime Minister would become spiritual, which he did.

Now the telephones in serene Surinam are ringing off the hook! More than 300 people have already registered for the Basic Course and they haven't even met Gurudev yet. The receptionist, the watchman, even the housekeepers are all busy doing one job: enrolling the people!

137. TOLERANCE AND ACCEPTANCE ARE NOT VIRTUES

Many people think tolerance is a virtue.

Tolerance is a negative term. Tolerance indicates a deep sense of dislike. If you like something, there is no question about whether you tolerate it.

When you are tolerating something, it means you are temporarily putting up with it. Tolerance is a potential volcano. If you are tolerating, it means you are still holding on to something.

At any time tolerance can turn into hatred. Tolerance indicates a sense of separateness, small mindedness, limited awareness.

Acceptance is also negative. You accept only that which is not lovable.

Question: Do you need self-assurance to love people?

Gurudev: Only the Self is always assuring – nothing else! This is our company–the Self-Assurance Company.

Question: Aren't we supposed to accept people as they are?

Gurudev: If you don't love them, then you will have to accept them.

These words tolerance and acceptance are thought to be positive; I say they are not. Tolerance and acceptance come with judgment and separation.

> *Don't accept people as they are or tolerate them. Just love them as they are.*

✍ News Flash:

From Surinam, the entourage moved on to Bogota, the capital of Columbia. After an interview for national television, the host of the show said she has to change her whole series, which was entitled "Tolerance."

Bewildered organisers were unprepared for the huge crowds at the evening talk.

In Panama, a minute-by-minute program was put together by Martine and her team. The celebration moved on to Costa Rica for a day, where, in contrast, the hall had enough space for three seats per person. Satsangs were just a dozen devotees, and Gurudev fed them all.

In Florida, Gurudev commented from the beautiful 28th floor accomodations, "I am staying in the second best place, the first being my Self!" Ronnie Newman organised a fabulous event sponsored by the Crime Prevention Unit of Nova Southeastern University, attended by scientists, researchers, therapists, and justice personnel.

138. FALSE SECURITY

False security does not allow your faith to grow. Faith grows only when you have dropped your securities.

False security is keeping faith where it doesn't belong. It is the illusion of security in having a job, a house, friends.

Even if you have all the material securities, without faith you will still reel in fear. When you buffer your life with securities, you keep faith away.

Faith is your greatest security. Faith brings perfection in you.

Keep money in the bank or in the pocket, not in the mind. Keep the house where it belongs, not in the mind. Keep friends and family where they belong, not in the mind. You have to let go of all possessions in the mind.

> *Your body belongs to the world.*
> *Your spirit belongs to the Divine.*
> *The Divine is your only security.*

Faith is realizing that you always get what you need. Faith is giving the Divine a chance to act.

✍ *News Flash:*

In the car to Verna's house after Satsang, Kumi said, "Lets take the long way home!" Gurudev replied, "I am making the ride home short, yet you want to take a long ride."

Gurudev gave a brilliant talk to over 200 people at the "World's Great Religions and Their Transformation in the 21st Century" symposium at the University of California, Los Angeles.

The Santa Monica Satsangs were filled with laughter, brilliant questions, and even more brilliant answers. Divya's voice lifted everyone's hearts.

One evening Scott invited over 80 people to come for the first time to hear Gurudev speak, but Gurudev did not say a word. Instead, he gave the entire talk in his own version of sign language. It was hilarious. Deaf people who were present shed tears at Gurudev's intuitive understanding of sign language.

David said, "Gurudev, you travel and work so much - 20 countries in one month! Do you ever take a vacation?" Gurudev said, "In between lifetimes!"

139. ORGANISATION AND DEVOTION

Organisation is control. Devotion is chaos! Organisation needs attention to details, a material awareness; organisation is being worldly. Devotion is getting lost, forgetting the world, being in ecstasy.

These are opposite in nature. They don't go together, yet they cannot be apart or exist without the other.

No organisation can arise without devotion. When you have so much devotion, you want to organise. Devotion brings faith, compassion, responsibility, and a desire to share knowledge, wisdom, and love. Then organisation happens. Organisation exists through devotion.

If you are devoted, you won't just sit. The nature of devotion is to give. If you think you are devoted and you are not caring for the world, then you are merely selfish. Real devotion means being one with the Divine, and the Divine cares for the world.

Often you lose devotion in organizing. And in the name of devotion you create chaos or disregard the organisation.

You have to be a saint to be in devotion AND in an organisation. With both, you are on the mark.

So... get lost – and be guided!

✍ **News Flash:**

Gurudev received a royal Hawaiian welcome from many new devotees when he arrived on the island of Oahu. John Osborne spoke on a local TV health show, and the largest course ever on Oahu was taught in Sir Sir's presence.

Satsangs continue on the Garden Island of Kauai, where Gurudev was ready for an adventure in the huge waves - but found himself surrounded by devotees at a safe beach instead.

140. When a Mistake is Not a Mistake

Blessed are those who don't see a mistake as a mistake... !!!

When you make a new mistake, it is not a mistake – you have learned a valuable lesson. But when you keep doing the same mistake over and over, it is a BIG mistake.

A mistake is something that brings misery to you in the long run, so why would someone knowingly commit a mistake? A "mistake" simply means you have "missed taking" a lesson that has come your way. Do not lament over your mistake. Just take the lesson from it.

It is hard not to see your own mistake. Outwardly you may justify yourself or plead innocence to someone else, but a mistake pricks your conscience.

Do not justify yourself. Instead, feel the prick of the mistake. That prick takes you out of the mistake.

When you point out a mistake to someone, do you see him as separate from you, or do you make him feel a part of you? Do your words make him more stressed, or do they create more awareness in that person?

Often you do not point out a mistake when it is required. This is also a mistake. Pointing out a mistake without consideration to time and place is also a mistake.

The fool keeps making the same mistakes again and again and never learns from them. Wise is the one who learns from his own mistakes. Wisest is the one who learns from others' mistakes!

> *You will not be judged by your mistakes, but by your virtues.*
> *Mistakes are of the earth. Virtues are of the Divine.*

✒ **News Flash:**

In Bali, we visited the ancient temple of Besaki, where, as in the old days, there is only the empty seat of the deity, signifying the divine beyond form.

The Indonesian Director of Religious Affairs and a member of the Ministry of Education welcomed Gurudev at the opening of our Jakarta Ashram.

Devotees from Jakarta have adopted an orphanage in Puncak. The director of the orphanage said that while other people bring money, clothes, and toys, our group supplied the missing nutrient the children need the most: love! The children also received packages of school supplies and goodies. We all laughed, sang, and danced as the director cried tears of gratitude.

The entourage moved to Singapore where more than 1000 people welcomed Gurudev at the packed SLF Auditorium. The evening commenced with a traditional Chinese lion dance. Later, Gurudev gave practical points on "Awakening the Beauty Within You".

141. RESPECT

When someone respects you, it is not because you possess some virtues; it is because of their greatness.

If you say God is great, it means YOU are great. God is already great–your saying so doesn't affect God.

When you respect someone, it shows your own magnanimity. However many people you don't respect in the world, that much less is your wealth. If you respect everyone, that much more is your value. Wise is the one who respect everyone.

Question: But *Gurudev*, you can't respect a terrorist!

Gurudev: You have to respect a terrorist, too, because he shows you the right way at his own cost.

Respect is a quality of refined consciousness. Respect for the Self is faith; faith is being open.

If you are open, you are close to me !
If you are close to me, you cannot but open up !

✍ **News Flash:**

Bhanu greeted the entourage with smiles and roses as we arrived in India at 1:30 AM. Touring through all the Ashram facilities, Gurudev personally saw to each one's comfort and accommodations until well past dawn.

The second symposium of the International Association for Human Values inspired people from 30 countries. Messages arrived from world leaders expressing their support and gratitude. A lecture on Ayurveda and talks by eminent spiritual leaders rounded out the program.

142. SHIVA AND VASHI

Often people think they are in control of their life, their situation, their world.

Control is an illusion.

The whole world moves according to the laws of Nature in an auspicious rhythm of innocence, intelligence, and divinity. That is *Shiva*.

Shiva is the eternal state of Being, the One without a second, the harmonious innocence that knows no control.

Control is *Vashi – Shiva* reversed. *Vashi* is of the mind. *Vashi* is weakness. *Vashi* is doing something by exerting unnatural pressure.

Vashi requires two, and duality is the cause of fear. *Shiva*, that harmonious innocence, dissolves duality.

> *Shiva means wholeness of the moment. When there is no regret of past, no want of future, the moment is whole and compete. Time stops, mind stops.*

✍ *News Flash:*

The International Association for Human Values conference continues.

The Ayurvedic Clinic is dispensing knowledge and remedies day and night.

In Gurudev's presence, live music performances under Sumeru's starry canopy enchanted us with recitals for sitar, bamboo flute, and Indian classical dance.

A number of devotees took a side trip to Mysore to visit the palace, Brindavan Gardens, the Mother Divine temple, and a school for the blind.

Last night's dinner featured a smorgasbord of Indian cuisine from around the country.

Today is Shivaratri. Devotees are flocking to the Ashram to witness the yagyas and receive the Master's darshan.

143. FORMALITY AND CORDIALITY

You cannot eliminate formality in society. It has its place. Formality improves communication. Yet communication is only necessary when there are two. Formality maintains duality.

Cordiality improves communion – oneness. Without cordiality, formality can be hypocritical and may appear uncaring.

Organisational structures are based on formality. An organisation cannot begin and orderliness cannot prevail if formalities are abandoned. All your plans of action are measured steps of formality.

Cordiality is one's nature, the core of one's existence; formality is the outer shell. When the outer shell is thin, like the shade of a lamp, the inner light can shine forth. But if the shade is too opaque, you cannot see the light.

Love and knowledge are rooted in cordiality. For these to blossom, you need an informal, cordial environment.

Devotion is informal... and totally chaotic. So, strike a balance between cordial formality and formal cordiality!

✍ *News Flash:*

Two planeloads of devotees flew en-masse to Ahmedabad where their hosts greeted them with singing and dancing at the airport, followed by dinner in a traditional Indian village setting and a riotous Satsang. The next morning, devotees joined in a Maha Kriya of more than 3000, personally led by Gurudev. Many toured Mahatma Gandhi's ashram, and the unforgettable day ended with a Maha Satsang of over 20,000. Darshan alone took four hours!

The group travelled north to new course facilities at an ashram in Rishikesh. At sunset, Gurudev led a dip in the Ganges. Devotees launched floating ghee lamps from the river banks to honour the auspicious occasion. The program continues in silence with visiting saints, profoundly deep meditations, and new levels of knowledge and experience.

144. You are the Tenth

Ten people were walking on foot from one village to another. On the way, they had to cross a river. Reaching the other shore, they wanted to be sure all had crossed safely. Each one counted only nine and left himself out. They were very distraught and began to cry for the loss of the tenth.

A wise man came along and asked them "Oh, my dear friends, why are you crying?"

"We were ten but now we are only nine," they replied. The wise man saw that they were ten, so he made them stand and count. To the last person he said, "You are the tenth!" They all rejoiced for having regained the tenth.

The five senses and the four inner faculties (mind, intellect, memory, ego) all lament when they lose sight of the Self. Then the Master comes and shows you that YOU are the tenth!

Count, but never stop until you find the tenth.

Finding the ever-present Self inside makes everything truly joyful.

Question: What did *Brahma* think when he made this creation?

Gurudev: He didn't think before doing, He didn't take anyone's suggestion. I would have given Him a few!

✍ *News Flash:*

Bhajans coming out from a locked suitcase! Was it a miracle? No... a tape recorder inside got turned on, delighting the late-night volunteers.

The course ended with the whole group joining Gurudev for another dip in the Ganges. An Advanced Course with 400 participants is now under way in Rishikesh while TTC 1 and 2 are having a hilarious time. Everyone is gearing up for Holi, the Festival of Colours.

145. Inside Out

Often people say, "be the same outside as what you are inside." I ask you, how is this possible?

Inside you are a vast ocean, an infinite sky. Outside you are finite-just a small limited form, a normal stupid person!

All that you are inside – the love, the beauty, the compassion, the Divinity – doesn't show up fully outside. What shows is only the crust of behaviours.

Ask yourself, "Am I really my behavioural patterns?" "Am I really this limited body/mind complex?" No... you are not the same inside as outside.

> *Don't mistake the outer crust for who you are inside.*
> *And don't show your infinite lordship outside for Divinity is not*
> *easily understood.*
> *Let there be some mystery.*

✍ *News Flash:*

Saints, merchants, and prominent people of Rishikesh joined our course participants to celebrate Holi, the Festival of Colours. With saints clad in orange and Gurudev in white, Gurudev said, "The heart is white, the sign of purity in life; the head is orange, the symbol of sacrifice; and life is all colourful!"

Later in the week Gurudev met with the Shankaracharya and other saints.

The Bangalore Ashram school celebrated its Annual School Day with parents and local dignitaries in attendance.

Among the healings reported this week from those practicing Sudarshan Kriya:

- *A 56-year old man who had lost his vision reported he can now read the newspaper.*

- *A man who suffered from abnormal blood pressure for 10-12 years was found to have normal blood pressure.*

- *The mother-in-law of a devotee, a 65-year old woman who has not even taken the course, had a brain hemorrhage and multiple injuries caused by a fall. She was hospitalized on January 10 and by March 2 showed no improvement. Unable to recognize her own son, her doctors said nothing more could be done and gave her six hours to live.*

Her daughter-in-law placed a photo of Gurudev on her bed, held her hand, and prayed. The next day, to the amazement of all – especially the doctors – she could recognize everyone, and her blood sugar report, EEG, ECG, and all other reports were completely normal. She is now home and manages the house while her daughter-in-law completes TTC.

146. DREAMS

When something is unbelievably beautiful or joyful, you wonder if it is a dream. What you perceive as reality is often not joyful.

When misery is there you never wonder if it is a dream. You are sure it is real.

This is knowing the real as unreal, and unreal as real. In fact, all miseries are unreal. A wise man knows that happiness is real, a quality of your very nature. Unhappiness is unreal, as it is only an affliction of memory. When you can see both as a dream, then you abide in your true Self.

Payal: What about nightmares?

Gurudev: A nightmare is mistaken as a reality only while you are dreaming.

Keep wondering whether your waking reality is a dream and you'll wake up to the real.

✍ *News Flash:*

Rishikesh: The Advanced Course, Teacher Training, and Art Excel courses ended amidst jubilee. Many shared their healing experiences. The last few days, Satsang has been graced by saints from neighbouring ashrams.

The trip from Rishikesh to Chandigarh was full of Gurudev's mischief. The entourage stopped past midnight at Paonta Sahib, a Sikh holy shrine. The next evening, Satsang enraptured seven thousand.

147. IMPRESSION AND EXPRESSION

Do not make an effort to impress others or to express yourself.

Your effort to express yourself is an impediment. Your effort to impress someone becomes futile.

When you do not try to impress, expression comes naturally.
And when you come from the Self, your expression is perfect and your impression lasts for ages.

Often you don't seem to have control over your expressions – or the impressions you take in. Wisdom is selecting your expressions and impressions. Enlightenment is when impressions do not stay at all, whether good or bad. Nature has inbuilt in us a system which releases impressions through dreams and through meditation.

Many impressions in the mind cause:

• Confusion

• Distraction

• Chaos

• Lack of focus, and finally

• Derangement of the mind.

Excessive expression makes you lose your depth, your lustre, and the serenity of Self.
Meditation erases the impressions and gives you mastery of your expressions.

✍ *News Flash:*

Due to increasing crowds, Nitin and Bharat mentioned to Gurudev that now he needs security guards. Watch out what you ask for in Gurudev's presence! The next day, the government of Himachal Pradesh provided pilot cars and security for his entire trip in the Himalayan state.

Gurudev had a whirlwind tour of Himachal Pradesh, with Satsangs in Kalka, Shimla, Nahan, Delhi, and Noida. Everyone marveled at Gurudev's stamina and love.

From huge banners, TV screens – even movie theaters – Gurudev smiled from every nook in Kolkata, the City of Joy, setting the stage for two grand Satsangs, where thousands are eagerly awaiting the Master.

148. TARKA, VITARKA AND KUTARKA

To know yourself or to judge your actions, you need to know *tarka*, *vitarka* and *kutarka*.

Kutarka is wrong logic. For example: The door is half open means the door is half closed; therefore, the door is fully open means the door is fully closed!

Another example: God is love; love is blind; therefore, God is blind!

Many people misuse logic in this way and get caught up in ignorance.

Tarka is sequential logic; it increases scientific knowledge. But scientific conclusions change. For example: Pesticides were considered to be very useful in the past, but are now proven to be very harmful. With *tarka*, the paradigm changes in time.

Vitarka is asking questions which have no evident answers: "Who am I?" "What do I really want?" These philosophical questions increase your awareness and bring forth knowledge of the Self.

The wise know how to distinguish between these three.

✍ News Flash:

The Commissioner of Human Rights in Assam received Gurudev in Guwahati.

The devotees trekked to a hilltop on the banks of the Brahmaputra River for a picnic with Gurudev.

Gurudev arrived the next day in Calcutta where the Ganguly home was enchantingly decorated in his honour.

Gurudev addressed the Calcutta Management Association and later enlightened ambassadors, officials, and politicians on Face to Face – a television program.

Eight thousand attended the Grand Satsang in Calcutta where Gurudev spoke little, but left everyone with happy smiles.

Gurudev's black bag was lost – complete with passport and visas – but was found miraculously after a week.

Easter Advanced Courses are in progress all over the world.

149. SOFTNESS AND FORCEFULNESS

Often people are soft from lack of courage and forcefulness. They suffer a lot, and at some time or other they become volatile.

Yet there are some people who possess a softness that comes from maturity, magnanimity, and the knowledge of the Self.

There are also two types of forcefulness in people: aggressive and assertive. Aggressive people are forceful out of weakness or out of fear. Assertive people are forceful out of care, love, and compassion.

David: Aggressive control and assertive support!

Gurudev: So look into yourself and become aware of what type of softness and forcefulness you have.

✍ *News Flash:*

Cherry blossoms and snow greeted Gurudev at the German Academy.

Bulgaria, Namibia, and the Dominican Republic joined the Art of Living map this month.

150. DO NOT FOLLOW ME

Do not follow me. In fact, you cannot follow me because I am behind you to push you forward. You have to leave everything behind and move ahead. All your experiences, your relations – everything – is part of the past. Leave the whole world of your memories behind – including me. Drop everything. I am there behind you. Move on. Stop looking for more and be free! Then compassion will flow from you.

Question: When people do not follow anyone, isn't it usually out of fear or rebelliousness?

Gurudev: One type of 'Do not follow' comes from fear or rebelliousness. Another type comes from heightened awareness.

You cannot follow me because I am behind you and I am in you.
For long you have been a sheep.
Now it's time to be a lion.

✍ **News Flash:**

Diplomats from various countries were touched to hear Gurudev at an elegant event beautifully organised by Stella and her Geneva team.

Then began the whirlwind Tour de France...

Gurudev and a bus load of gigglers travelled to five major French cities spreading waves of joy. The Master who lives in the present took us to the Futuroscope (a famous fun park). Gurudev asked Denise, "Isn't this most beautiful?" Denise winked in reply, "It is only second."

In the car, Gurudev gave the directions to the driver. Nathalie asked, "How can you know this place better than we do?" Gurudev laughed and said, "I just guess!"

Opposite values are complementary; the lighthearted tour ended in a thought-provoking interfaith conference in Paris.

During the Weekly Knowledge meeting, Marcel asked, "How come I cannot follow the discussion sometimes?" Gurudev said, "Well done!"

So, if you have not followed this Knowledge Sheet – well done!

151. CONFUSION AND DECISION

A decision is required only when there is confusion. When there is no confusion, then there is no need of a decision.

If on your desk there is a piece of wood and a biscuit, you don't have to decide which to eat, do you? Decision is always about choice, and choice is always confusing. The more decisions, the more confused you are, swinging always between pain and pleasure. So, all decision-makers are confused! (Laughter)

In you, there is an actor and there is a witness. An actor is either confused or decisive, but the witness just observes and smiles.

Action is spontaneous (no decision) when there is no actor. The more the witness grows in you, the more playful and untouched you are. Then trust, faith, love, and joy all manifest in and around you.

Are you confused, decisive, or happy now?

Eberhard: Confusion is too strong of an expression. Is it not rather that we need to make a choice?

Urmila: We are decided that choice is confusion. (everyone laughs)

Hans Peter: Is there any freedom without confusion?

Gurudev: When you are confused, there is no freedom.

Hans Peter: Then what is freedom of choice?

Gurudev: Confusion! (Laughter)

✑ *News Flash:*

There was a big discussion about whether Gurudev should wear a plain white shawl or a white shawl with gold for the evening Human Values Conference. This choice confused everyone, but provided lots of laughter!

152. YOU ARE PRIVILEGED

Among all the planets in our solar system the earth is privileged to host life in so many forms.

Among all the species, humans are most privileged, for they can host the Knowledge.

Among all the knowledgeable ones, you are the most privileged... guess why?

The underprivileged are those who do not realise that they are privileged. They also host, but they host all the negativity.

Again and again, remember that you are peace, you are love, you are joy, and that you host the Creator. If you don't realise you are the host, you live like a ghost.

> *Like the birds returning to their nests, again and again come back to your Source; only there can you realise that you host the Divine.*

✍ **News Flash:**

A happy crowd greeted Gurudev with loud applause after a debate and short meditation at the Inter-Faith Conference on Human Values, held in the prestigious Hamburg University Auditorium.

The Indian Ambassador in Vienna hosted a Satsang at his gracious home.

Gurudev and his ideas delighted nearly 150 diplomats and U.N. officials at a meeting organised by Mary and her team in Vienna.

May 6 marks Gurudev's first visit to Rome in eleven years.

153. The Value of Chanting

When you sing *bhajans*, the vibration of sound energy gets absorbed into every atom of your body. This enkindles the energy in you and brings up the consciousness. Your entire body gets soaked in energy. Transformation happens.

A microphone absorbs sound and converts it into electricity; the body absorbs sound vibration and converts it into consciousness.

If you sit and listen to gossip or violent music, then that energy gets absorbed by your body and does not give a nice feeling.

> *When you hear the Knowledge or chant with all your heart, that elevates your consciousness.*

An ancient proverb in Sanskrit says that the words of *rishis* and enlightened ones are translated into experience immediately.

Bawa: We have read and heard from so many people, but when *Gurudev* speaks the same knowledge, it straightaway hits home.

✍ *News Flash:*

A family of devotees found, within a few weeks of doing Sudarshan Kriya, that their cat – whose diet had been exclusively dried fish – has turned vegetarian and will not even look at fish anymore!

One of our teachers had an operation, and later discovered that the absent-minded surgeon had left a metal clip inside her abdomen. In addition, a large stone developed in the gall bladder which caused an internal abscess. She had planned to go to the Bangalore Ashram, but instead had to be scheduled for surgery on the day of her intended departure. Upon examination, the doctors were surprised to discover that there was no clip, no stone – and no abscess!

Gurudev was not born, but 2000 people came to the Bangalore Ashram to celebrate his birthday. Everyone applauded Prashanth and his housing team for the way they avoided chaos.

P.S. Ishani and Bawas dogs also turned vegetarian.

154. INTENSIFY YOUR LONGING

Attainment of the Divine depends on the intensity of longing and not on the time or qualification.

A proverb among the villagers in India says, "It may take some time to pluck a flower, but it takes no time to meet the Divine!" Your abilities or qualifications are not the criteria – it is simply the intensity of your longing.

Intensify your longing for the Divine right away. This happens when you know that you are nothing and that you want nothing.

Suneeta: If we are nothing and we want nothing, then how can longing come?

Sidappa: Knowing you are nothing and you want nothing brings belongingness...

Gurudev: ... and belongingness intensifies longing.

Bill: What is the difference between desire and longing?

Gurudev:

> *Desire is the fever of the head.*
> *Longing is the cry of the heart.*

✍ **News Flash:**

The Ashram is buzzing with Advanced Courses, the Indian Teachers Meeting, Teacher Training, and Art Excel! Housing has overflowed into neighbouring resorts and hostels. Huge tents were pitched for meditation. Everyone felt a dire need for a bigger meditation hall and dining room.

Even with this shortage, Gurudev came up with yet another Seva project: Health, Hygiene, Home, and Human values – the four H's. In less than an hour, inspired devotees took up Seva projects to provide drinking water, sanitary facilities, prayer halls, and over 600 homes for the homeless in rural districts all over India.

Vikram: Someone should take up a similar project for the Ashram!

155. FAITH IS YOUR WEALTH

If you think your faith in god is doing a favour to God, then you are mistaken. Your faith in God or Guru does nothing to God or Guru. Faith is your wealth.

Faith gives you strength instantly. Faith brings you stability, centeredness, calmness, and love. Faith is your blessing.

If you lack faith, you will have to pray for faith. But to pray, you need faith. This is a paradox. (Laughter)

People put their faith in the world, but the whole world is just a soap bubble. People have faith in themselves, but they don't know who they are. People think that they have faith in God, but they really do not know who God is.

There are three types of faith:

1. Faith in yourself: Without faith in yourself, you think I can't do this; This is not for me; I will never be liberated in this life.

2. Faith in the world: You must have faith in the world or you can't move an inch. You deposit money in the bank with faith that it will be returned. If you doubt everything, nothing will happen for you.

3. Faith in the Divine: Have faith in the Divine and you will evolve.

All these faiths are connected; you must have all three for each to be strong. If you start doubting in one, you will begin to doubt everything.

Bill: Atheists have faith in themselves and faith in the world, but not in God.

Gurudev: Then they don't have complete faith in themselves. And their faith in the world cannot be constant because there are always changes. Lack of faith in God, the world, or yourself brings fear.

Faith makes you full – faithful.

Rajesh: What's the difference between faith and confidence?

Gurudev: Faith is the beginning. Confidence is the result. Faith in yourself brings freedom. Faith in the world brings you peace of mind. Faith in God evokes love in you.

Having faith in the world without faith in God does not bring complete peace. But if you have love, you automatically have peace and freedom. People who are extremely disturbed should only have faith in God.

✍ News Flash:

During a late afternoon Satsang at Sumeru Mantap, Gurudev started chanting. Suddenly, people started pointing to a huge thundercloud in the western sky filled with brilliant colours of unusual intensity. The trees had been crying for water, and within a few minutes, the wind came up and a delicious rain began to fall. But what were these colours? It was not a rainbow. We contacted the weather observatory, but they had no idea of this phenomenon. When we asked Gurudev for an explanation, he replied, "Nature is our friend".

After hectic activities in Bangalore, Gurudev tried to escape to Mangalore for 24 hours, but it turned into another party!

Art of Living representatives, headed by Sharada Lavingia, were invited to the G-8 Summit reception in Birmingham, U.K.

Art of Living was also represented in the World Health Organisation Conference in Geneva, Switzerland.

Teachers presented programs in St. Petersburg, Russia.

Women's prison programs have started in Bangalore.

Reports of more Seva projects are arriving from all over the world.

156. WHO WAKES UP FIRST?

Who wakes up first – you or God?

YOU wake up first – while God is still asleep!

When you wake up, you experience pleasure and pain. You become aware of the beauty and the shortcomings of the world. Then, when you seek the ultimate, your cry for help wakes up God. And when God is awakened in you, there is no "two."

> *God is asleep in every particle of this universe. God is in you in seed form. When He wakes up, neither you nor the world remain.*

The *rishis* made a mock practice of awakening God every morning. They call it *Suprabhatam* service. Many people find this ridiculous because they don't understand the depth of it. Only awakened God can see that God is everywhere asleep! (Laughter)

Brenda: Why should we wake up?

Gurudev: Because you are not asleep. If you are asleep, how can you ask the question?

Bill: Once you are awake, can you go back to sleep?

Gurudev: If you have not had tea, of course.

Bill: Who wakes us up?

Gurudev: You figure that out.

✍ News Flash:

A tree-planting program has taken root at the Bangalore Ashram.

Gurudev met with local people, inaugurated the 4-H program (Health, Hygiene, Home, and Human values), and initiated Satsang groups in the villages around the Ashram. Bombay was plastered with big billboards that attracted over 5000 to the Satsang. Arriving at the airport for the trip to Mauritius, Gurudev and entourage were told the flight was overbooked. Gurudev showed his "Guru Card" and suddenly all seven travellers had seats.

Mauritius hosted many events: interviews with television and radio, two Satsangs, a lecture at the University, audiences with the President and Prime Minister, a meeting with wardens and other prison officials, and, as part of a local Seva project which the Art of Living organisation has adopted – a visit to an old-age home (which is where you may be by the end of this sentence).

Vikram recorded Seeds of Wisdom at a local radio station, which will broadcast one quote each day over the next month.

This completes the third year of Weekly Knowledge.

Homework for next week: Everyone write a Weekly Knowledge sheet.

157. Breaking Beyond the Rational Mind

You usually do only that which is purposeful, useful and rational. Everything you see, you see through the rational mind.

But an intuition, a discovery, a new knowledge goes beyond the rational mind. Truth is beyond reason.

The rational mind is like a railroad track that is fixed in grooves. Truth needs no tracks. Truth can float anywhere like a balloon.

Some people step out of the rational mind in order to rebel against society. They want to break social law, but it is for the sake of ego – out of anger, hatred, rebelliousness, and wanting attention. This is not stepping out of the rational mind (though they may think it is).

We step out of the rational mind when we do something that has no purpose. If there is no purpose, the action becomes a game. Life becomes lighter.

If you are stuck with only rational acts, life is a burden. But if you play a game without a thought of winning or losing, if you do something without any purpose attached to it – just act irrationally – it is freedom, like a dance.

Just step out of the rational mind and you'll find a great freedom, an unfathomable depth, and you'll come face-to-face with reality.

Reality transcends logic and the rational mind. Until you transcend the rational mind, you will not get access to creativity and the Infinite.

But remember: if you do an irrational act in order to find freedom, then you already have a purpose. It is no longer irrational. This Weekly Knowledge note has already spoiled its own possibility!

Break the barrier of the rational mind and find freedom for yourself.

✍ *News Flash:*

That old Guru Magic worked so well and got Botswana and South Africa in its spell. Gurudev's talk made headline news in Johannesburg and Durban.

Senior government officials and prominent religious leaders met Gurudev at our International Symposium on Human Values. The Premier of the Kwa-Zulu Natal Province offered to organise courses in the local prisons. Our International Association for Human Values 1998 Award was given to President Nelson Mandela. The African tour left crowds reeling.

Gurudev moved on to crowds in Atlanta and New York, and tomorrow he will address the Values Caucus at the United Nations.

158. IF YOU CANNOT MEDITATE - BE STUPID!

If you are unable to meditate, if your mind is chattering too much and nothing works, just feel that you are a little stupid. Then you will be able to sink deep.

Your intellect is a small portion of your total consciousness. If you are stuck in the intellect, you miss a lot.

Happiness is when you transcend the intellect. When you feel stupid or in awe, you transcend the intellect.

Have you noticed how mentally retarded people are more happy?

Question: How do you go beyond the intellect?

Gurudev: By acting stupid! Everyone avoids being stupid – no one wants to look dumb. That is really stupid.

Stupidity should be followed by meditation, otherwise depression may follow.

Question: Can I ask a stupid question?

Gurudev: All questions are anyway stupid.

Mikey: How do you become stupid?

Yash: By asking the question.

Rajshree: Just be yourself.

✍ *News Flash:*

Torrential rains hit New England as Gurudev and his entourage gave talks in Boston. The mayor declared a state of emergency. Many true seekers travelled for hours through the storms and, miraculously, the rain stopped for three hours while Gurudev gave a Satsang.

Gurudev attended the Baltimore conference on Breaking the Cycle of Violence. Dr. Ganesh Prabhu, Tom Duffy, Odyl Wittman, and Ronnie Newman gave presentations on the health benefits of Sudarshan Kriya and the Prison Smart Program – including the women's program and ground-breaking independent research on juvenile offenders. Our panel stirred up a storm of interest with the enthusiastic audience.

159. Give Away Your Rights

Those who fight for their rights are weak; they do not know their inner strength, their magnanimity.

The weaker you are, the more you demand your rights. Asserting your rights makes you isolated and poor. People take pride in fighting for their rights. This is an ignorant pride. You need to recognize that no one can take away your rights: they are yours.

Courageous people give away their rights. The degree to which you give away your rights indicates your freedom, your strength. Only those who have rights can give them away!

Demanding rights does not really bring rights to you, and giving away rights does not really take them away.

Poor are those who demand rights. Richer are those who know that their rights cannot be taken away. Richest are those who give away their rights.

> *Demand for rights is ignorance, agony.*
> *Knowing that no one can take away your rights is freedom.*
> *Giving away your rights is love, wisdom.*

✍ *News Flash:*

Heavy cyclones hit the coastal areas of Gujarat, India. More than a thousand people were killed; five thousand are missing. Art of Living chapters sent teams of volunteers with ten tons of grain, ten thousand garments, and medicines to the villages of the Jamnagar District – the hardest hit. Volunteers raised a fund of 250,000 rupees in just two days.

Four successful courses for women prisoners in Bangalore reported miraculous experiences. Cases of hernia, asthma, and appendicitis were completely cured. Participants reported visions of Gurudev.

Veena Gandhi, a relative of Mahatma Gandhi, hosted a Satsang in Philadelphia.

In Pittsburgh, Gurudev enjoyed a university professor who attempted to disrupt the meeting, but whose heckling only added charm.

160. GENEROSITY IS A QUALITY OF SPIRIT

When you feel stuck in life not growing, bombarded by desires, dry, lacking enthusiasm, no juice – what do you do?

Here is the solution:

FEEL GENEROUS... right away, not tomorrow.

Generosity is a quality of spirit. A prince or a pauper can both feel generous. When you feel generous, your life becomes abundant, full of compassion and love.

Question: Is generosity the same as being grateful?

Gurudev: No, gratefulness always has self-concern. Why are you grateful? Because you have something or you will get something.

Generosity is independent of external circumstances. No one else can make you feel generous. It is something you have to do by yourself. Generosity is a state of consciousness. Generosity is not an act, but it always finds its expression in an act.

Question: What about passion?

Gurudev: Passion indicates scarcity; dispassion is abundance.

But dispassion without generosity makes you self-centered and causes dryness.

> *Don't think about what you've done in the past; that only brings doership. Just feel generous.*

✍ *News Flash:*

A successful prison program is now in progress following Gurudev's visit to South Africa (see Weekly Knowledge #157).

Gurudev came to Chicago for inspiring talks and intimate Satsangs. As the Knowledge flowed, each devotee felt Gurudev was speaking personally to them.

In Jackson Hole, Wyoming, the weather was cool while the volunteers were hot arranging packed talks.

In Vancouver, Gurudev was again met by sunshine – in the sky and on the faces of devotees.

161. THE PATH OF LOVE IS SURRENDER

Krishna first tells *Arjuna,* "you are very dear to me." Then *Krishna* tells *Arjuna* he must surrender.

Surrender begins with an assumption. First you must assume you are the most beloved of the Divine; then surrender happens.

Surrender is not an action, it is an assumption. Non-surrender is ignorance, an illusion.

Surrender has to begin as an assumption and then it reveals itself as a reality. And finally, it reveals itself as an illusion, because there is no "two" – no duality.

No one has any independent existence! That is it!

Question: Do you have to go through surrender to realise surrender is an illusion?
Gurudev: Yes, absolutely.

Question: Where is choice then?
Gurudev: The choice is your destiny. *Krishna* doesn't tell *Arjuna* in the beginning that he must surrender. First he says, "You are so dear to me." Later he tells him, "There is no other choice for you – you must surrender. Either do it now, or you will do it later."

This is the path of love.

✒ *News Flash:*

Hundreds of grateful devotees greeted Gurudev under a full Guru Purnima moon at beautiful Lake Tahoe. During the evening celebration, devotees floated across the stage for blessings from Gurudev to the sweet chant of Om Namo Bhagavate. A huge brown mama bear and her cub came out of the mountains to join the festivities.

162. It Takes Courage to Say "I Am"

The Divine comes only in deep rest – not by doing.

All your spiritual doings are to help you become silent. You will go further when you do not stop to enjoy the bliss or the peace, otherwise cravings may arise.

If existence wants to give you peace and bliss, then fine; your true nature is bliss. But by trying to enjoy the bliss, you step down from "am-ness" to "I am something" – "I am peaceful," "I am blissful" this is followed by, "I am miserable." It takes courage to simply say "I am – period." "I am" is dispassion.

Dispassion means welcoming everything. You can be anywhere and be dispassionate. Dispassionate centeredness brings energy, a spark. Indulgence in bliss brings inertia.

If you are dispassionate, the bliss is still there. When the freezer is full of ice cream, you need not bother about it.

Dispassion takes away a sense of scarcity. Passion is a sense of lack of abundance.

Whenever everything is in abundance, dispassion happens.
And when dispassion is there, everything comes in abundance.

Question: What do we do when we catch ourselves indulging in bliss?
Gurudev: Just this understanding creates a shift. There is no effort. Knowledge is better than action to make you free.

✍ *News Flash:*

Under crystal skies, surrounded by the snow-capped mountains of Alpine Meadows, the week-long gathering included an Advanced Course, a weekend and six-day Basic Course, Teacher Training 1-3, Parenting the Angels, and ART Excel. The teenagers kidnapped Gurudev for an afternoon of ice-skating and laughter.

163. Do You Know I Have No Mercy?

Mercy indicates lack of intimacy – a distance, a lack of belonging.

You don't have mercy on your near and dear ones. You don't hear parents say, "I have mercy on my children."

You have mercy only on those whom you think are not yours. Mercy indicates anger, judgment and authority.

When you ask for mercy, you are self-centered. You want to be excused from the law of cause and effect. It indicates lack of courage and valour.

At times, mercy is an impediment to growth. Mercy, of course, brings some comfort and relief, but can impair a transformation. If the leaves were to ask for mercy from falling, what would happen to the tree?

Patti and Victoria, high on bliss, did not stop at a stop sign, so the police mercilessly gave them a ticket. Victoria said, "Thank you," but the police woman told her to go to court and beg for mercy! (Laughter)

> *When you know and trust the process of creation, you will simply rejoice.*

You only ask for mercy if you think that God is angry and judging you. This is the small mind superimposing itself on the Divine mind. The Divine is all-knowing and all-loving – there is no chance for mercy.

Do you know I have no mercy? There is intimacy here and no place for mercy.

✍ *News Flash:*

The summer tour continued in the San Francisco Bay area and Santa Cruz, where sold-out talks swept away the crowds with knowledge and grace.

Gurudev Visited the infamous "Mystery Spot" and, of course solved the mysteries.

Record-high temperatures and record-high bliss followed the entourage to three Colorado cities for standing-room-only crowds and joyous Satsangs.

164. Ego Is Only an Atom

The "I" or ego in you is a tiny atom. It can either become associated with matter or with spirit. Whatever it becomes associated with, it identifies with that. When associated with matter, it identifies with the body; when associated with Being, it identifies with the infinite Self.

When this atom, this ego, is associated with the material world, it becomes mundane. When it is associated with the spirit, it becomes Divine. It becomes *shakti* when associated with the Being, the Self. It becomes miserable when identified with the body.

You see, in a huge atomic reactor, it is just one tiny atom that is exploded. In the same way, in our whole body there is just one little tiny atom of "I." And when this "I" explodes, then it becomes the light of the Self.

Usually we say, "I am miserable," or "I am happy."

Shift this atom from identifying with the body and the conceptual world, to identifying with the Real World.

✍ News Flash:

Ottawa, Canada's capital, was graced with the Master's presence for two action-packed days this past week, where his public talk on Human Values at the elegant Chateau Laurier made the TV evening news, and the Hindu temple experienced a tidal wave of joy and bliss.

Then our caravan moved on to the Advanced Course at the Montreal Ashram, where we set new attendance records with 450 course participants. All are amazed at how smoothly things have gone, and there is no question that this is all due to the Guru's grace. A group of devotees from Central America had everyone dancing at the lively Satsangs this week in our spacious and colourful tent by the lake. Nature has cooperated by providing perfect weather all week, and no bugs. Everyone is happy amidst great celebration. Fireworks at the lake on Thursday night will mark the grand finale of the North American summer tour, as Gurudev prepares to leave for Germany.

165. LOYALTY

Loyalty is the way in which a mature and integrated mind behaves. Loyalty indicates undivided wholeness of consciousness and shows richness of the mind. When the mind, is not integrated it is feverish, disloyal and opportunistic.

Disloyalty comes out of opportunism. Opportunism is being short-sighted about one's destiny. Integrity or wholeness is essential to be healthy. A divided mind will gradually lead to schizophrenia and other mental and physical disorders. Loyalty is a real strength and will have the support of nature in the long run.

Fear and ambitions are impediments to loyalty. Loyalty is needed both in the material and spiritual plane. To destroy, create or maintain any institution, group or society, loyalty is essential.

Loyalty means believing in the continuity of commitment. Honouring commitment is loyalty. It takes you beyond the duality of craving and aversion.

Responsibility, dedication and commitment are the limbs of loyalty.

A loyal mind is a "yes"-mind. The purpose of asking questions is to get an answer. The purpose of all answers is to create a "Yes!"

"Yes" is an acknowledgment of knowledge. The "yes"-mind is a quiet, holistic and joyful mind. The "no"-mind is an agitated, doubting and miserable mind. Loyalty begins with a "yes"-mind and starts to perish with a "no"-mind.

166. Do You Love Someone Because They Are Great or Unique?

I tell you, you are hopeless! Why do you love someone? Is it because of their qualities? Or is it because of a sense of kinship or intimacy?

You can love someone for their qualities and not feel a sense of kinship. This type of love gives rise to competition and jealousy. Such is not the case when love arises out of kinship. If you love someone for their qualities, then when the qualities change or when you get used to the qualities, love also changes. However, if you love someone out of kinship, because they belong to you, then that love remains for lifetimes.

People say, "I love God because He is great." This is no big thing. If God is found to be ordinary, just one of us, then your love for God collapses. If you love God because He is yours, then however God is, whether He creates or destroys, you still love Him. The love of kinship is like the love for yourself.

Question: Many people do not love themselves, so...?

Gurudev: No! It is the other way around. They love themselves so much that they want better qualities and a better appearance for themselves. This love of qualities makes them hard on themselves.

If love is based on the qualities of a person, then that love is not stable. After some time the qualities change and the love becomes shaky. Loving someone because of their greatness or uniqueness is third-rate love.

Loving someone because they belong to you, great or otherwise, is unconditional love.

Knowledge, *Sadhana*, *Seva* and *Satsang* help to bring about a sense of belonging in no time. When love springs forth from a sense of belonging, then the actions and qualities do not overshadow the love.

Neither qualities nor action can be perfect all the time. Love and a feeling of kinship alone can be perfect.

✍ *News Flash:*

*Atit and his team are teaching a Basic Course in Ahmedabad for 765 people ......
record breaking! Also, an Art of Living Course will be offered at Nova University
in Florida as part of their regular curriculum.*

*After the first Advanced Course in Germany, everyone went to the waterfalls
for a full moon Satsang.*

167. SINGING, COMMUNICATION AND EGO

There are three modes of communication: in head-to-head communication you talk, in heart-to-heart communication you sing, and soul-to-soul communication happens in silence.

When you meet with people, often you communicate from head to head. When you are with nature, you start singing, you communicate with nature from your heart. Often when you are with people, you keep talking, blabbering and you keep the communication on the level of the head only. But when you are with nature, you start humming and your communication comes through the heart. And when you are with the Guru, you go blank and forget all the questions. Then communication comes through the soul in silence.

When you meet with people, you like to remain in the head. You seldom sing with people other than when it is organised. Your ego obstructs you from singing. Many do not feel comfortable singing with people.

When you sing with people, then you descend to the heart level or feeling level.

Some feel comfortable just listening to music. Some feel comfortable singing only when they are alone. Some sing to attract attention or to charm others. Some only want to join in when all the others are singing. All this singing comes from ego. *Bhajan* means sharing, sharing from the deepest level of our existence. *Bhajan* is authentic sharing.

If you could sing with people, then your ego shatters.

Children can sing with people for they do not have ego. To sing with a stranger you have to be free of ego. Ego doesn't let you sing with a stranger.

Head level is safe for the ego; heart level breaks the ego; soul level dissolves the ego. All communication gaps happen because of ego.

Exercise: When you are with people, rather than chatting, just start singing and feel the shift of energy that happens. If you want to have more fun, greet a stranger with a song.

✍ News Flash:

The Art of Living hosted a United Nations Round Table in Geneva on the Art of Making Peace.

Krishna's birthday was celebrated in the ashram with the conclusion of the Advanced Course.

A prison program is starting in Denmark. Several research scientists came and met with Gurudev. A beautiful talk on happiness in daily life was given by Gurudev in Copenhagen.

There were too many seats in Copenhagen and too few in Oslo. The whole hall was so packed that people sat on the floor, which is unusual in Norway.

The Chandigarh Advanced Course swept course participants off their feet.

168. Expansion of Consciousness is Peace

Consciousness moving on the surface of the body is stimulus, which causes pleasure. When consciousness shrinks, then the sensation of pain and suffering arises. Suffering is the shrinking or contraction of consciousness.

When consciousness moves through the body in limited channels, pleasure is experienced. Repeated enjoyment of stimuli causes inertia and dullness. Often cooks don't enjoy their own food. The same piece of music heard over and over loses its charm. People in the sex industry don't enjoy sex.

If the stimuli are observed, then consciousness expands and becomes peace. With awareness, the stimuli lose their significance; whether they exist or not makes no difference. When the sun is shining, then it makes no difference whether or not the candle is lit. To realise that all pleasures are just stimuli, and that you are more than the stimuli, brings freedom.

Pain is nothing but consciousness wanting to expand and to become free. Freedom is liberation from the craving or the stimuli. Pain is not a permanent state.

The natural tendency of consciousness is to expand, to become bliss. Like the natural tendency of water is to flow downward and the natural tendency of air is not to be under pressure, the natural tendency of consciousness is to expand and to be at peace. Like the insomniac who has forgotten how to sleep, most of us have forgotten how to be at peace and in bliss.

Question: What about the pleasure in *Satsang*?

Gurudev: The pleasure of *Satsang* takes you towards expansion.

✍ *News Flash:*

A beautiful course in the picturesque mountain setting of Norway, a visit to the Tamil SriLankan temple in Aslant, public lectures in Sweden – it was always the same: everyone blissfully cried out, "Please stay longer."

Gurudev visited Finland for the first time, staying for a total of 15 hours. In this short time he made the headline news on the main television channel. Several people dreamed of Gurudev even before hearing about him.

In Hamburg, Gurudev addressed the oldest Rotary Club of Europe and held a blissful Satsang in a fully-packed church that left everyone spellbound. In his welcome to Gurudev, the priest said, "It is time to open the church doors for real spiritual knowledge."

169. DEPENDENCE, INDEPENDENCE, INTERDEPENDENCE AND ONENESS

The body is dependent on the whole creation. In society somebody has to make clothes, produce electricity, drill for oil. The body cannot be independent of the world. For the body, dependency is absolute. When the Spirit identifies with the body, then it gets pinched and looks for independence. Mind, intellect, ego - they all look for independence.

In looking for independence, you often get stuck in the ego and become more miserable. Most people are not aware of their dependency. When they become aware of their limitations and dependency, the desire for independence arises. Independence cannot be achieved unless you start moving from within. When you move within, you discover that you are interdependent. Individual Self/Soul/*Jeeva* is interdependent and in fact every wise person knows that everything is interdependent and that there is no such thing as independence.

On one level dependency is a harsh reality. On another level, it is an illusion because there is nothing else but the Self. It's only when you don't feel oneness, belongingness that you want independence.

The Self being non-dual, there is no question of dependence or independence. One who asks for independence is a beggar. One who knows that it is an illusion is a king.

When the sense of belongingness is not well-founded, there is a volatile state in the life of a seeker. Then the ego finds some excuse to revert to smallness. It is not yet totally soaked in the totality of knowledge. As it is not used to it, the mind finds every little excuse to revert back to the ego and to be aloof, independent and separate; and it finds any small fault and blows it out of proportion.

Be aware of these tendencies and come what may, be strong in the commitment to the *Satsang*, to the path.

Question: How about self-sufficiency?
Gurudev: Self is sufficient and efficient. (Laughter)

✍ *News Flash:*

In the past 240 days, Gurudev visited 92 places. In the ashram in Germany, the Teacher's Training Courses were in jubilation; the Basic Course was like an Advanced Course.

Assisted by the official Polish government interpreter, Gurudev addressed an enthusiastic audience of 1,700 in Warsaw. There were about 1,000 people, including VIPs and the TV crews, who could not get in. It took great skill and effort for the organisers to pacify them. From there 450 people have moved to the scenic Muszyna camp for an Advanced Course.

September 10, 1998
Bangalore Ashram, India

170. REST AND ACTIVITY

Activity and rest are two vital aspects of life. To find a balance in them is a skill in itself. When to have what, and how much to have, is wisdom. Finding them in each other - activity in rest and rest in activity - is the ultimate freedom.

More tiring than the work itself is the memory of hard work. Thinking you have worked hard interferes with the quality of rest. Some people take pride in working hard without any results. And there are others who crave for long rest, not knowing that the rest is in non-doership. It is the quality of rest, even if it is short, that recuperates.

When rest is needed, your body will automatically take it. Resting, without thinking about the need for it, is more restful. Desirelessness, dispassion and *samadhi* are the deepest rest.

Question: Our work is very stressful. We don't get enough time for the family. What should we do?

Gurudev: Do you spend quality time with your family? Even if you spend half an hour, are you cordial and fully attentive to the needs of your family? It is not the length of time you spend with your family that matters. What matters is the quality of time that you spend with them.

Thinking you need rest makes you restless.

Thinking you have to work hard makes you tired.

Thinking you have worked hard brings self-pity.

✑ News Flash:

The Polish Advanced Course bid farewell to Gurudev with a candle dance.

Bombay saw an unannounced Satsang of over 500 devotees.

Gurudev arrived at the ashram on a full moon day and launched the paddle boat on the lake, much to the delight of all devotees. The Bangalore Ashram is getting dressed up for the Navaratri celebrations.

171. DO IT UNTIL YOU BECOME IT !

Virtues have to be practised until they become your nature. Friendliness, compassion and meditation should continue as practises until you realise that they are your very nature.

The flaw in doing something as an act is that you look for a result. When it is done as your nature, you are not attached to the result and you continue doing it.

An action that arises from your nature is neither tiring nor frustrating. For example, daily routines like brushing your teeth or bathing are not even considered actions because they are so integrated into your life. You do all this without doership. When *Seva* is made part of your nature, it happens without doership.

Question: When do you realise that compassion, meditation and *Seva* are your nature?

Gurudev: When you cannot be without them.

Wise men continue their practises just to set an example, even though for them there is no need for any practises.

✍ *News Flash:*

The Art of Living family has taken up a "Clean Guwahati" Program. The Mayor of Guwahati, who recently did the course, actively assists the Seva teams in their drive to clean the city.

Seventeen boulevards in Calcutta have been adopted by the local chapter under the 5-H Program. Enthusiastic volunteers carried food, clothes and other necessities for the flood victims of Malda, West Bengal. The Advanced Course in Junagadh had 500 people. Gurudev attended 4 to 5 Satsangs each day in different parts of the city.

Excellent teamwork and arrangements made for an electrifying Satsang in Rajkot with over 7,000 people. Gurudev made a great escape after tearing the decorations, jumping off a wall, getting into his car without his sandals and driving through fields.

The latest news from Bangalore is the Advanced Course in the ashram and Gurudev's series of talks on the Bhagavad Gita in the Kannada language.

172. SILENCE

As *Gurudev* is in silence this week, he requests that everyone write their own Weekly Knowledge and read it out loud.

173. Do Not Correct Your Mistakes!

Wanting to correct a mistake brings doership and doership is the foundation for mistakes. Often those who are trying to correct mistakes get caught up in more mistakes. Those who recognize their mistakes are freed from them.

Often when we acknowledge a mistake, we try to justify it without taking responsibility for it. And sometimes we accept that we made a mistake and start justifying it or feeling guilty about it. Mistakes get dropped when one is troubled by one's conscience (*viveka*) or by grief.

There may be flaws in any action, any situation or any person. Treat a flaw as you would treat a flower. Just as a flower has to wither away after some time, so does a flaw.

✍ News Flash:

Hope all of you enjoyed last week's knowledge; written on paper that is space, with ink that is love, in a language that is silence. How many of you got it?

Navaratri was celebrated in the ashram by hundreds of devotees from all around the world. Silence made way for celebrations that got louder and louder, culminating in a wave of bliss.

Serious discussions are under way for expanding the facilities in the ashram. Even though the volunteers and the housing team did an excellent job, the need for more rooms and a larger meditation hall was sorely felt.

174. YAGNA

Yagna creates energy and energy creates consciousness, awareness. Heightened awareness brings you close to reality and reality is a witness. To realise that everything is happening, you need heightened awareness. And to bring about heightened awareness, you have to increase the *prana*.

Prana can be increased through:

1. Fasting; fresh food.

2. *Pranayamas*, *Kriya*, Meditation.

3. Silence.

4. Cold water baths.

5. Total exhaustion; not letting sleep take over.

6. Emotional peaks.

7. Presence of the Master.

8. Singing and chanting.

9. Giving without givership; serving without doership.

All of these together are *Yagna*.

✒ *News Flash:*

Every corner of the Bangalore Ashram resonated with the energy of Navaratri celebrations. Many service projects were taken up by the devotees on Dashera (Victory Day). Many people from different cities of Nepal came to the ashram for the first time to join the Advanced Course.

Gurudev inaugurated the Women's Empowerment Camp organised by Adichunchungiri Swamiji. More than 900 women participated in that camp.

On his way to Canada, Gurudev stopped in Switzerland for a beautiful Satsang in Lausanne.

175. THE DIFFERENT KINDS OF UNDERSTANDING

There are three kinds of understanding: intellectual understanding, experiential understanding and existential realisation.

Intellectual understanding says "yes," it agrees. Experiential understanding feels, is obvious. Existential realisation is irrefutable. It becomes your very nature.

All you hear will simply remain a jumble of words if there is no experiential understanding, which is more on the feeling level. You can know intellectually that you are hollow and empty, but sitting and feeling that you are hollow and empty is totally different.

When one gets an experience, one wants to understand more about it and becomes a seeker. If you have only intellectual understanding, you will think you know it all. Most theologians are in this category.

Existential realisation contains within it both experiential and intellectual understanding. But it is beyond both of these.

Question: How do we get there?
Gurudev: There is no way. When the fruit becomes ripe, it falls.

Question: What is doubt?
Gurudev: It is one part of the mind challenging the other part of the mind.

✍ Bonus knowledge Flash:

Although "there is no way," Gurudev nonetheless gave some interesting clues about "the way" in a spontaneous discourse this week on the eight limbs of yoga. Following a noontime meditation, in which some practitioners must have been busy "doing" or otherwise impatient for the final "Jai Guru Dev," Gurudev said: "You have to rejoice in the means. You have to love the means. Love is the goal; the means must also be lovable. Love springs when there is no effort, when all activities are shunned." More on this in the next Weekly Knowledge.

✍ News Flash:

Gurudev theoretically is on vacation this week at the Montreal Ashram. To the untrained eye, however, his so-called vacation appears no different from his usual hectic schedule. Streams of visitors flow through his kutir all day long and invariably come out beaming. How this happens continues to he the greatest mystery.

Gurudev surprised the devotees of Halifax with an unexpected visit. Halifax is far from Montreal and many devotees were unable to come to the ashram to see him. Gurudev continually confirms in so many ways that he is indeed the embodiment of love and compassion.

176. THE CAUSE OF RETURN

Most of us come into this world with the seed in us – "It's not OK." And all our life we try to correct events, people and situations. How much can you correct? Is like trying to rearrange the clouds in the sky. This seed does not allow you to be happy, to smile from your heart, to be loving and lovable. It's there all the time like a thorn - irritating, irritating.

This seed – "It's not OK" – brings you back into this world again and again. How do you burn this seed?

1. First recognize that it is there. This can happen in deep introspection and meditation.

2. Sometimes you feel your body, mind, intellect, memory and ego are also not OK. You justify them or find fault with them. These are also part of the world. Acknowledge what you see as an imperfection and offer it to the Divine.

3. Have faith in the infinite organizing power of the Supreme Intelligence and have the sincere feeling, "Let Thy will be done." Then the seed – "It's not OK" – gets burned. "Thy will be done" is a state of total contentment, a state of just love. We need not even make it a statement about the future: "Thy will alone is happening now".

Question: So everything that happens is God's will?
Gurudev: Yes, including the thought, "This shouldn't be happening."

Last week's Bonus Knowledge Flash Continued.

You have to rejoice in the means. You have to love the means. Love is the goal; the means must also be loveable. Love springs when there is no effort, when all activities are shunned. As long as there is karma - the impression to act, you have to act. When this tendency to act eases up, total effortlessness happens. In effortlessness, unconditional love dawns. And every life is aching for that love.

News Flash:

One evening this week, Gurudev took a very long walk through the forest after dark. For the flock of devotees following him, the experience seemed to be a metaphor for the spiritual path: following the Guru blindly along a steep and narrow trail, through the pitch-black darkness, without any idea of how to find our way, yet laughing merrily anyway.

Diwali (The Festival of Lights) was celebrated in fine style with fireworks over the lake, a candlelight procession and the Light of Lights illuminating our hearts. The trees are now nearly bare, but the colorless landscape of late fall is not nearly as bleak as the prospect of Gurudev's departure this weekend.

We are happy to report that Art of Living Courses have now begun in El Salvador and Zimbabwe.

177. Appreciation

When do you appreciate someone? When they do something that is unusual, not ordinary and not their nature. Isn't it so?

For example, when a wicked person doesn't create a problem, then you appreciate him. Or, when somebody you think is not good does a good act, then you appreciate him. Also, when a good person does something extraordinary, then you appreciate him. If a child made you a cup of tea, you would appreciate it, but if a mother made the same cup of tea, most likely you would not appreciate it, because it is a normal act for her. In the same way, you appreciate getting a ride from someone you don't know, but you don't necessarily appreciate it from a bus driver.

In all these cases, the acts are temporary, out of character, or not that person's nature. So when you appreciate someone for something, you imply that it is not the way they usually are.

Question: What if a person wants to be appreciated?

Gurudev: That means that it is not in their nature and that is why they want to be appreciated. If it is not coming from their nature, it is an imposed act. So when you appreciate someone, you simply imply that it is not their nature, it is not the way they usually are. It is a rare act or quality. Appreciation implies a sense of separateness or distance, so watch out when you appreciate someone!

✍ *News Flash:*

During the last week of Gurudev's very busy vacation at the Montreal Ashram, the only way he could have an uninterrupted meeting was in a boat out in the middle of the lake. The pink sky in the blue water was reflected in everyone's heart.

In Calgary, some instant gopis and gopas were born, who had not even taken the Basic Course. On a walk around Lake Louise, Dean was taking pictures and Gurudev reminded Dean that the sun was on the camera. Dean said, "It's amazing, you always know where the sun is." Gurudev laughed and said, "Who does not know where the sun is? What an appreciation!"

178. WHAT ARE THE SIGNS OF LOVE?

When you love someone you don't see anything wrong in them. Even if you see some fault in them, you justify the fault and say, "Well, everyone does it! It is normal." You think you have not done enough for them. The more you do, the more you want to do for them. They are always in your mind.

Ordinary things become extraordinary, for example, a baby winking at its grandmother. You want them to be yours exclusively. When you love someone you want to see them always happy and you want them to have the best. You get hurt even over small things.

33% extra knowledge! (Laughter)

Gurudev: You wish someone what they don't have, right?

Answer: Yes!

Gurudev: When you say, "Best wishes," you imply that they are not best. NOW, I tell you, NOW is the best. If you realise this, tomorrow can only be better.

✍ *News Flash:*

Gurudev visited Japan for three days. A group of 25 people travelled with Gurudev to Kakagoa International Centre for a wonderful talk.

Kobe had a beautiful Satsang, then the group went to Tokyo where Gurudev stayed with his former classmate. Laudable teamwork made possible exuberant Satsangs filled with tears of love and gratitude. It was amazing to see people from all walks of life and culture simply melting in love.

From there the group went to Hong Kong. The new Hong Kong International Airport reverberated with sounds of "Jai Jai Radha Ramana Hari Bole" by enthusiastic devotees. Lots of devotees flew from mainland China and Taiperi to be with Gurudev. A well organised Satsang was attended by about 1,000 people.

Gurudev arrived at midnight in Delhi amidst singing of bhajans by around 100 people at the airport.

A prestigious venue, Indian Habitat Centre, is awaiting a talk by Gurudev, on "Spirituality in the New Millennium" to be attended by leading dignitaries. Two other large Divya Satsangs are planned during Gurudev's short stay at Delhi.

November 12, 1998
Bangalore Ashram, India

179. THE PURPOSE OF LIFE

Our first and foremost commitment is to do *Seva* (service) in the world.

If there is fear in your life, it is because of a lack of commitment. If there is confusion in your life, it is because of a lack of commitment.

The very thought, "I am here in this world to do *Seva*," dissolves the "I" and when the "I" dissolves, worries dissolve. *Seva* is not something you do out of convenience or for pleasure. The ultimate purpose of life is to be of service.

An uncommitted mind is miserable. A committed mind may experience rough weather but will reap the fruits of its toil.

When you make service your sole purpose in life, it eliminates fear, brings focus in your mind and purposefulness, action and long-term joy – and may be short-term problems!

✍ News Flash:

At the India Habitat Centre, policy makers, the elite and the intellectuals were spellbound in a brilliant dialogue with the Master. The atmosphere was charged with love and awe.

Anand Vihar (Abode or Bliss) lived up to its name as several thousand queued up for a divine embrace.

Pune witnessed a grand Satsang with over 8,000 people. The Monday Puja saw a revolutionary shift with 66 women chanting the Vedic hymns. Civic receptions were given to Gurudev by mayors of Pimpri-Chinchwad and Pune. Then Gurudev was received warmly at the Sadhu Vaswani Missions by the Spiritual leader J.P. Vaswani, and there was silent wisdom and blissful singing.

Finally, it was on to Bangalore where Teachers' Training Course Phases I and II are in full swing.

180. AUSTERITY

Austerity is often mistaken to be poverty or self-denial. It is neither. Austerity comes out of maturity. It is a sign of social health.

Often people who practise austerity are resentful of richness. This is a very pitiable state. Such austerity is not born out of maturity but out of compulsion. True austerity has tolerance for richness and is never resentful.

In fact, one who is mature will have pity for one who is not austere. Austerity is not opposed to celebration, and vanity alone is not celebration. Celebration dawns in the spirit. Only one who is rich in spirit can practise austerity. One may be rich materially but if he is poor in spirit, he can neither celebrate nor evolve.

Poverty of spirit is vanity. Austerity brings freedom from the pride of vanity. But taking pride in austerity is again vanity!

Austerity comes out of abundance, and austerity brings abundance. If you feel a lack in any area of life, immediately start austerity. Austerity not only brings freedom but also nurtures sharing and caring.

✍ News Flash:

Alerted by some noise at midnight, our gardener rushed out with a torch and was amazed to find five wild elephants in the garden! He just said "Jai Guru Dev" and prayed to them and the elephants didn't damage the garden - though they did break the fence.

Meanwhile, Gurudev's cat has stopped catching mice - it leaves the job to us!

Bangalore saw its biggest Basic Course of 230 people and Gurudev gave a series of inspiring talks on the Bhagavad Gita in the local language.

November 26, 1998
Bangalore Ashram, India

181. Focus And Expansion

Focus sharpens the mind and relaxation expands the mind. Just an expanded mind without sharpness cannot bring holistic development. At the same time, just a sharp mind without expansion causes tension, anger and frustration.

The balance between the focused mind and expanded consciousness brings perfection.

Sudarshan Kriya and the Advanced Course techniques are aimed at developing such consciousness which is both sharp and unbounded.

Seva and commitment play major role in this. Also food and attitude have an effect.

Expanded consciousness is peace and joy. Focused consciousness is love and creativity.

A point of focused consciousness is individual self.

When every atom of the expanded consciousness becomes sharp and focused, that is the awakening of Divinity.

✍ *News Flash:*

Make your own news!

December 3, 1999
Cochin, India

182. Sublimating Lust

Lust is one of the main botherations that many face. Lust grips the mind, tires the body and dulls the intellect.

Lust when indulged brings inertia, and when suppressed brings anger. Lust is nothing but primordial unharnessed energy. The same, when harnessed, manifests as enthusiasm, sparkle, sharpness of intellect and love.

What are the factors which can sublimate or transform lust into love?

1. Playfulness — People who are in the grip of lust cannot he genuinely playful. When you are genuinely playful, then there is no lust.

2. Generosity — When you realise that you are here only to give and give, and you feel that you are very generous, then lust is sublimated. Lust makes one possessive and not generous.

3. Moderate to small intake of food.

4. Remembrance of death.

5. Divine romance.

6. Cold water baths.

7. Undertaking creative challenges.

✍ *News Flash:*

Creation returned to the source as Gurudev visited Shimoga, the birthplace of the Art of Living, to a tumultuous traditional welcome. The course participants from 1982 met Gurudev saying that their every wish has been granted and thanked him for the enormous grace and joy that fills their lives. A grand Satsang there began a hectic, fun-filled week for Gurudev and all of us.

Gurudev stopped in Shringeri overnight and met with the Shankaracharya. They had a silent dialogue!

Gurudev's first ever Satsang in Mangalore had over 4,000 people and an elaborate welcome with the sound of huge horns.

On to Kerala, known as "God's own country," where the picturesque countryside and thousands of enthusiastic devotees greeted the Master ecstatically. Thallassery had its first ever Satsang, and Calicut saw thousands thronging the hall. On this trip, Gurudev has astonished organisers and delighted audiences by speaking in the local language (Malayalam) -which he is not supposed to know!

Trissur, the cultural capital of Kerala, welcomed Gurudev with caparisoned elephants, traditional drums and horns, and a moonlit, open-air Satsang of over 10,000! Of course, many healing experiences are being reported. Even as Gurudev is making headlines in all the leading newspapers, many amazing and amusing incidents have been "happening." Gurudev stopped the car at a small village and was immediately surrounded by the locals. One of them said that after seeing Gurudev's photo in the newspaper, he had been praying to Gurudev ever since. His joy knew no bounds when Gurudev visited his tiny shop and blessed him.

Earlier, an autorickshaw driver was doing pranam to Gurudev's poster - imagine his surprise when he turned and saw Gurudev smiling from the car next to him!

183. UNCERTAINTY

You can be at ease with the uncertainty of the world when you realise the certainty of consciousness. Often people do just the opposite. They are certain about the things in the world and uncertain about God. They rely on something that is not reliable and get upset. Uncertainty causes craving for stability and the most stable thing in the universe is the Self.

The world is of change; the Self is of non-change. You have to rely on the non-change and accept the change. If you are certain that everything is uncertain, then you are liberated. When you are uncertain in ignorance, then you become worried and tense. Uncertainty with awareness brings higher states of consciousness and a smile.

Bharat: A certain smile!

Gurudev: Often people think that certainty is freedom. If you feel the freedom when you are not certain, then that is "real" freedom. Often your certainty or uncertainty is based on the relative world. Being certain about the uncertainty of the relative makes you certain about the existence of the absolute and brings a "certain" faith in the absolute.

Nitin: Yes, to understand this you certainly need to have awareness!

Question: Can we still be enthusiastic when we are uncertain?

Gurudev: Yes. In knowledge you can be enthusiastic in uncertainty. Often people who are uncertain don't act; they simply sit and wait. Acting in uncertainty makes life a game, a challenge. Being in uncertainty is letting go. Certainty about the relative world creates dullness. Uncertainty about the Self creates fear. Uncertainty about matter brings certainty about consciousness.

✍ News Flash:

In Cochin, by the ocean, a grand open-air Satsang of over 12,000 had a full moon shining on the sea of devotees. The next day, Kollam, the cashew hub of India, saw thousands flock to the noontime Satsang despite it being a working day.

Then the party zone moved to Trivandrum, the capital of Kerala, where Gurudev was welcomed with caparisoned elephants, umbrellas, deepa balikas (girls holding lamps) and the King. Over 15,000 people were present and yet there was pin-drop silence during meditation. The program was telecast live.

Then on to Varkala for a morning Satsang en route to Kanyakumari, the southernmost tip of India, where the three seas meet. The next day the entire town of Udayankulangara celebrated Gurudev's brief stopover and a fest was arranged for the entire township. A very famous painter who was making a portrait of Gurudev for a billboard felt strong currents in his body as he was giving the finishing touches and started crying. He joined the next Basic Course. All the teachers are busy with hundreds taking the course.

Throughout Kerala there were arches built welcoming Gurudev. Our devotees and the District Administrator took the task of cleaning Ambaji, a pilgrimage centre of Gujarat.

184. ORGANISATION

The entire creation is a huge organisation. Everything is made up of atoms. The whole world is nothing but organisation where the atoms have decided to organise themselves in a specific pattern to form a particular substance. And those particular patterns bring them specific qualities.

Death, decay, transformation happen when the atoms get bored with patterns and decide to reorganise themselves. For example, when the atoms of the apple say, "Enough of being an apple," that's when the rotting starts. If there is no boredom with patterns, there can be no decay.

The movement from one organised state to another is also organised. This is the transient organisation which we call chaos. This transient organisation may need a catalyst. Knowledge is such a catalyst. So, you have absolutely no escape from organisation.

✍ News Flash:

This week's highlights:

An overflowing ashram.

Inauguration of a youth wing of the Art of Living.

Jubilant Teachers' Training Course Phases I and II.

Opening of a research project in Trivandrum.

Plans to expand ashram facilities.

Service projects.

And people wondering how Gurudev copes with all this without any sign of tiredness!

185. RECYCLING AND HYGIENE

Everything here is recycled. The earth is 200 million years old - the Alps, the water, the air. Billions of people have breathed the same air. All the particles in your body are old; you are recycled. Your thoughts and emotions are recycled; mind is recycled.

You are a recycled person. Everything here is recycled. Consciousness is recycled - it's the same old consciousness. Remind yourself that everything here is recycled material - so relax! Everything goes to where it came from. Recycling brings back purity and hygiene. Knowledge recycles the mind.

Tarah: Recycling makes everything new and therefore a mind that is recycled by knowledge finds everything fresh.

Gurudev: Knowledge keeps everything fresh. That is why you can keep recycling the same creation. A mind in knowledge finds everything fresh.

If you don't put knowledge into the mind, the mind gets rotten. Knowledge brings the mind back to purity. Recycling brings purity and hygiene.

Hygiene supports health but too much hygiene destroys health. In too hygienic a situation, the immune system in the body becomes like lazy, unequipped soldiers. People who live in slums often don't get sick because their immune system becomes like a well-trained soldier. Often people who are too fussy about hygiene have poor health. Sometimes unhygienic conditions create health. It keeps your immune system active, alive and strong, while knowledge keeps your mind fresh.

✍ News Flash:

After a grand Satsang in Madras the group went to the Chidambaram temple, the place of the cosmic dance of Siva. Then on to the temple town of Kumbhakonam, also for a big Satsang where Gurudev honoured many Vedic pundits and meditations were held in many ancient temples.

Then the Satsang army marched on to Papanasam, Gurudev's birthplace, where everyone played in the water - shooting missiles of bliss. Then on to Trichy for an invigorating Satsang. People were well-fed in the temples. Despite the tour being hectic, the whole group of 80 was energetic and enthusiastic. Gurudev was received by the temple authorities at the Sri Rangam temple and honoured by the pontiff of the Vaishnava tradition, who was visibly moved.

Then the troupe moved on to Madhurai where the elephants garlanded Gurudev to the beat of the drums on the premises of the famous Minakshi temple, for a jubilant Satsang with more than 8,000 people who were spellbound in a great meditation.

Next morning the entire town of Rajapalayam celebrated a long-awaited (seven years) Satsang with Gurudev. Before noon the group left for Udimalpet, where many Seva projects had been launched. Again a big Satsang with several thousand people.

The next morning there was a live Kriya and Satsang for about 2,500 people and the group went to Pollachi for the grand, final Satsang of the tour.

Then the caravan of buses and cars left for Bangalore and Gurudev left for Madras, where a gentleman came to meet him with an ancient, 5,000-year-old palm leaf script which mentioned the name of Gurudev and the immense grace that flows through him and protects and transforms the lives of millions.

Then Gurudev came to the European Ashram in Bad Antogast, Germany. Several Advanced Courses and Seva projects are happening around the world this week - as usual - not to mention the joy and celebration.

The message for the New Year: Be in touch with the source and make your life a celebration!

186. Bliss

Bliss cannot be understood. It is extremely difficult to get into bliss. After many lifetimes you get into bliss. It is even more difficult to get out of bliss. All that you seek in your life is bliss, that divine union with your source, and everything else in the world distracts you from that goal. There are a zillion things to distract you from that goal in so many ways. So many unexplainable, incomprehensible ways of not coming home.

The mind is kept alive by cravings and aversions - shoulds or should nots and wants. Only when the mind dies, does bliss dawn. Bliss is the abode of all divinity, all *devas*. It is possible only in this human body to comprehend, to uphold. And having had a human life and having known this path, if you still do not realise this, you are at the greatest loss.

The cravings and aversions make your heart hard. There is no use in being polite in your behaviour. You can be rude in your behaviour but you cannot be rough in your heart. If you are rude in your behaviour, it is acceptable, but not if you are rough in your heart.

The world does not care how you are inside - It only looks to your behaviour. The Divine does not care how you are outside - It only looks to your inside. Never let any tiny bit of dislike or craving house in your heart. Let it be fresh, soft and fragrant like a rose.

It is such an illusion - you dislike someone or something, and this only makes you hard, and your hardness takes a long time to soften, to disappear. It is such a trap for keeping you away from the treasure.

Nothing in this material world can give you contentment. An outer-looking mind seeking contentment gets discontented, and the discontentment grows. Complaints and negativity start hardening the brain, clouding the awareness (the aura) and forming a huge cloud of negative energy. When the negativity reaches its peak, like an overloaded balloon, it bursts and comes back to the Divinity.

You can never escape the Divine, the long route of negativity, or the instantaneous positive approach. When the Divinity dawns, in no time the shift happens from the untruth to truth, from darkness to light, from the dull inert matter to the sparkling spirit. When the heart is hard, there is no fun. You cannot experience fun.

✍ News Flash:

In Poland, as the mercury dipped to -25 centigrade, 100 huge bags of warm clothes and sleeping bags were collected for the poor and homeless people. It took four lorries to transport the clothes and sleeping bags to the homeless people.

The Polish police sent a plainclothes policeman to investigate the courses in the city of Rzeszow. The policeman liked the course so much that he is now arranging for the whole police force in Rzeszow to do the course.

Prison courses are starting in West Bengal and Gujarat.

In Slovenia two courses were conducted for people suffering from multiple sclerosis. Senior doctors from the Institute of Republic of Slovenia for Rehabilitation conducted research when the course was in progress and have come out with good results.

187. DO YOU TEST GOD, OR DOES GOD TEST YOU?

Testing is part of ignorance. You only test that of which you are not sure, if God is testing you, that means God doesn't know you well enough. How could people ever think that God is testing them?

God does not test you, because He knows you in and out- your past, present and future. He knows your strengths and weaknesses, and He alone gives you strength. He doesn't test you.

Only you can test yourself. Only when you do not have confidence, then you test, if you are confident, why would you test? It you are testing yourself, you do not know yourself.

Are you testing God?

God will never pass your test because He will never show up for your test. If He shows up for your test, then He is not God. (Laughter)

Whether you get this or not - just laugh!

✍ News Flash:

The Poland Art of Living distributed 76,000 kgs of milk powder to homeless children. Russia reports that the Art of Living Course is now a part of the curriculum at the University of Irkutsk in Siberia, Russia.

Gurudev's tour of the Netherlands began with a noontime talk at the University of Maastricht to an overcrowded hall with no room even to stand. The group continued to Amsterdam, where he gave an inspiring talk on human values to 140 diplomats, ministers and ambassadors representing 20 countries. The next evening, a public talk was held in a beautifully-decorated hall with melodious music and marvelous meditation, and everyone was in bliss. There was an art exhibit on human values and the atmosphere was filled with joy and enthusiasm.

The group then moved on to Rotterdam, where Gurudev completed the tour with a talk to the Indian community and everyone present was shining as brightly as the decorations.

188. WELCOMING AND RESISTING

Do you welcome all that comes to you or do you resist it? If you cannot resist anything, you cannot welcome anything! You cannot resist everything and you cannot welcome everything!

You don't welcome all thoughts that come to your mind. When you welcome a thought, it means you find it good and act on it. If you act on all thoughts that come to your mind, you will end up in a mental hospital or in prison. So, you resist or ignore some thoughts and welcome other thoughts.

You need discrimination in life. Welcoming and resisting is a swing in life.

Welcoming is essential for expansion and growth and resistance is essential for maintenance.

Audience: But what you resist persists!

Gurudev: If you resist a cold, it does not persist!

If there is no resistance in your body, you cannot survive. Your body resists some things and welcomes others.

Where the resistance is weak, the persistence happens. A weak resistance makes the opposition persist. A strong resistance erases the opposition. Strong resistance leads to valour, power and *samadhi* (equanimity). It brings in you the strength of a warrior. Nothing can tempt you, nothing can obstruct you. Then the victory is gained without fighting. Where there is strong resistance or total welcome, the victory is gained without any fighting.

✍ News Flash:

Laughing clubs started this week in Europe.

Today the Art of Living will be delivering a half-hour presentation at the United Nations World Health Committee in New York.

The Sikh priest from the Sikh temple of Frankfurt came to the ashram for chanting of the Holy Book (Sukhmani Sahib).

There was a roaring laughter session in the ashram later in the afternoon. Only those who were there would know the cause and effect of it

Holland television has made a documentary on Gurudev.

189. STIMULATING THE SOUL

When a part of the body is stimulated, pleasure arises. When your soul is stimulated, love arises. Love has no end, but pleasure ends. Often people think pleasure is love. The distinction between pleasure and love has to be understood. Only the luckiest one will understand.

Just as you eat sugar and stimulate the tongue, music stimulates the ears and sight stimulates the eyes. And what stimulates the soul? *Sadhana* and *Satsang* are what stimulate the soul!

All that one wants is the stimulation of the soul. Even a faint idea of it keeps life going. Every other stimulus is on the surface. The stimulus of the soul energises and the stimulus of the body brings tiredness. Every stimulus should lead you to the Self so that when you listen to music you transcend the music, and when you listen to knowledge it takes you to silence.

✍ *News Flash:*

Gurudev's longest-ever stay in Bad Antogast made the ashram shining and vibrating with joy and bliss. Amazing talks were followed by crazy walks in the darkest night where the only light shining was Gurudev.

Ronnie Newman presented a paper on the Art of Living at the United Nations which was applauded by one and all.

190. Stretching the Emptiness

Stretching the Sound is Music.

Stretching the Movement is Dance.

Stretching the Smile is Laughter.

Stretching the Mind is Meditation.

Stretching the Life is Celebration.

Stretching the Devotee is God.

Stretching the Feeling is Ecstasy.

Stretching the Emptiness is Bliss.

Question: What is emptiness?

Gurudev: Emptiness is the doorway between the material and spiritual worlds. It is where you come to understand the nature of the spirit, if you do not know emptiness, then you cannot know the joy of the Being. The knack for experiencing the Being causes emptiness. From the emptiness begins the fullness.

On one side of emptiness is misery and on the other side of emptiness is joy.

That is what Buddha said: "The whole world is misery and what is to be achieved is emptiness".

✍ *News Flash:*

Clothes were distributed to about 500 villagers as part of the Sri Sri Seva Project of the ashram.

191. LOVE'S WISDOM

I chant the name of my beloved in every breath.
The beloved is faultless - perfect.
But being in love I have lost my reputation.

When there is so much love, you take total responsibility for any misunderstanding. You may express dismay for a moment on the surface. But when you do not feel that in your heart, you arrive at a perfect understanding. You are in a state where all problems and differences slide away and only love shines through.

Usually we get stuck in our differences, because we have lost sight of ourselves. In the name of love we try to manipulate and control the other person. It is natural that when we love somebody, we want them to be perfect.

You never see the holes in the ground from the top of a hill; from a plane the earth looks so smooth. So also from a state of elevated consciousness, you do not see the pitfalls in others. But if you come to the ground, you always see the holes. And when you want to fill the holes, you have to see them. You cannot build a home being airborne. You cannot till the land without looking at the holes, filling them, removing the pebbles.

That is why when you love somebody, you find all the faults in them. But finding faults destroys love, instead of filling the holes, we run away from them. When you love somebody and see their faults, stay with them and help them fill the holes. This is wisdom.

✍ *News Flash:*

The Shankaracharya of Elenir Mutt (Ashram) enthralled the Satsangees with his mellifluous rendering of bhajans. After our devotees started singing, Swamiji was so inspired that he forgot the time, grabbed the mike and started singing again.

It has been proposed to open an International School of Journalism in the ashram to give a positive effect to journalism. Those who are experienced in this field are invited to provide input.

192. Becoming Defenceless

Whenever a boundary is broken, it creates some fear. The fear creates dislike. This dislike puts us back within the boundary. And to keep yourself within the boundary you put forth defences. When you try to defend your position, it is such a stress, isn't it? And every time you try to defend your position it makes you weaker.

On the path, people even use the knowledge as a defence against criticism! Don't use knowledge as a defence.

The knowledge is like an umbrella for you - a shelter, not a weapon. Of course, sometimes "Don't use knowledge as a weapon" becomes an excuse of not being in knowledge! (Laughter)

I say, drop all your defences. Anybody can make a mistake. Even you!

Don't defend your mistakes. Just accept them and move on. When you are totally defenceless, that's when you'll be strong.

✍ News Flash:

Maha Shivaratri celebrations at the Bangalore Ashram held everyone spellbound. Three Rudra Pujas in two days and a magnificent Satsang of 4,000 devotees awakened the Cosmic Dancer within. Consciousness became so alive and vibrant, and celebrations continued late into the night.

Gurudev inaugurated several community halls that were built in the neighbouring villages.

The Indian Teachers and Organisers Meeting filled everyone with joy and enthusiasm on seeing the way the knowledge is spreading in every part of the country. There are huge plans for the coming millennium, with many Seva projects already underway.

193. DIKSHA

Initiation is called *diksha*. In Sanskrit '*di*' means intellect,'*ksha*' means the horizon or the end. *Diksha* means transcending the intellect.

Education is called *shiksha*, the horizon of discipline, total discipline. Discipline is needed for education. *Diksha* is needed for meditation.

A teacher gives *shiksha*. A Guru gives *diksha*. A Guru takes you beyond intellect to the realm of Being. It is a journey from the head to the heart.

Blossoming beyond the intellect is *diksha*. If you do not go beyond the intellect, you will not smile, you will not laugh. Once *diksha* happens, you are happy, blissful and contented and the thirst for knowledge is quenched.

Totality of discipline is *Shiksha*.

Totality of intelligence is *Diksha*.

✍ News Flash:

Major Seva projects were started in various parts of India.

Gurudev declared a two-month training program for volunteers who would like to be involved in the 5-H Program in India.

In Mangalore, the ex-Chief Minister of Karnataka, Sri Veerappa Moily, the Education Minister and other dignitaries inaugurated an open-air theater named after Gurudev.

As Gurudev arrived at Hyderabad after a hectic schedule in Bangalore, the airport reverberated with Vedic chants, clarinets, drums and enthusiastic devotees.

Gurudev was given a grand reception at the Shirdi Sai Baba Ashram. Over 10,000 people came to a grand Satsang at the Nizam College Grounds. Everyone took Gurudev's blessings and expressed their gratitude.

194. LOVE AND LUST

In love even an object gains life. Stones speak to you, trees speak to you, the sun, the moon and the whole creation become alive and divine.

In lust even a living being becomes a mere object. You want to even use people like objects.

Here are some salient attributes of love and lust. They are so different yet so close! If you find more, you may add to the list.

Lust brings tension; love brings relaxation.

Lust focuses on the part; love focuses on the whole.

Lust brings violence; love brings sacrifice.

In lust you want to grab and possess; in love you want to give and surrender.

Lust says, "All I want you to have is what I want."

Love says, "I want you to have what you want."

In lust there is effort; love is effortless.

Lust causes feverishness and frustration; love causes longing and pain.

Lust imprisons and destroys; love liberates and sets you free.

Lust demands; love commands.

Lust gets you mixed up and confused. In love you are focused and spaced out!

Lust is only dark and monotonous; love has many modes and colours.

If someone's lust is interrupted they get angry and start hating. Hatred in the world today is not out of love, it is out of lust.

Love is playfulness, and in lust there is cunning and manipulation.

Shiva, the embodiment of innocence and love, was meditating. His meditation was disturbed by an arrow of flowers from the lord of lust. As soon as *Shiva* woke up he opened his third eye and the lord of lust, *Manmatha* (one who churns the mind), was reduced to ashes.

Everybody celebrates by throwing colours on each others, realizing that life is full of colours.

We play many roles in our lives. If all the roles get mixed up, it becomes dark, like when you mix all the colours. The wise play each role distinctively side by side, like the colours displayed side by side form a rainbow.

✒ *News Flash:*

Only 10,000 people attended the Calcutta Satsang! - as public transport was closed down by a statewide bandh (strike). The decorations, Satsang and Gurudev's talk all combined to create a dream world. People are still in a daze after so many days...

On to the Pink City – Jaipur – for a dignitaries meeting, followed by a wonderful Satsang where the thronging crowd played with flowers. On this tour a couple came up with a unique way of showing their gratitude – a giant rose garland weighing over sixty pounds!

Now the celebration continues in Rishikesh. People from all over North India came to celebrate Holi, the festival of colours, with the Master.

195. DOUBT AND CLOSENESS

Doubt cannot come where there is a sense of closeness. Doubt needs distance to appear. You never doubt something that is dear to you, close to you.

The moment you doubt, it is no longer dear to you; a distance has come. You may doubt yourself, but you do not doubt that which is yours.

Self-doubt is a lack of closeness to oneself. A sense of belonging, closeness, intimacy are all the antidotes for doubt.

✍ *News Flash:*

Knowledge is flowing from the source, on the banks of the Ganges. Waves of love are overwhelming the Advanced Course participants and teacher trainees –everyone is in BLISS.

196. INTELLIGENCE

The first sign of intelligence is not to begin anything! Not to be born at all!

Having lost this first sign, the second sign of intelligence is this: once you have started something, see it through to the end. The short-sighted ones look for short-term benefits. Far-sighted ones look for long-term benefits.

Whether you consider yourself intelligent or not, there is no escape from *Seva* (service), for *Seva* gives immediate satisfaction as well as long-term merit.

✍ *News Flash:*

Each country is asked to choose one particular month in a year to organise a community lunch or dinner once each week.

197. ATTAINING SELF-KNOWLEDGE

Desire, awareness of the Self and action are all manifestations of the same energy that is you. Among these three, one of them dominates at any one time. When you have many desires, you are not aware of the Self. When desire dominates, Self-awareness will be at its lowest, and that is why philosophers all around the world have always advocated renunciation and dropping of desires.

When the awareness is dominant, then happiness dawns. When desire dominates, stress and sorrow result. When action dominates, restlessness and disease are the result.

When your actions and desires are sincerely directed to the Divine or to the welfare of society, then consciousness is automatically elevated, and Self-knowledge is sure to be attained.

News Flash:

India has stepped into the 52nd Century of Krishna's time. The 18th of March began our year 5101 and a great celebration is happening everywhere. The "sun" of knowledge dawns ever brighter in this holy valley of Rishis and sets in a Kaleidoscope of laughter, joy, celebration and bliss. The purity of the holy waters has inspired a new "wave" of pranayama.

Many healing experiences have been shared amidst tears of gratitude - "cancelled" cancers, disappearing depressions. A heart patient spent Rs. 4 lakhs in a hospital in Bombay and was given five months to live. But after Rs. 500, a five-day Art of Living Course and two years of enthusiastic living, he is still going strong - hale and hearty!

A program to teach 400 youths has been launched all over rural India for the implementation of the 5-H Program.

Many new books of Gurudev's precious knowledge have now been released in Hindi.

April 8, 1999
Bangalore Ashram, India

198. You And Your Time

When you feel time is too short, you are either restless or in a state of expanded awareness. When you feel time is too long, you are either miserable or you have a keen mind.

When you are happy and when you love what you are doing, you don't feel time. Similarly during sleep you don't feel time.

In deep meditation, you are time and everything is happening within you. Events are happening in you like clouds passing in the sky.

When you are ahead of time, it is dragging and boring. When the time is ahead of you, then you are surprised and shocked. You cannot digest the events.

When you are with the time, you are wise and at peace.

Narayana Sharma says, "Gurudev, you spend a good time with us!"

Next week we will see how to manage time or how the time manages us.

✍ *News Flash:*

Bus loads of people arrived in Rishikesh for Mahakriya and MahaSatsang - a grand finale for Gurudev's Rishikesh visit. At the India Habitat Centre in Delhi, Union Cabinet Ministers, Members of Parliament, judges, other dignitaries and public servants attended Gurudev's talk and were so happy that they all came back the next day for a jubilant Satsang in a hall packed to three times the normal capacity.

Gurudev's first visit to the mountain kingdom of Nepal – he was received at the airport by the Prime Minister's Emissary and later had a meeting with the Prime Minister. An impressive dignitary's meeting was followed by an ecstatic Satsang of nearly 3,000.

Over to Chennai in Southern India – Gurudev presided over India Heritage '99, a special conference of Temple Administrators. In his sparkling keynote address, he enlightened the guardians of Temple Heritage on the newer ways to bring about fusion of spiritual and cultural dimensions.

199. A PRAYER

Give me not thirst if you cannot give me water.

Give me not hunger if you cannot give me food.

Give me not joy if I cannot share.

Give me not skills if I cannot put them to good use.

Give me not intelligence if I cannot perceive beyond it.

Give me not knowledge if I cannot digest it.

Give me not love if I cannot serve.

Give me not desire that doesn't lead me to you.

Give me not a path that doesn't take me home.

Give me not a prayer if you don't want to hear it. (Laughter)

Question: When you pray, to whom do you pray?

Gurudev: To myself! In prayer the mind goes to its source, the Self. God, Guru and the Self are the same.

Dean: Give me not time if I don't know how to manage it.
Daniel: *Gurudev* says, "You're all out of time..." (Laughter)

✍ *News Flash:*

Gurudev arrived in Singapore for a big Satsang in the football stadium. As usual, nature cooperated by providing good weather.

Then on to a Satsang in Kuala Lampur.

In Japan people called together others on their cell phones - a spontaneous cellular Satsang!

Gurudev is now in Kauai, Hawaii, where the laughter here is competing with the waves on the ocean.

200. THE NOISE OF NONVIOLENCE

Often violence comes with noise. Nonviolence happens in silence. People who are violent make a lot of noise; they make it known. People who are nonviolent are quiet. But the time has come for people who are nonviolent to make noise so that the violence will quiet down. The message of nonviolence has to come loud and clear so that it can be heard from a young age.

A sense of shame has to be connected with anger and violence. The reason for violence in young people is a sense of pride in anger and violence, not a sense of shame. People feel proud that they are violent or angry. They think it is prestigious or a status symbol to be aggressive.

Aggression is not considered a quality to be ashamed of. This promotes aggression and violence in the whole society, and when aggression and violence are promoted, human values diminish. Some movies and modern music glorify frustration, anger and revenge and make these a role model for children.

We need to promote human values loudly and clearly, especially love, compassion and a sense of belongingness. Speak to groups or through your local media in the newspaper and on TV and create as many ART Excel and Art or Living Courses in your area as possible.

David: If people are ashamed to be angry, won't that keep them unnatural and set up resistance in them that will persist?

Gurudev: If they are not ashamed, they will feel they have a license to get angry and violent. Sometimes resistance is a good thing, like resistance to disease or resistance to bad habits.

✍ News Flash:

Gurudev continued on from Kauai, Hawaii to the island of Oahu, Hawaii where an Advanced Course, public Satsangs and meetings with government leaders awaited him. The Hawaiian Prison SMART Program continues to flourish and other new programs for government agencies are being planned. Gurudev spoke at a luncheon honoring volunteer service leaders, was interviewed on NBC-TV and was invited to speak at a youth conference with delegates from over 100 countries. The traveling Satsang then made its way to the mainland to a warm welcome from our Art of Living community in Apple Valley, California.

201. LIFE IS TOO SHORT; LIFE IS ETERNAL

The realisation that life is very short brings dynamism in your life. Unwanted things will fall off as well as distractions. When you have to act or put out effort, know that life is short. When you realise life is short, procrastination falls away. When you are expecting a result, know that life is eternal.

The ignorant person does it the other way: he hurries for the result and is impatient and frustrated. Impatience goes away when you know that life is eternal. When you are looking for a return of a favour or a result from your good deed, you want it quickly. But when you know that there are many lifetimes, you realise that if you don't get it sooner, you get it later.

WAKE UP AND SEE YOUR LIFE IS TOO SHORT! Time is running, so what are you doing with your life? Is it being useful to you and the world around you? Realise life is too short.

WAKE UP! LIFE IS ETERNAL!

When you want to enjoy the fruit of action, know that life is eternal. When it comes to hope, you should know that there are many lifetimes. When you are looking for results, know that time is eternal. If someone doesn't thank you or takes advantage of you, thank them because they will pay you back later with interest. So no one needs to feel sorry that they are unappreciated or have been taken advantage of. Know that you will have to be paid back in the future with interest!

When it comes to enjoying the fruit of your actions, good deeds or even blessings, know that life is eternal. Anytime that you are in a hurry, you cannot enjoy. So know that life is eternal.

✍ News Flash:

In addition to the jubilant Satsangs in Apple Valley, Los Angeles, Santa Barbara, Monterey, Berkeley and San Jose, Gurudev spoke on human values in the 20th century at the University of California in Santa Barbara. A new initiative has begun to promote ART Excel in high schools and colleges throughout the USA. New schools sponsored by the Art of Living in tribal areas in Bihar, India have been inaugurated with 90 students. Volunteers interested in promoting the ART Excel project can send their bio-data to the ART Excel coordinator in care of their national office.

May 6, 1999
Boston, Massachusetts, United States

202. A Deep Rest

You cannot rest when you have to do something which you cannot do. And you cannot rest when you feel you have to be someone whom you are not. You are not required to do what you cannot do. You will not be asked to give what you cannot give. Nothing is expected of you that you cannot do. Doing service involves only doing what you can do. And no one wants you to be someone whom you are not.

This realisation brings you deep rest. You cannot rest if you have either ambition or lethargy. Both are opposed to good rest. A lazy person will toss and turn at night and be "rest-less" and an ambitious person will burn inside. This rest brings up your talents and abilities and brings you closer to your nature. Even a slight feeling that the Divine is with you brings deep rest. And prayer, love and meditation are all favours of deep rest.

✍ *News Flash:*

Gurudev's American tour picked up speed as it moved first to San Jose with a day-long Advanced Course and an evening program for the Indian community and then to a weekend Advanced Course is Wisconsin where tears of joy were shed.

Next the traveling Satsang moved on rapidly to Kansas City, New Jersey and New York. The following day took on the feeling of an adventure as Gurudev cruised north through New England, with a picnic lunch in New Haven, several wrong turns and a happy arrival in Boston in late afternoon.

Tomorrow Gurudev speaks at Harvard University on the topic of children, violence and our ART Excel Program.

203. Blessing

Make your home Gods home and there will be light, love and abundance.

Make your body God's abode and there will be peace and bliss.

Feel your mind as a toy of God and you'll watch and enjoy all its games.

See the world as play and as a display of God Himself and you will repose in the non-dual Self.

Blessing comes to you in many forms:

If you are generous, blessing comes to you as abundance.

If you are hard-working, blessing comes to you as happiness.

If you are lazy, blessing comes to you as hard work.

If you are pleasure loving, blessing comes to you as dispassion.

If you are dispassionate, blessing comes to you as knowledge of the Self.

✍ News Flash:

Gurudev gave a talk at Harvard University in Boston and there was a jubilant Satsang in the evening.

Then on to Virginia and Washington D.C. In addition to the grand Satsangs, Gurudev also addressed doctors and scientists at the National Institutes of Health, where Dr. Janakiramaiah, who has done research on Sudarshan Kriya, presented his paper. The response was overwhelming.

A Human Values Conference was held in which diplomats and officials from many countries participated. A joyful finale to the American spring tour took place at Great Falls.

There has been a great rise in the German ashram in all aspects – four times its capacity and still everyone is happy.

The Art of Living Basic Course has been approved for the employees of the judiciary in Wayne County in the state of Michigan and the ART Excel Program is in full swing in several states in the USA.

Big news....Gurudev looks much younger!

May 20, 1999
European Ashram, Germany

204. SHORTCUT!

If you think you are stupid

Then ... you know who you are.

And if you know who you are ...

You are enlightened!

And if you are enlightened,

Then ... you certainly are not stupid,

If you think you are intelligent,

Then you don't know who you are.

And if you don't know who you are ...

Then you really ARE stupid!

Better realise your stupidity . . . and be enlightened!

✍ *News Flash:*

The Guru as usual, with his love and grace, charmed the French people in their capital city. After the wonderful course in Paris everyone attended Satsang aboard a boat on the River Seine.

The following evening many ambassadors and dignitaries attended a conference on human values which Gurudev addressed.

205. FAITH; NATURE OF CONSCIOUSNESS

Whatever you have faith in, do not make it an object of knowing. You do not need to know about that in which you have faith.

If you have faith in God, do not try to know God. God and Self are not objects of knowing. And you cannot have faith in that which you have made into an object of knowing.

A child has faith in the mother. The child does not try to know the mother; it simply has faith in the mother. You cannot make love an object of knowing. If you try to do so, the love will disappear.

Curiosity to know obstructs faith by making into an object of knowing that in which you have faith. Often when people fall in love with each other, they don't let go of curiosity. Curiosity slowly erodes their faith and love.

Faith is non-analytical. Knowledge is analytical. God, love, Guru, sleep and Self are beyond knowing. If you try to analyse, you get confused. And the moment you make something into an object of knowing, analysis starts.

Nick: Does God have faith in us?

Gurudev: I don't know! (Laughter, very non-analytical)

To know whether God has faith or not, you have to analyse. And in asking this question, you give God a mind which is not there.

Barbara: Can you have faith without being aware of it?

Gurudev: Yes. You have faith. Faith is the nature of a relaxed and undivided consciousness.

✍ **News Flash:**

Seva Camps are in full swing in Bangalore with a particular focus on disabled children. Seva Camps are also held in other areas.

206. SUCCESS

Question: How was yesterday's program? Was it successful?

Gurudev: There is no question of success if you have nothing to gain. There is nothing to gain if you have only come to give and serve. Success indicates non-supremacy. Success means what? It indicates that there are chances of failure. If something is supreme, there is nothing to lose. People running after success only exhibit their limitations.

Success means crossing a limit. To cross a limit you need to assume that you have a limit. Assuming a limit is underestimating yourself. If you have no boundaries, then where is your success? If you have limitless access, then there is no success. You don't say that you successfully drank a glass of water, because it is well within your capabilities. But when you do something that is beyond your perceived limits, you claim success.

When you realise your unboundedness, then no action is an achievement.

Anyone who claims to be successful only reveals his limitation. If you feel very successful, it means that you have underestimated yourself. All your gains can only be smaller than you. Taking pride in any gains is belittling yourself.

Sheila: What if you feel that you are not serving successfully?

Gurudev: When you serve others, you may feel that you have not done enough but you will not feel that you have been unsuccessful. Real service is when you feel that you have not done enough.

Kai: You are not very successful! (Laughter)

Gurudev: I am just full!

✍ **News Flash:**

The Scandinavian whirlwind tour started with a lively Satsang in Denmark and Finland.

In Sweden, the Swedish television filmed Gurudev for one hour for a millennium program. Gurudev gave a hilarious talk in Stockholm and as usual the best talks are not recorded.

Then on to the land of the midnight sun, Norway. Over 200 diplomats and officials attended the Human Values Conference in Oslo, followed by a grand Satsang in a beautiful hall.

207. MESSAGE

Question: *Gurudev*, what is your message?

Gurudev: I have no message. In order to give a message you have to be far away. Message needs a distance. Message is of the past or of the future. Message is impersonal and lifeless. Knowledge cannot be a message. The wise one will not give you a message, but will simply awaken you.

God will not give you a message. For God to give you a message, God has to be so far away from you. God is closer to you than your breath. How can He give you a message?

The wise neither need a message nor give a message. The unwise would give a message and want a message and would be unable to use the message anyway. Whoever needs the message will not use it. And one who can use the message wouldn't need it!

Jim: What is the difference between "knowledge" and "message"?

Gurudev: You can read about living in the moment so many times, but it becomes knowledge only when you experience it. You can read the ingredients, but when you taste the food the information becomes knowledge.

Jim: These Knowledge Sheets really cut down on our communication. (Laughter)

✍ News Flash:

For the first time Gurudev visited Argentina, Chile and Brazil to deliver people from messages! There was great enthusiasm everywhere and government officials of several departments were eager to adopt the programs. South America was in jubilation!

208. BLESSED ARE THOSE WHO ARE BORED

Only a conscious, alert and dynamic person can get bored. A dull and inert person doesn't get bored. If you get bored, it indicates you are more alive and human. It is a sign that you are growing, that you are evolving.

An animal, for example, keeps doing the same thing. It never gets bored. Cows, horses, birds do the same things over and over all their lives.

People eat, watch television, change jobs, change partners to escape boredom. And they get frustrated. Frustration takes them back to inertia and unconsciousness.

Only in two states does the boredom not occur: in a state of total inertia or in a state of Divine Consciousness. If you are bored, it indicates you are evolving. Boredom moves you.

Jim: Boredom moves you towards the Divine.

Gurudev: Yes. Be proud of your boredom and celebrate!

✍ *Volcanic News Flash:*

May be you are bored listening to "the hall was packed" all the time.... Well, in Bogota, Colombia, about 100 people showed up for a morning lecture at the university. The microphone came at the end and so did most of the people! About 12 showed up for another university talk, but Gurudev was not there. In contrast, the evening Satsang was very crowded and there was much confusion. The meditation was reduced to five minutes as many had to keep standing. [McQueen went on strike and refused to write this News Flash because it was too factual. (Laughter)]

The Dominican Republic's devotion and organizing power pulled Gurudev on an 11-hour marathon journey to reach them. After his last minute trip to the ocean, Gurudev boarded the plane soaking wet.

In Panama the warmth of the Latin American hearts and songs lit up the Satsangs.

In Costa Rica Gurudev had a diplomatic reception and a motorcycle escort, and his talk was co-sponsored by the University of Peace and the National Commission for Human Values. The First Lady, on behalf of the President, received Gurudev at the palace and extended her full-hearted support for Art of Living activities in Costa Rica.

Gurudev was fascinated by the orange fire spewing down the side of the volcano as we drove through the rain forest at midnight. Today the Weekly Knowledge erupted at the foot of the volcano.

209. RELIGION AND POLITICS

The role of religion is to make one righteous and loving, and politics means caring for people and their welfare. When religion and politics don't coexist, then you have corrupt politicians and pseudo-religious leaders.

A religious man who is righteous and loving will definitely care for the welfare of the whole population and hence becomes a true politician. And a true politician can only be righteous and loving. He can not be anything but religious. All the avatars and prophets have been caring for people and so were in politics. You can find many examples to this effect.

When religions restrict the freedom to worship and restrict modes of worship, they become unsuitable for creating a harmonious society. When religion becomes all encompassing and gives full freedom to pray and worship in any manner that religion will bring righteousness and peace in people and will be suitable for any society.

People think politics and religion have to be kept separate because many religions did not give freedom to worship and did not care for all people equally. History has shown that religion has created conflict. But irreligious societies (e.g., communism) have created chaos and corruption.

Today both religion and politics need reform. Religion has to become broader and more spiritual to allow freedom of worship and to encompass all the wisdom in the world. And politicians have to become more righteous and spiritual.

✍ *News Flash:*

Fantastic Satsangs in Florida, Raleigh, North Carolina and New York. One hundred or so liberated Satsangees went on a cruise to bless the Statue of Liberty.

210. LOVE AND RENUNCIATION

Only one who has renounced can truly love. To the degree you have renounced, to that degree you have the ability to love.

Often people think those who renounce cannot love, and those who love cannot renounce. This is because so called renunciants do not seem to be in love, and so called lovers are very possessive and seem to be in love are in need.

True love is non-possessive and brings freedom, and renunciation is nothing but freedom. Only in freedom can love fully blossom. When in love you say, "I want nothing, I just want this." Renunciation is, "I don't want anything. I am free." In love there is no other need. Renunciation is having no need. Love and renunciation, although appearing to be opposites, are two sides of the same coin.

McQueen: They are the same side of the same coin. (Laughter)

Tara: Does this mean the lover renounces his beloved?

Gurudev: You renounce the attachment, the possessiveness. Renunciation doesn't diminish love; it enhances it. Only renunciation can sustain love and joy. Without renunciation love turns into misery, possessiveness, jealousy and anger. Renunciation brings contentment and contentment sustains love. Without renunciation one gets discontented, frustrated, sad, fearful, suspicious, analytical. And the whole soap opera begins. And this is what we find in society - don't we?

The so-called renunciants have run away from life frustrated and disappointed. Real renunciation is born out of knowledge and wisdom, knowledge of life in the background of time and space and in the context of this magnanimous universe.

✍ *News Flash:*

There was such a contrast in Shakti Kutir as Gurudev created the Weekly Knowledge this week. Profound wisdom was flowing along with the debate and laughter of devotees. Eventually the discussion went haywire.

Belma said, "Gurudev, you have the purest intellect. Why do you ask us for our opinion? Then it only gets all messed up." Mikey said, "Those who know will know and those who don't won't." Tommy said, "Those who don't get it are free!" Finally roaring with laughter some devotees renounced the Weekly Knowledge sheet to go to dinner.

Last night, at an electrifying Satsang full of uncontrollable laughter and dance, Gurudev gave paradoxical knowledge that enlightenment is a journey from heart to head. (Of course the talk wasn't taped.)

The Clean Gujarat Project has been launched by the devotees from Gujarat. A Yagna was performed in the Bangalore Ashram to bring peace in Kashmir. Two of our teachers will be going to Belgrade and Kosovo.

July 8, 1999
Montreal Ashram, Canada

211. CHANGE AND LOVE

There are some who are longing for change. Feeling that everything is stagnant in their lives, they want to change partners, careers, dwellings. And there are some who are scared of change. They feel secure the way they are.

There are some who see the change, but don't acknowledge it out of fear. There are some who do not notice the change at all. There are some who do not think there is anything to change.

And there are some who realise that everything is changing, yet see there is something that is non-changing. Those who recognize the non-changing amidst the change are the wisest of all.

Question: Must love as well always change?

Gurudev: Love is your nature. What is your nature cannot change. But the expression of love changes. Because love is your nature, you cannot but love.

The mother has total love for the child, but sometimes she feeds the child, sometimes she is strict with the child. "Come on, sit and write!" Sometimes she slaps the child. She does this out of love, and these are all different modes of love. So the expression of love changes. But love itself does not change, because love is your nature.

✍ *News Flash:*

There is nothing new. Everything is the same, meaning everything is changing, everything is recycled. Gurudev this week, has spoken beautifully on the four pillars of knowledge. Canadian Broadcasting Company crews followed Gurudev around for two days and taped a high-energy Satsang complete with wild dancing and Carla's raucous laughter, to be Broadcast on national television.

Admissions to our schools in India continue to increase. The enrolment in our Bangalore school has grown to more than 700 children. Three more schools have been established in underdeveloped regions in Northern India.

212. THANK SUPERFICIALLY

Gurudev: Which is better, to thank deeply or superficially?

Everyone in unison: Deeply!

Gurudev: No, superficially. (Everyone is baffled.) Thanking needs a separation. Thanking means there are two. If you are deeply thankful, it means you deeply feel the separation.

Deep within there is no need to thank, because there is oneness. But superficially you can thank. Thanks are like ripples on the surface of the water.

When you say, "Thank you," you complete something. You are finishing a transaction, a relationship, a process. "Thank you" is like "Good-bye". You can complete all transactions at a surface level, but deeper inside is only oneness.

Thankfulness always exists in relation to something else.

You don't thank for nothing at all, you thank for something. But in this case, something is less than nothing!

At the deepest level, thanking has no meaning. Does one hand thank the other hand? The deeper you go, you see there is no "other" to be thanked.

John: So we should thank superficially and feel deeply?

Gurudev: Feeling is also superficial. If you think the feeling is the depth, then you have not gone deep. Feeling is deeper than thinking. But feelings change. Whatever is the deepest doesn't change.

So thank superficially, not from the depth. Deep thanks indicate deep separation!

Steve: Maybe we should say, "I thank you from the tip of my tongue!" (Laughter)

✍ *News Flash:*

A trip to a nearby waterfall by 200 course participants marked the grand finale of the Advanced Course at the Canadian Ashram. (And Gurudev got thoroughly splashed!)

The trip to Canada's capital was cancelled - but the show went on anyway and all went well. The Satsangs in Toronto were beautiful and the hospitality was warm.

Then off to the USA West Coast, where the Satsangs and warm hospitality continue. Tomorrow the Art of Living caravan will leave for Portland.

213. SATYAM PARAM DHIMAHI

Satyam Param Dhimahi — Truth and the Divinity of the transcendental I uphold in my awareness. It is the intellect that divides the world, and the same intellect can bring it together by soaking itself in Divinity. When the intellect discusses mundane things, it starts dividing the existence. When the intellect starts discussing knowledge, wisdom, truth, then it starts uniting. It brings forth the transcendental. It rediscovers its true nature, which is non-dual.

Whether you complain, compose a poem, or speak knowledge, you are a witness to the flow. Suppose someone is complaining or justifying. They are simply saying things spontaneously. In the same way, when you speak knowledge of the Self, or spontaneously compose a poem out loud, there is a flow from the intellect.

Anything can flow from the intellect, and you are a witness to the flow, whether it is garbage or wisdom.

And all that you can do is pray to the Divine, "Let wisdom, divinity and truth flow through this intellect."

Exercise – Give away your names: Give the same name to all the members of the *Satsang* for one month. The name is up to you. You could choose a name like Chris, Michael or *Krishna* that could refer to anybody.

Question: What is the purpose of this exercise?

Gurudev: Your identification with your name is very deep and strong in the consciousness. When you can let go of the name, you experience freedom.

✍ **News Flash:**

Over 250 Art of Living teachers have gathered at Lake Tahoe for the Teachers' Fiesta, a truly ecstatic celebration and feast of sublime knowledge.

The snow-covered peaks of the Sierra Nevada Mountains are not nearly as high as the energy here nor the knowledge that is flowing from the Master.

In India, a mass food and clothes distribution for the poor took place at the Bangalore Ashram.

214. GURU IS THE GOAL

Guru is nothing but wisdom and love.

Guru is that principle which is wisdom and love, and that is awakened in each one who has stepped onto the path. You also call that person a Guru in whom there is no gap between life and wisdom and love.

Often one recognizes wisdom but sees a gap between wisdom and one's own life. The purpose of becoming a disciple is to bridge that gap.

Being with the Guru means spontaneous integration of life and wisdom.

✍ News Flash:

Miracle in Tahoe: Finally all the diverse personalities in the Art of Living are saying, "I agree with you." It is the latest buzz word! Agree comes from the Sanskrit word "agra" which means to be in the forefront.

At the Teacher's Fiesta all rose to a new level of wisdom. One thousand people have assembled for the Guru Purnima Celebration at Lake Tahoe with Vedic chanting and tears of gratitude.

Advanced Courses and Guru Purnima celebrations happened all over the world.

215. How to Conquer Jealousy or Envy

There are many ways to conquer jealousy or envy.

1. Know that the person of whom you are jealous or envious has done some good karma in the past and is now reaping the fruit.

2. See it as an inspiration to gain merit yourself.

3. Create a sense of belongingness with them. See that they are a part or you.

4. Think of all you have that they do not have and feel grateful.

5. Observe the sensations.

6. Join hands and form a team with them.

7. Realise that in the current of moving time all will perish.

8. Think of everyone who is jealous of you for what you have and see that what they envy has not brought you joy.

9. Go and ask them, "Are you happy?"

Caroline: And what if they say, "Yes"?

If the answer is "yes" then they must be in the Art of Living! (Laughter)

Ananda: What should you do if others are jealous or envious of you?

1. Praise them in superlatives.

2. Create a sense of belongingness in them by your kind actions.

3. Know that their feelings are temporary.

4. The best is not to recognise their envy or jealousy at all. If you recognise a feeling as a reality, it only makes your ignorance grow.

5. Know that all feelings and emotions are just passing clouds.

6. Do not show off your talents to them.

7. Know that they are puppets. They will all perish like apples and tomatoes - just with a longer shelf life. (Laughter)

✍ *News Flash:*

Question: *With all the talk of the eclipse on the 11th of August, what should we do?*

Answer: *The time during an eclipse is an auspicious time for doing spiritual practices. Make sure your stomach is fairly empty. You should stop eating at least a couple of hours before the beginning of an eclipse and you may do your spiritual practices such as meditation, Kriya and Satsang.*

It is advisable that pregnant women and nursing mothers (for the first three months) stay indoors during the three to four hours of an eclipse.

The Art of Living and the Human Values 5H Program brochures were so nice that the Government of India borrowed the content word-for-word and made it into their own ... but we are not jealous about it!

As usual, Bad Antogast is filled with celebration.

216. ANU VRAT

The mind lives on "more." Misery starts with "more and more." Misery makes you dense and gross.

Self is subtle. To go from gross to subtle you go through the finest relative - the atom. To overcome aversion, hatred, jealousy, attraction or entanglements, you have to go to the atom. Going to the atom means accepting a teeny tiny bit of all this.

It may be difficult to accept something that you do not like but you can definitely accept a teeny tiny bit of it - an atom. The moment you accept that one atom, you will see change happen. This has to be done in a meditative state.

Suppose you love someone. You want more and more of them, yet there is no fulfilment. In *Anu Vrat* - the vow of an atom - you take just one atom of that person and that is enough to bring fulfilment to you.

Though the river is vast, a little sip quenches your thirst. Though Earth has so much food, just a little bite satisfies your hunger. All that you need are tiny bits. Accept a tiny bit of everything in life - that will bring you fulfilment.

Stephano: What about trouble?

Gurudev: There is so much trouble in the world, you can accept just a tiny part of it.

Tonight go to bed feeling that you are satisfied, taking a tiny part of divinity with you. Satisfaction comes from the subtle and not from "more and more."

Question: What about giving?

Gurudev: You take a tiny part, and the rest you give away.

✍ *News Flash:*

For a teeny tiny two minutes there was midnight at noon at Bad Antogast during the solar eclipse.

Celebration is in full swing with people from 22 countries at the European Ashram in Bad Antogast.

ART Excel teachers became teenagers and felt a big transformation in their Teacher Training Course.

The Delhi chapter of the Art of Living inaugurated the "Clean India" Seva project in Delhi.

217. KNOWLEDGE AS A BURDEN

Knowledge is a burden if it robs you of innocence.

Knowledge is a burden if it is not integrated into life.

Knowledge is a burden if it does not bring joy.

Knowledge is a burden if it gives you an idea that you are wise.

Knowledge is a burden if it does not set you free.

Knowledge is a burden if it makes you feel you are special.

✍ News Flash:

We are accustomed to all kinds of systems - financial systems, operational systems, management systems, social systems. But we are oblivious to the cosmic system that has always been present.

Transition from our little systems of functioning to the cosmic system of functioning is what we call chaos. The little mind blasts into the cosmic system around Gurudev, giving out laughter, pain, tears, gratitude and other emotions.

All our ashrams run on the cosmic system, and the devotees' homes are also switching to this mode of functioning.

Gurudev's return to India saw a frenzy of joyous celebration with a crowd of 3,000 at the Mumbai Satsang - amazing for a weekday afternoon, with virtually no publicity. From masti (ecstasy) in Mumbai, it is now bliss in Bangalore!

218. PROTECTION AND TRANSFORMATION

Only that which is temporary, small or perishable needs protection, while that which is permanent, big or vast does not.

Your body needs protection; your soul does not.
Your mind needs protection; the Self does not.

Protection simply means prolonging the time in that state; hence, protection also prevents transformation. Transformation cannot happen in protection. At the same time, without protection the desired transformation cannot happen. A seed needs protection to transform into a plant; a plant needs protection to become a tree. Protection can aid or hamper transformation. The protector should have an idea to what extent he should protect.

Kashi: Grace brings transformation with protection.

Gurudev: Truth does not need any protection. Both protection and transformation fall within the purview of time and space and these laws have to be honoured in order to transcend time.

We are both protected and transformed. This is *Hari* and *Hara*: *Hari*, the protector and *Hara*, the transformer.

Protection is limited to time, to perishable things. How long can a doctor heal or protect someone? Forever? No. Peace and happiness do not need protection because they are not temporary.

✍ *News Flash:*

Onam was celebrated in the ashram with full Kerala pomp ana splendor. The moon blushed and went into hiding after seeing the Divine in all His glory.

The 5H Youth Training Program is in full Swing, and SH volunteers are going into village after village.

A renowned saint of Ratnagiri Temple - who is always dressed in only a loin cloth, observes strict silence, and never moves anywhere - was eagerly awaiting Gurudev's visit as ancient scriptures written 5,000 years ago had predicted his visit there.

Today Gurudev begins a series of discourses on the Bhagavad Gita.

219. WHO WINS?

Many people quit doing *Seva* as they put their self image, prestige, respect, comfort and convenience ahead of their goal.

People shy away from *Seva* when they do not receive a good position, when they get insulted, when they feel they are not getting what they expected out of it and when they consider working towards their goal a struggle rather than a challenge.

And that is why only a few people in the world succeed in reaching their goal.

What is more important to you?

✍ News Flash:

Eighty-two enthusiastic new teachers have taken off this week to spread the knowledge!

220. TWO ANECDOTES

Once somebody made a mistake and Gurudev asked him, "What punishment can I give you?"

The person replied, "Don't punish me, *Gurudev*, I won't make the mistake again."

After some time, Gurudev asked another person who had made a mistake, "And what punishment can I give you?"

With a bright smile Nityanand replied, "Any punishment, *Gurudev*."

At this Gurudev turned to the rest of us with a smile and said, "See, he is so confident of my love for him that he is not afraid of any punishment."

Where there is love, there is no fear.

Do not be afraid of being punished by God.

Trust in the love that He has for you.

It was Arun and Chitra's wedding anniversary. They presented an ornate fan to Gurudev, saying, "A fan from two grateful fans."

At this Gurudev said, "Devotees are the fan; God is the air. The air is always there, but the fans make you feel it. God is always there; devotees make His presence felt!"

✍ *News Flash:*

And three more miracles ...

On a domestic flight in the U.S., Manjesh's mother fainted. A checkup later showed that her aorta had dilated and the doctors suggested an immediate operation. She visited Gurudev in San Jose, and when she went for a checkup again, her aorta was back to its normal size! The doctors could not believe this miracle.

Mr. Sardana from Delhi could not even walk - he was advised to have a heart transplant and total bed rest. He somehow made it to both the Basic and Advanced Courses, and his doctors were amazed to find his heart absolutely normal! Now he walks happily all over the ashram.

In Deesa, Gujarat, a boy who was deaf-mute since birth, started speaking and hearing after his first Sudarshan Kriya!

Many such experiences are being reported from all over.

Lord Krishna's birthday was celebrated in all gaiety at the ashram. Devotees danced and played - transported back 5,000 years!

Bangalore saw its biggest ever Satsang this week.

221. COMPASSION AND *KARMA*

There are two types of compassion. One is the compassion of the wise, one is that of the ignorant.

An ignorant person's compassion is toward the fruit of an action - the sickness or suffering that he witnesses. But a wise person's compassion is toward the lack of knowledge – the underlying reason for sickness or suffering.

Compassion for suffering shows ignorance. Suffering comes because of *karma*, and if you believe in *karma*, where is compassion? One reaps the fruit of one's actions.

If a judge has compassion for all the offenders, then the jails will be empty. At the same time, are the judges cruel to the offenders? No. The judges' compassion is for the lack of knowledge, not for the suffering of the criminals. It is the criminals' *karma*. Often people think compassion is an act, an action. Know that compassion is your very nature. Then you will see that *karma* and compassion are not contradictory but complement each other.

Suppose two people come to a hospital. One is suffering from starvation, the other is ill from overeating. What type of compassion should the doctor have toward each of them? This is a riddle for you to solve!

✍ News Flash:

The Youth Training Program ended this week on a jubilant note as 230 Yuvacharyas set forth on their mission to transform rural India. In less than three weeks, these youngsters acquired skills in disciplines as varied as martial arts, organic farming and directing plays. They presented a splendid cultural program on the concluding day. This course showed once again that grace and knowledge have the power to transform raw material into polished gems!

The festival of Lord Ganesha is being celebrated with gusto all over India. In two districts in Karnataka, senior government officers have advised all schools to conduct ART Excel courses.

222. Negativity Needs An Anchor

Negativity cannot remain without a support.

Positivity, happiness can exist without any reason.

The mind goes on trying to find support for its negativity. It looks for a hook on which to hang its negativity - if not this person, then that thing or that person. This perpetuates Maya!

The creeping vine or negativity needs a support in order to grow. But negativity or aversion for even one person can guarantee a one-way ticket to hell - you need nothing else!

All negativity is an indicator for you to move to the centre and to broaden your vision to cosmic intelligence. Instead of focusing your attention on support for your negativity, look at the seed of negativity.

With meditation, silence and *Kriya*, the source of negativity is nipped at the root.

✍ News Flash:

Bangalore saw its biggest and best ever Satsang - nearly 2,000 people were outside the jam-packed hall, but were smilingly watching the proceedings on a large screen!

A new Seva project was inaugurated by Gurudev in Urugahalli, a village adopted by the Art of Living. The project helped over 200 young women become Self-employed.

Several other villages have benefited from our Seva projects as we provided water supplies, electricity and buildings under the 5H Program.

The ashram is bursting with joy with more than 800 blissful faces!

223. LIFE IS A WAR

Life is a war.

Doctors fight against disease.

Lawyers fight against injustice.

Teachers fight against ignorance.

Depression happens when you lose the will to fight. *Arjuna* was depressed; he did not want to fight. His bow fell from his hands and his fingers trembled. *Krishna* urged him to wake up and fight! The decision to fight can take away your depression as it did for *Arjuna*.

Bharat: Fight until you give up.

Prashant: Not give up ... give in! *(Laughter)*

Even your body is a battlefield.

✍ *News Flash:*

There were two glorious Advanced Courses and a fantastic Teacher Training Course. The ashram was lit up with more than 2,000 happy faces. Two Shankaracharyas met Gurudev. Swami Swatantranandji regaled us with stories from the Puranas. The ashram is getting ready for the Navratri celebrations that will start early next week.

224. Spirituality And Celebration

Celebration is the nature of the spirit.

Any celebration has to be spiritual.

A celebration without spirituality has no depth.

Silence gives depth to celebration.

Some people think being silent is spirituality. For example, many meditators feel that laughing, singing and dancing are not spiritual.

Some people think only celebration is spirituality. For example, in some parts of the world, such as rural India or Africa, celebration means loud music; there is no silence at all.

Spirituality is a harmonious blend of outer silence and inner celebration; and also inner silence and outer celebration!

✍ *News Flash:*

His Holiness the Dalai Lama was in Bangalore and met Gurudev. He was all praise for the help Art of Living programs have provided to India and the world. He lauded Gurudev for his success in reviving the ancient Indian Vedic heritage and presenting it to the world in such an accessible way in a modern context.

At the recent International Youth Meeting on Human Values organised by the United Nations in Seoul, South Korea, the Art of Living Foundation played a stellar role. Out of the nearly 1,000 non-governmental organisations participating, the Art of Living was the only workshop mentioned in the plenary session.

Navratri celebrations at the ashram were a combination of bubbling joy, deep meditation and profound silence. Among the many saints who graced the occasion were the Shankaracharya and Swami Swatantranand with his humor-filled discourses on the Bhagvatam. Thanks to the excellent video arrangements, the thousands who came were able to participate fully in all the celebrations. Next year we plan to go live on the Internet.

225. SOUND FAITH

Have faith in sound and move on to have faith in silence. Have faith in sound when it is pleasant and have faith in silence when sound is unpleasant.

When someone says something bad, you immediately believe it and the mind becomes more disturbed. Believing in an unpleasant sound creates more turmoil in the mind. In that situation shift your faith to silence.

Have faith in sound, like the chanting of mantras.

People seem to have more faith in chatting and gossip rather than chanting and knowledge. Have faith in knowledge and chanting, and have faith in silence.

Anecdote

On the day of the full moon, Gurudev visited the ancient temple or Kollur where there was an elaborately decorated chariot of the goddess being pulled around the temple. Explaining its significance, Gurudev said that each one of us is like a chariot carrying the power of God within. We are the real chariot of the Divine. Our body is the chariot and the soul is the deity that is being pulled around to purify the world.

News Flash:

Steady rains could not stop over 8,000 people in Mangalore and over 1,000 people in Mysore from singing, dancing and soaking in Gurudev's presence.

November 4, 1999
Bangalore Ashram, India

226. ALWAYS?

How can you always be happy? Forget about "always," then you will be happy.

In always wanting to be comfortable, one becomes lazy.

In always wanting perfection, one becomes angry.

In always wanting to be rich, one becomes greedy.

Fear comes when we do not realise that only life is for always.

This projection of the nature of self - which is "always" - onto the temporal - which can never be "always" - is called *Maya*.

All ways do not lead you, only one way leads you.

If you remove "always" from your dictionary, then everything is "all right." Drop "always" and all will be right - that is intelligence.

✍ *News Flash:*

Gurudev was the chief guest at a Muslim gathering where he spoke on "Human Values and the Prophet Mohammed."

Gurudev initiated a revolutionary movement among 24 prominent saints of India to welcome His Holiness Pope John Paul II to India, an event that was publicized in several national newspapers.

In the week that passed, Gurudev said that it was a "free" week with not many appointments but he ended up being busier than when he was supposed to be "busy."

227. BEING IN UTTER LOVE

An example inspires and brings confidence in the application of knowledge, and the visible sign of it is an undying smile.

The Self knows neither sorrow nor death, yet in it flow all the relative events.

It is easy to be detached when you are not in love. Being in utter love, and yet undisturbed, caring yet not worried, persistent yet not perturbed, are all the obvious signs of the Self shining through!

News Flash:

Diwali celebrations saw unbounded joy and Gurudev gave full expression to it with a spellbinding dance! One renowned Swamiji commented, "I have narrated the Bhagvatam for decades, but now I have experienced Dwapar (the age of Krishna) for the first time."

This tidal wave continued from the banks of the Ganges at Rishikesh to Varanasi, where more than 4,000 swayed in bliss. There is a saying - "Kashi Dhama Marnat Mukti" - dying in Kashi (also known as Varanasi), you attain salvation. Gurudev won over everybody's hearts by commenting that now, even while living in Kashi, people could attain salvation.

The Touring Tornado held a hurricane Satsang at Delhi and then moved on to Hardwar for the immersion of Amma's ashes.

HOMAGE TO AMMA

Gurudev's mother, our beloved Amma, left her physical body in a peaceful and meditative state at 1 p.m. on November 9, 1999 in Bangalore, just as Gurudev set foot in the holy city of Varanasi, precisely as he had predicted a few days earlier. For those present around Gurudev, it was an amazing experience to feel the depth of love and not an iota of grief. It was a celebration of knowledge never before experienced. Even as the news came, Gurudev kept meeting people and addressed the big Satsang with the same smile as always.

All her life Amma served with love, humour and dynamism, extending her motherly love to one and all. She had an unparalleled love for Gurudev and shared a unique relationship with him - he was not only a son, but also a mentor. Hundreds of people bid a moving farewell to Amma, singing Jai Jai Radha Raman.

Amma's mortal ashes were brought to Delhi and Gurudev accompanied them to Hardwar and immersed them in the holy Ganges there. Some of her ashes were also immersed in the river Cauvery, on whose banks Amma grew up.

On November 9, Gurudev was the chief guest at the consecration of the Vishalakshi temple at Varanasi, an invitation that had come two months earlier. At this very temple, Gurudev's grandfather had prayed 73 years ago and was blessed with Amma. Creation returned to its source as Gurudev reinstalled the very same ancient deity from whom Amma got her name, on the very same day that she left for her heavenly abode.

The Art of Living family is greatly indebted to Amma and seeks her blessings. The memorial service was held on November 21 and all chapters were requested to have Satsangs that day. Through this event the Art of Living has shown to the world that not only life, but death, can be a celebration.

228. DEATH AND SPIRITUALITY

Death brings you in touch with the reality of life. Death creates a vacuum, a void.

Void is fertile ground for the spirit to manifest.

All talents, inventions and creativity spring forth from the void.

Creation has a tendency to return to the void.

Bharat: All problems come when you avoid the void. *(Laughter)*

All the places of worship in all religions are connected with places of burial or cremation because the awareness of death alone can bring dispassion and make you well grounded in knowledge.

According to Indian mythology, the abode of *Shiva* is in Mount *Kailasa*, as well as in *Smashana* - the cremation ground. *Kailasa* means "where there is only celebration" and *Smashana* is "where there is only void."

Thus Divinity dwells in the void as well as in celebration. In you there is void; in you there is celebration.

✍ *News Flash:*

ART Excel children avoided sweets, colas and fireworks this Diwali festival and saved the money to sponsor children in the tribal school.

In the Rishikesh Advanced Course hall there is no void, only celebration! Profound knowledge and immense love radiate from Gurudev.

In a devotee's house in Bhubaneshwar, Odisha, Gurudev's photograph turned red just before the cyclone and returned to normal after the cyclone was over. Some devotees from Odisha actually made it to Rishikesh despite the catastrophic conditions in the state. One lady shared that she was in a meeting with about 50 people, when she felt that Gurudev was sending her a message. Closing her eyes, she prayed to Gurudev and then immediately advised everyone to evacuate the city. Later it was discovered that the entire area, including that building, was Submerged in the deluge. She thanked Gurudev with tears of gratitude for saving their lives.

Our volunteers are already engaged in Seva and relief work in Odisha.

229. AGGRESSION AS A WAY TO OVERCOME DEPRESSION

Lack of idealism is the main cause of depression among youth today. Life appears to be so meaningless to these children, who are either too scared of the competitive world or too bogged down by heavy stimuli. They need an inspiration, and spirituality is the inspiration that can keep the spirit up!

Aggression is the antidote to depression.

Depression sets in if there is a lack of zeal to fight.

Depression is the lack of energy; anger and aggression are a bolt of energy.

When *Arjuna* was depressed, *Krishna* inspired him to fight and thus reinstated life back into *Arjuna*.

If you are depressed, do not take Prozac - just fight for any cause.

If aggression crosses a certain limit, it leads you back into depression. That is what happened with King *Ashoka* who won the *Kalinga* war but became depressed. He had to take refuge in *Buddha*.

Wise are those who do not fall either into aggression or depression. That is the golden rule of a Yogi.

Just wake up and acknowledge you are a Yogi.

✍ *News Flash:*

The two Advanced Courses in Rishikesh were simply out of this world. Gurudev flew to Bangalore for a day for the memorial service of his most beloved Amma. People had come from all parts of India to pay homage to the great lady who gave Gurudev to this world. Gurudev did Aarti to Amma's portrait, singing the same song that Amma used to sing when she did Aarti to him. Tears flowed from everyone. Gurudev shared a few anecdotes about Amma. It was no coincidence that Amma left the body on Yama Dwitiya and that Vaikuntha Samaradhana fell on Vaikuntha Chaturdashi Day (the day when (Godliness wakes up).

He then flew back to Delhi where he addressed thousands in a mind-boggling Satsang, then on to Indore where huge cutouts and welcome arches greeted Gurudev. The indore stadium was packed to its capacity of 20,000. The following day saw over 40,000 people spellbound in meditation at the open-air stadium. This was telecast live on local TV. Gurudev has devised a new way of giving darshan – all 40,000 were satisfied. Guess how!

230. Think Fresh

To think fresh you need to be free of all impressions. Let go of all impressions right this moment and be hollow and empty. When you hear a word, the sound conveys the meaning instantaneously. Similarly, the knowledge that you are sitting, standing or talking needs neither confirmation nor proof.

Just an intention to be free makes you free right away. Realisation that freedom is your very nature brings enormous *"Shakti"* (energy).

Forget about this knowledge sheet and be fresh! *(Laughter)*

✍ *News Flash:*

Mumbai media provided excellent coverage of Gurudev's visit there. The football stadium at Cooperage held over 50,000 people spellbound in meditation and Satsang. Everyone was welcomed with sandalwood paste and sweets. Gurudev visited blind women in a shelter named after him.

Then on to Cochin in Kerala, where an interfaith convention was attended by thousands. The Imam of Trivandrum and the Bishop of Cochin praised the Art of Living Foundation's work in elevating human values. Several senior government officials and dignitaries took part in the program.

A traffic policeman in Cochin suddenly got a glimpse of Gurudev and started giving wrong signals ("with a blissful smile on his face," Raghu adds). In the evening, Gurudev served dinner for all the volunteers before leaving Kottayam. Even though there was a political strike throughout Kerala, only Art of living vehicles plied smoothly on the roads and only Art of Living Satsangs were held as scheduled.

231. THE FIVE SECRETS

There are five secrets that are sacred and are guarded by the subtle beings and angels in this creation. They are:

Jananarahasya (the secret of birth) - Birth is a secret. How a soul takes a body, the criteria for selecting the place of birth, time of birth, type of body and parents are all a secret.

Maranarahasya (the secret of death) - Death is a highly guarded secret. Death remains a mystery. The process of separation of spirit from matter and its journey from then on is a secret.

Rajarahasya (the royal secret, the secret of ruling) -The principles of governing, the principles of maintaining orderliness in creation are a secret.

Prakritirahasya (the secret of nature) - Nature is a mystery. The more you know about nature, the more the mystery deepens. The more a scientist knows, the more he feels there is much more to know. Science, though appearing to resolve the mystery in creation, has deepened it. The knowledge of particles, wave functions, black holes, the vacuum state have only deepened the mystery.

Mantrarahasya (the secret of mantras) - The mantras and their effect, influence, method and mode of working are all a mystery. Mantras are the impulses or rhythms of consciousness, which itself is a mystery.

Usually in the West, a secret is shameful and dishonest. But in the East, it is honoured and regarded as sacred.

✍ *News Flash:*

Gurudev's tour of seven cities in Kerala saw thousands of people coming to Satsangs, culminating in the grandest ever Satsang and meditation of the millennium. Over 75,000 people sat enraptured in meditation for half an hour in pin-drop silence in Thiruvananthapuram, the capital city of Kerala.

Our teachers Nitin Limaye and Bharat Shirur, representing Gurudev and the Art of Living Foundation, addressed the World Parliament of Religions in Cape Town, South Africa this week.

Want to see wild elephants? You do not need to visit Africa. These days 40 to 50 wild elephants have been visiting the ashram school and lakes by night.

232. The Wisdom Of Secrets

A wise person makes no effort to conceal a secret. But he does not make an effort to reveal a secret either. For example, you do not talk about menstruation or death to a five-year-old, but as they grow older these things are not hidden from them anymore. They become known as a matter of course.

An unenlightened one tries to protect a secret; and he also reveals the secret at the wrong time, to the wrong person, in the wrong place, and makes a big fuss about secrets.

Trying to protect a secret causes anxiety and discomfort.

An ignorant one is not comfortable with a secret, whether revealed or unrevealed, but the wise one is comfortable with a secret, whether revealed or unrevealed.

News Flash:

Prominent leaders of the Jain community are meeting in the Bangalore Ashram to discuss Ahimsa - nonviolence - on the 2,600th anniversary of Lord Mahavira.

233. INTENTION

Intentions keep the tension in. Being hollow and empty means dropping all intentions. Within tension, rest does not become deep. But devotion dissolves intentions.

Intention pushes you to the future yet bliss is always in the present. The one who wakes up to this truth is wise. Occasionally, if an intention arises in a state of bliss, the intention manifests effortlessly.

The more intentions you have, the more "in tension" you will be. To minimize your intentions could be your last intention.

✍ *News Flash:*

Gurudev's stay in India concluded with a grand celebration with more than 7,000 people from all over Bangalore. The Bangalore devotees published a bhajan cassette and a beautiful pictorial book in memory of Amma. The Art of Living was invited by leaders of the Jain community to join them in celebrating the 2,600th anniversary of Mahavira's birth. We were also invited to participate in the millennium celebration with the Dalai Lama at Varanasi.

The brightest moon of the millennium lit up the snow and the smiling faces that welcomed Gurudev to his home in Europe.

234. THE NATURE OF THE FIVE SENSES IS KNOWLEDGE

Every cell in your body has the ability of all five senses. You can see without the eyes. Vision is part of consciousness. That is why in dreams you can see without the eyes. You can feel without the skin. That is why people without limbs can still feel sensations in their missing limbs. You can smell without the nose and taste without the tongue.

When someone says something, you are all ears - you are listening with every cell of your body. There is the expression "looking with a thousand eyes" - one is all eyes.

The five senses and the ability to think are all present in consciousness. So each cell of the body has the potential to perform all the functions of the senses.

All cells are made of the same tissue - each DNA molecule contains all functions of the body. Consciousness is inherent in all the cells.

Every sensory stimulus brings knowledge, which is the nature of consciousness Sight brings some knowledge - blue, red, green. Knowing is the nature of consciousness.

Vikas: Some people who have lost one of their senses find that the others become heightened.

Gurudev: You do not have to lose one to sharpen the others. You can sharpen all of them in deep silence.

Mikey: What happens when you have no sense?

Gurudev: You become like Mikey! *(room explodes with laughter)*

✍ **News Flash:**

Two new books, the fourth volume of An Intimate Note to the Sincere Seeker and Wisdom for the New Millennium, have been released.

A huge Christmas tree adorned the meditation hall in Bad Antogast for the glorious Christmas celebration with gifts of wisdom and grace; everyone was gift wrapped in smiles and knowledge.

The Massachusetts Institute of Technology (MIT) in Boston has introduced the Art of Living program as part of its curriculum.

Thirteen hundred people have assembled on the Mediterranean in an indoor stadium with the master to celebrate and welcome the new millennium.

*Available to the reader through the Divine Shops

235. FIVE FACTORS THAT INFLUENCE THE MIND

There are five factors that influence the mind: place, time, food, past impressions, and associations and actions.

Every place you are in has a different impact on the mind. Even in your house you can see that you feel differently in different rooms. A place where there has been singing, chanting and meditation has a different influence on the mind. Suppose you like a particular place; you may find that, a little later it will not be the same.

Time is also a factor. Different times of the day and year have different influences on the mind.

Different types of food that you eat influence you for several days.

Past impressions - *karmas* - have a different impact on the mind. Awareness, alertness, knowledge and meditation all help erase past impressions.

Associations and actions or the people and events you are associated with, also influence your mind. In certain company your mind behaves in one way and with others your mind behaves in a different way.

Question: Should we worry about them?

Gurudev: No need to be paranoid about it. Just know these factors.

Though these five factors influence life and the mind, know that the Self is much more powerful. As you grow in knowledge, you will influence them all.

✍ **News Flash:**

About 1,300 people from over 41 countries gathered to celebrate the New Millennium Satsang and Advanced Course at Massa di Carrara, Tuscany, Italy. As the sun set, everyone gathered on the shore of the Mediterranean with Gurudev, chanting Om to say goodbye to the passing millennium. They were uplifted and inspired by a silent meditation at midnight and Satsang with bhajans in many languages. The Advanced Course participants were so blissed out that the French translator spoke into the Italian earphones for 40 minutes and the French had no translation, yet no-one commented.

Satsangs and New Years Advanced Courses were held around the world in over 93 countries to welcome the new millennium.

On January 6, Gurudev spoke on Italian national television as part of the continuing celebration.

Dog Story: There was this man who walked his dog every day for seven years. On this particular day he goes to walk the dog and the dog misbehaves and runs away from him, and runs for about ten minutes. The dog had never done this before! The man finds him standing under a pole with a poster announcing the Milano Satsang. So the man sees him standing there and the dog won't move. This forces him to read the poster. He decides that the dog ran away because he wanted the man to see the poster. The man called about the Satsang and said he and his friends were coming. The dog led the men and his friends to the Divine.

"Ever New Happy You!"

236. REASONS TO BE WITH A GURU

There are six main reasons to be with a *Guru*.

1. You would like to have your wishes fulfilled, and being with the *Guru* is more pleasurable.

2. Everything else looks more painful to you and you come for comfort.

3. You want to evolve and become enlightened; you want to attain higher knowledge.

4. You have a vision or goal that you share with the *Guru*, whom you see as a missionary or visionary.

5. You are there just to serve and to give comfort to the *Guru*.

6. You are with the *Guru* because you belong to the *Guru*. There is no choice.

✍ *News Flash:*

The President of Italy sent a message congratulating the Art of Living Foundation for its contributions and wishing success with our program.

The Art of Living Foundation also received an unofficial message from the Vatican saying they cannot officially support our activities but they will not interfere.

It was a moving scene at the completion of the Central Jail prisoners program in Bangalore. The State Inspector General of Police had boundless praise for the selfless service of the Art of Living teachers and volunteers.

237. EVOLUTION: NOT PART OF THE SELF

Are you evolving? If you are evolving, you are not in the Self. But you are not out of the Self, because nothing can exist out of the Self, *(Laughter)*

There are six distortions that do not exist in the Self.

1. Expansion - *Prasarana*. Expansion implies there is something into which to expand. That which expands cannot be the basis for expansion.

2. Contraction - *Akunchana*. Contraction means something shrinks from something else. Self does not withdraw or shrink from anything, so contraction does not exist in the Self.

3. Evolution - *Vriddhi*. Evolution is the process of becoming something that does not already exist. Self is always the same, so it cannot evolve.

4. Decay - *Kshaya*. There is no devolution or decay in the Self. It does not get old or stale. That is why when you are close to your Self, you do not feel that you are aging.

5. Beginning - *Anaadi*. Self has no beginning. If God has a beginning, then He is not God.

6. Lack - *Abhava*. Self has no lack. Whatever lacks something is not complete. Self does not lack anything; it is complete. Lack indicates the existence of something outside itself that does not exist for the Self. So if you feel you have not grown at all, do not worry, you are close to the Self, *(Laughter)*

When your mind is with the Self, then you do not worry about evolution, if you are thinking about evolving, then you are stuck in the mind. Mind is part of the matter, and matter evolves and decays.

That is how the experience of contraction and expansion is all play and display of the mind. Mind expands and contracts. When it expands, it comes close to the truth, which has no expansion.

Are you still evolving? Good luck!

✍ *News Flash:*

A distressed devotee went to Gurudev this week when her pregnant daughter began to hemorrhage and the baby was thought by the doctors to be dead.

The next day news came that the bleeding had stopped and the body's heartbeat was again detected.

After a weekend of intimate Satsangs with the devotees in Holland, Gurudev returned to Bad Antogast at the European Ashram.

238. VARIETIES OF SPIRIT

Why should you think God is only one? Why cannot God also be many? If God made man in His own image, what image is He? African, Mongolian, Caucasian, Japanese, Filipino? Why are there so many types of man and so many varieties of things?

There is not just one type of tree, not just one type of snake, mosquito or vegetable. There is not just one type of anything, so why should God be only one? How could this consciousness that manifested this whole creation and that loves variety, be monotonous ? God loves variety, so He must be infinite variety Himself. God manifests in many names, forms and varieties.

Some schools of thought do not give God the freedom to appear in His many forms. They want Him in one uniform!

You change your appearance to suit the occasion. When such is the case, how could you think there is no variety in the Spirit? Ancient people knew this and that is why they cognized the Divinity as infinite qualities and forms. The Spirit is not dull and boring.

The Spirit that is the basis of creation is dynamic and ever changing. God is not only one, but many!

When you accept the variety of Divinity, you cease to be a fanatic or a fundamentalist.

Tommy: God is many, God is one, He made so many just for fun.

✍ *News Flash:*

Howdy ya'll! After an intimate East Texas Advanced Course, Gurudev's entourage took the Alamo (San Antonio, Texas) by storm. Satsang -brimming with bliss, laughter, the flow of knowledge and love - washed over the devotees. After ten years, Gurudev is back at home deep in the heart of Texas.

239. THE PROBLEM'S TAIL

Gurudev: There is no problem that cannot be solved.

Someone: I have a few I can give you. *(Laughter)*

Gurudev: When you have a problem and you think it cannot be solved, you have accepted it. Then it is no longer a problem, it is a fact.

For example, suppose you think it is a problem that the ocean in Norway is too cold. Obviously, you cannot heat the ocean. If it cannot be solved, you accept it and it is no longer a problem. Only when you are searching for a solution is there a problem and so there is no problem that cannot be solved. The moment you realise there is no solution, a problem ceases to be a problem.

The solution is the tail of every problem. Solutions come to you when:

- You are calm and collected.
- You use intelligence.
- You are not lethargic but active.
- You have strong faith in Divine Law.

Kai: If you don't want any problems, you can have a *Guru*.

Sheila: If you want all the problems of all the people, become a *Guru*.

Tom: You cannot solve a problem when you focus on the problem alone. But when you step up to your real need, your real goal, to the higher Self, you find many solutions.

✍ News Flash:

Snow followed Gurudev from Dallas to Oslo.

Spontaneous ana contagious laughing meditations followed Gurudev's public talks in Hamburg and Oslo.

Riding the waves of bliss, Gurudev's giggling Gopi Gang went ice skating.

On to Copenhagen tomorrow.

240. DO NOT WORSHIP OR IDOLIZE

Worshipping or idolizing without a sense of belonging is always futile. Such worship only causes fear and distance.

There are others who are paranoid about worship. They get irritated when they see others worshipping.

The modes of worship or idolizing may be different in different parts of the world. Some worship the Pope; others worship pop stars; some are crazy about politicians. Look at all the children; they worship their heroes on posters all over the walls.

Adoration alone makes you a fan. A sense of belonging and seeing the divinity in those whom you adore makes you a saint.

Raghu: You mean we can see divinity in a pop star or a politician?

Gurudev: If you can, it is a divinity that is distorted. *(Laughter)*

Those who worship without a sense of belonging and those who are against worship are in the same boat, as both are clogged with fear.

The Bible says, "I am your God. You shall have no other gods before me." The same is said in the ancient Indian scriptures. "One who worships God as separate from the 'I am' consciousness is dull-headed," and *"Poojo aur na deva"* - do not worship other gods.

The offering, the offered and the offerer are all ONE.

✍ News Flash:

In Copenhagen, a thrilled audience of 900 was enraptured with Divya's and Craig's music. The excellent teamwork of the Denmark Art of Living made a memorable Satsang.

About 18,000 people did the Basic Course over a three-week period in Ahmedabad, a city in Gujarat, India. One of our youth leaders addressed a gathering of 20,000 people and inspired them about the 5H program.

After ten years of developing the Prison SMART program, one of our teachers, Tom Duffy, will be acknowledged by the Lower Cape Youth Congress with an Outstanding Achievement Award for Service to American Youth.

241. FEEL THE PINCH

A devotee asked Gurudev: Please forgive me if I have committed a mistake.

Gurudev: Why should you be forgiven? You are asking for forgiveness because you feel a pinch and you want to be free from it, is this not true? Let the pinch be there. The pinch will not let the mistake happen again. Forgiveness removes the pinch and you keep repeating the mistake!

Question: How do you know a mistake is a mistake?

Gurudev: A mistake is something that gives you a pinch. If it has not pinched you, it is not a mistake at all. It is the pinch that irks the consciousness and that pinch disallows the mistake to be repeated. Be with the pinch and not the guilt. It is a very fine balance.

Question: What is the difference between guilt and a pinch?

Gurudev: Guilt is about a specific action and a pinch is about a specific result or happening. You can only feel guilty about what you did - not about what happened.

But whatever happened, whether because of you or someone else, it can cause a pinch in you.

Question: How do we get over the guilt?

Tom: Just blame the boss! *(Laughter)*

Gurudev: You can get over the guilt through wisdom, by knowing the nature of mind, the nature of consciousness and by having a broader perspective of the phenomenon.

Question: Can we learn from our mistakes without feeling the pinch?

Gurudev: Learning is at an intellectual level while you feel the pinch at an emotional level. The drive of your emotions is much stronger than your intellect, so a pinch will not let the mistake recur.

Bharat: We feel guilt where we have control, at the intellectual level. But a pinch is at the emotional level where we do not have control.

Question: So, should we discard the intellect?

Gurudev: You cannot be driven by your emotions alone. Your intellect acts as a brake for your emotions.

Feel the pinch. The pinch will create an awareness that what happened was beyond your capacity. The awareness will bring you to surrender. Surrender will free you from guilt.

So, the steps of evolution are from pinch to awareness to surrender to freedom.

✍ *News Flash:*

Chinese New Year - the Year of the Dragon - was celebrated in the ashram. The International Advanced Course began in jet lag and ended in bliss!

242. Skill In Praising

Often when you praise, you praise in comparison to someone else. In order to praise one person, we put down someone else and when we want to point out somebody's mistake, we praise another.

Some are stingy in praising, and some are shy.

Some are simply not accustomed to praising.

Some praise with motives, and some praise just to elevate.

Others praise themselves in order to hide their low self-esteem.

But real praise dawns in a blossomed state of consciousness.

The praise that comes out of an elevated state of consciousness is simply its nature and is quite different. Normally praise comes out of craving and pride. Praise that comes from a heightened consciousness always comes out of fulfilment.

Praising can no doubt elevate the consciousness and bring enthusiasm and energy. At the same time it can also bring arrogance. Praising is a skill.

When someone praises you, do you take it without shying away? Accepting praise without shyness is also a skill.

✍ *News Flash:*

The hot weather at the Bangalore Ashram was dispelled by cool showers of grace. Agastya Nadi - a system of prediction through 5,000-year-old inscriptions on palm leaves - was brought to the ashram and amazed people by very accurate readings of their past.

Adi Chunchungiri Swamiji, one of the renowned pontiffs of South India, visited the ashram.

Sixty enthusiastic people bid a loud fare well to 100 very lucky people "flying" by train with Gurudev to Belgaum near Goa.

243. NEWS FLOOD

This week we had so much news that we are sending just a news flood.

It has been an unusually hectic week even by Gurudev's standards. Last Friday, Gurudev addressed three Satsangs in a single day, starting with a rural Satsang among thousands of poor people of Inchilla, a brief stopover with the enthusiastic devotees of Belgaum, and on to the urban elite of Goa, with the sound of our bhajans reverberating everywhere.

Ahmedabad was all keyed up as Gurudev returned after a two-year gap - teachers from all over Gujarat had been working together to make this the biggest Satsang ever. In the morning, over 25,000 people did the Sudarshan Kriya conducted live by Gurudev. A cosmic rhythm was set in motion. Intense experiences, strong fragrances, and changes in the weather pattern occurred as three eagles circled directly overhead, joined by a flock of other birds. Many people stated that their entire life until now was on one side and this event on the other - such was the magnitude of the experience for them. Kriya was followed by an elaborate lunch for the participants - the network of volunteers had organised 60 counters to feed everyone.

In the evening the same cricket stadium was transformed, with a huge lotus constructed in the stands for Gurudev to sit in, and video screens all over the grounds. Streams of people flooded in, excited and happy even before the program began. The crowd totaled nearly 200,000. The traffic diversion for the event was announced by the traffic police well in advance, and the event took place without any chaos.

Following 27 minutes of total, still meditation, the entire crowd was on its feet, singing and dancing. The subinspector of police remarked that even though a meager force of 500 was deployed, they had nothing to do, so blissful and orderly was the crowd. The policemen hugged people and confessed that only their uniforms prevented them from joining the dance. The high priests of the ancient city of Dwarka (Krishna's capital) came all the way to invite Gurudev and placed a resplendent turban from the temple deity on his head.

The next day was the foundation-laying ceremony of the Gujarat Ashram on the banks of the river Mahi. After a brief Satsang in Vidyanagar, Gurudev addressed over 3,000 ART Excel youth - it was the best ever question-and-answer session, with witty one-line exchanges between the little ones and the wise one.

Enthusiastic devotees with a live hand awaited Gurudev at 4 a.m. in Jamnagar. Gurudev visited the ancient capital of Krishna in Dwarka for a Vishnu Yagna in the ancient Dwarkadheesh Temple.

The entire city danced as Gurudev was taken in a horse-drawn carriage through the streets of Dwarka - it was a nonstop celebration.

That evening, we had another divine Satsang in Jamnagar, before returning to Ahmedabad. The blissful ones are now in Delhi, en route to Rishikesh.

Postscript: The three-year-old daughter of one of our devotees fell from a three-storey building recently. Later she said to her parents, "That bearded uncle whose photo we have at home - he caught me!" She escaped totally unhurt. (Caution: Please do not try this at home!)

244. FORM AND FORMLESS, AGGRESSION AND INTUITION

Form And Formless

Life is a combination of form and formless. Feelings have no form but their expressions have form. The Self has no form but its abode has form.

Similarly, wisdom and grace have no form but are expressed through form.

Discarding the formless, you become inert, materialistic and paranoid.

Discarding the form, you become a lost ascetic, a space cadet or an emotional wreck!

Aggression and Intuition

Aggression and assertiveness overshadow intuition.

Often, people who are sensitive tend to become aggressive in order to avoid being hurt.

In this process, they lose sight of their fine intuition.

Fine intuition needs sensitivity, but sensitivity is often painful.

In order to avoid pain one becomes aggressive and assertive, and in turn loses one's intuitive ability.

Intuition is close to the truth.

Often, aggression and assertiveness thrive on the idea of truthfulness - an aggressive person is convinced of the tightness of his position.

To be truthful, you do not need to be aggressive and assertive.

✍ *News Flash:*

At the World Presidents' Organisation (WPO), Gurudev delivered the keynote address which was lauded by a standing ovation.

Over 3,000 people participated in the Shivratri celebrations at Rishikesh, where the all-night Satsang and darshan line culminated in a live Kriya at dawn.

Following Gurudev's visit, 28 Basic Courses with nearly 8,500 participants started this week in Ahmedabad.

Around 60 Art of Living teachers are in Rishikesh, planning strategies to develop various areas. Prison programs and 5H programs are in full swing all over India.

March 16, 2000
Rishikesh, India

245. THE GOAL OF ALL ANSWERS

Some questions can only be answered in silence. Silence is the goal of all answers. If an answer does not silence the mind, it is no answer.

Thoughts are not the goal in themselves. Their goal is silence. When you ask the question "Who am I?" you get no answer, there is only silence. That is the real answer. Your soul is solidified silence and this solidified silence is wisdom, knowledge.

The easy way to silence the thoughts is to arouse the feelings, for only through feelings will peace, joy and love dawn. They are all your very nature.

To the question "Who am I?" the only relevant answer is silence. You need to discard all answers in words, including "I am nothing" or "I am the cosmic self" or "I am the Self." Just stick to the question "Who am I?" All other answers are just thoughts and thoughts can never be complete. Only silence is complete.

> *"You cannot betray people unless you gain their trust. A wicked person first gains trust and then betrays. But even the deception of a wise man will only do the highest good."*

> *"To be afraid of the wicked is a sign of a weak society and to be afraid to do bad is a sign of a strong society."*

✍ **News Flash:**

B.R. Ambedkar Marathtvada University has included the Art of Living Course in their curriculum. All those seeking higher education will get college credits by taking the course.

Twenty-five hard-core militants were totally transformed and they pledged to Gurudev to drop violence.

246. SURRENDER

The main impediment of many seekers on the path is that they want to surrender. Do not say that you want to surrender; know that you already are surrendered.

Wanting to surrender becomes an impediment on the path. This is like a child saying to its mother, "I want to love you." No child ever tells its mother, "I want to love you." Love is self-evident.

Surrender is not an act; it is a state of your being. Whether you acknowledge it or not, it is there. The wise wake up and see; the unwise take a longer time.

Know that you have no choice, you are in a state of surrender deep within you.

Anecdotes

A four-year-old child in an ART Excel meeting told Gurudev, "I love you very much."

Gurudev asked, "Why?"

She replied, "Because God has sneaked into your heart, and you are in God's heart."

In Satsang, a man asked Gurudev, "I do not feel the need for a Guru. What is your opinion of people like me?

Gurudev replied, with a twinkle in his eye, "Don't take my advice!" (Laughter)

So, if he takes the advice, he has done what the master said and has become a disciple anyway! And if he does not take the advice, even then has he become a follower! It is a paradox.

✍ News Flash:

Enthusiastic devotees celebrated Holi, the festival of colours, with song, dance and laughter in the divine presence of the master in Rishikesh.

Our 5H program has benefited 1,050 villages in India in the first quarter alone.

The Gurumobile is on its way to Panchkula after a jubilant Satsang in Chandigarh.

247. How To Handle Feverishness

When you are in the grip of feverishness about the result of your actions, what should you do?

Have faith and confidence that the result will be much better than you can ever imagine. With faith you can get rid of the feverishness of action and achievement. Feverishness can also be a hangover from over activity. Then sleeping, listening to flute music, and bathing in cold water can help.

Have dispassion. Know the whole thing will be over one way or the other, and it does not matter. Meditation and breathing can calm you down. Drop whatever you are doing and do something completely irrelevant. For example, while decorating your house, take some time to mow the lawn or go shopping. When you are doing something very important, take a moment to do something totally irrelevant and insignificant. This enhances your creativity. Relevant action keeps you bound to the action. Irrelevant action makes life a game.

✍ *News Flash:*

One of our devotees tricked two rival groups of hardcore terrorists and brought them to meet Gurudev. Twenty-five of them belonged to one group, and the other 20 were their rivals. One meeting with the master and the transformation in them, was total. The same people who had been responsible for chaos, disruption and killings in their state now took a vow to give up violence and to spread peace.

A jubilant Advanced Course with over 1,000 people concluded in Rishikesh yesterday.

248. How Does A Desire Arise?

- A desire arises with the memory of a pleasant experience and past impressions.

- A desire might arise through listening.

- A desire can be triggered through association with certain people or a place.

- Someone else's need or desire may manifest in you as your own desire, (for example, when someone is hungry and you get a desire to feed them, or someone wants to talk with you and you get a spontaneous desire to talk with them.)

- Destiny or a happening in which you have a part to play may trigger a desire, but you are not aware of the reason for your actions. For example, a gentleman in Quebec, Canada kept making roads and working on a farm for 30 years, not knowing for what – the farm was destined to become our Montreal Ashram.

✍ *News Flash:*

After a brief halt in Delhi, Gurudev arrived in Dharamshala as a state guest of the Government of Himachal Pradesh, a picturesque place with temples, snow-clad mountains and mango trees. His Holiness the Dalai Lama warmly received Gurudev at his residence and had an hour-long meeting. Later he met all thirty Art of Living teachers and devotees and lauded their contribution to society. It was a treat to be in that atmosphere of love, laughter and a total sense of belongingness.

The second 5H Youth Training Program has begun in Rishikesh with 240 participants. Of the planned 3,000 villages, work has already begun in 1,200.

Today is the Hindu New Year 5101 (52nd Century). Happy New Year to all.

249. RAM NAVAMI

"*Ra*" in Sanskrit means "that which is radiant" and "*ma*" means "myself."

That which shines forth within me is *Rama*. That which is radiant in every particle of the being is *Rama*.

Rama was born to *Dasharatha* and *Kaushalya*. *Dasharatha* means "the ten-chariotted one" in Sanskrit. It signifies the five sense organs and the five organs of action. *Kaushalya* is Sanskrit for "skilled." The skilful driver of the ten chariots can give birth to *Rama*. When the five sense organs and the five organs of action are used skilfully, radiance is born within.

Rama was born in *Ayodhya*, which in Sanskrit means "the place where no war can happen." When there is no conflict in our mind, then radiance can dawn.

Lakshmana, brother of *Rama*, was born of *Sumitra* - The good friend. When the ten are cooperating with you, awareness is born.

Often we try to look for radiance within. Just realise that you are radiant. Once when Gurudev was 5 or 6 years old, he closed his eyes and said to a visiting saint, "*Swamiji*, I do not see any light." The saint replied, "You are the light! How can you see the light?"

✍ *News Flash:*

Vishu, the Kerala New Year, was celebrated with a grand pooja in the Bangalore Ashram.

250. Desire Kills Joy And All Desires Aim For Joy

This couplet needs to be pondered over and over - a whole lifetime is not sufficient to digest this knowledge: desire kills joy and all desires aim for joy.

Whenever happiness has disappeared from your life, look deeper and you will see it is because of desire. And all that we desire is happiness!

No person, animal or creature desiring unhappiness is ever born; never has it happened before and never will it happen in the future.

When your small mind gets tired of running here and there, of wandering everywhere, it reaches the conclusion, "My desires have killed my happiness." A person who has conquered his desires is called "*mahavira*".

✍ News Flash:

Gurudev had a Satsang in Wayanad with over 12,000 people. Later he gave an address in a Catholic church on Easter Sunday.

On his way back to Bangalore, Gurudev addressed a congregation organised by the Muslim League in Sultan Batheri.

May 4, 2000
Bangalore Ashram, India

251. YOU ARE NOTHING

Each experience completes. Completion means being led to void or nothing. In the progression of life, you will leave behind every experience saying, "This is nothing." Anything that is completed loses its importance. That is to say, it leads you to void - this is nothing.

A sign of intelligence is how soon you arrive at this understanding. Examine everything in life and say "This is nothing" and what remains is love, and that is everything.

When "This is nothing" does not come out of knowledge, it comes out of misery. Either through knowledge or through misery, you come to the point of "This is nothing, this is nothing." The choice is yours.

If you got this, it is really NOTHING. If you did not get this, never mind - this is nothing. *(Laughter)*

✍ *News Flash:*

Gurudev addressed the annual meeting of the Confederation of Indian Industry in New Delhi and was well received.

Gurudev visited Ulaan Bataar, capital of Mongolia, on a two-day state visit and was received by the first President of the Mongolian Republic and a few members of parliament. Though the flight was delayed by five hours, thousands waited at the National Opera House, where Gurudev was driven straight from the airport. Even though he had travelled such a long distance, there was not a trace of tiredness as he greeted the cheering crowd. Gurudev tricked the security guards several times and mingled with the crowd.

Meetings and Satsangs at Ulaan Bataar were filled with gratitude. A ten-year-old boy who was deaf for several years regained his hearing! A lady who had suffered a paralytic attack felt sensations all through her body on seeing Gurudev's picture in the newspapers. Three days later, with some help, she came walking to attend Gurudev's Satsang!

On April 29, Gurudev was received by Mongolia's highest Buddhist leader, His Holiness the Hamba Lama Choijamts at the Gandan Monastery. The Lama, in his welcome address, noted that Gurudev's work has brought much peace and strength to the people of Mongolia.

252. DESIRE FOR TRUTH

Buddha said that desire is the cause of all misery. If your desire does not get fulfilled, it leads to frustration and causes misery. Even if it does get fulfilled, it leaves you empty.

Vasishta said that desire is the cause of pleasure. You get pleasure from an object or a person only when you desire them. When you do not desire an object, you do not get pleasure from it. For example, when a person is hot and thirsty, a sip of cold water gives him pleasure; but there is no pleasure if he is not thirsty. Whatever gives you pleasure binds you and bondage is misery.

Gurudev says when you desire truth, all other desires drop off. You always desire something that is not there. But truth is always there! Desire for truth removes all other desires; it dissolves and what remains is bliss.

✍ News Flash:

Teacher Training Courses ended on a celebrative note and with that began Gurudev's South Asian tour. A well-attended live Kriya, followed by a Satsang in a packed auditorium the next day, highlighted the Singapore visit.

A lady reporter asked Gurudev how many followers he has, pointing to the people sitting in front of him. He replied, "I don't have any followers; they are all in front of me and 1 wont turn my back on anyone.

An Art of Living group presented the scientific research on mental health benefits of Sudarshan Kriya to the United Nations Non-Governmental Organisation Mental Health Committee. It was so well received that the discussion was extended an extra half hour.

253. Seekers Beware

You can only seek that which you know and when you really do know, you already have it.

You cannot seek something you do not know.

Whatever you are seeking and wherever you seek, it is always only One; and the One is what you already are.

So, you cannot seek something you do not know and when you know what you are seeking, you already have it. When you seek the world, you get misery and when you want to find the way out of misery, you find the Divine.

A man lost a penny and was seeking it in a bush when he found a huge treasure. He was not seeking treasure but only for his lost penny. In the same way, when you seek something, you may get something else.

The truth, or Self, cannot be sought directly.

Dean: Many people come to the Art of Living seeking some mundane thing and find something else. *(Laughter)*

✍ *News Flash:*

Gurudev's tour through Asia continued with nonstop Satsangs and celebrations with enthusiastic crowds in Jakarta, Hong Kong and Taipei.

Gurudev met with President Lee Teng-hui of the Republic of China on Taiwan. The enthusiastic president started talking about Art of Living activities to our own delegation. He sought blessings for his people and his continuing work on social programs.

254. IS THE *GURU* RESPONSIBLE?

Is the *Guru* responsible for your enlightenment?

If yes, and you do not get awakened, then the *Guru* is to be blamed. If you get freedom, then the *Guru* is also to be blamed because he has been partial to you. If the *Guru* could set you free, he could have done it to the whole world.

So the *Guru* is not responsible for your awakening. And yet freedom is next to impossible without the *Guru*. So the *Guru* is responsible and yet not responsible. This is a mystery.

✍ *News Flash:*

The police force in Slovenia is participating in an Advanced Course.

Reports of rural service projects are coming from all corners of India.

255. LIFE WITHOUT WISDOM IS INCOMPLETE

Wisdom that does not give rise to feeling is incomplete.

Feeling that does not translate into action is incomplete.

Action that does not give rise to fulfilment is incomplete.

Fulfilment is returning to the Self.

✍ *News Flash:*

The Art of Living is actively involved in protecting the environment. About 80 full-grown 100-year-old trees were saved from illegal felling through the prompt action of the Art of Living. In North Gujarat, where thousands of cattle were dying of starvation and lack of water, the Art of Living has started a huge "Cattle Camp" to accommodate around 1,500 cattle.

June 7, 2000
Bangalore Ashram, India

256. EDUCATION

Education has five aspects:

1. Information - Often we think information is education, but it is only one aspect of education.

2. Concepts - Concepts are the basis for all research. You need to conceive in order to create.

3. Attitude - An integral aspect of education is cultivating the right attitude. Proper attitude at the right time and place determines your actions and behaviour.

4. Imagination - Imagination is essential for creativity, for the arts. But if you get stuck in imagination, you can become psychotic.

5. Freedom - Freedom is your very nature. Only with freedom do joy, generosity and other human values blossom, Without freedom, attitudes become stifling, concepts become a burden, information is of no value and imagination becomes stagnant.

✍ *News Flash:*

Our volunteers have initiated a drought relief program in Gujarat. Cow Camps are on the way. This year the students in our rural school at Ved Vignan Mahavidyapeeth (VVMVP), Bangalore scored 100% on achievement tests.

257. TRUTH

Truth is that which does not change. Examine your life and identify all that changes as not truth. With this outlook, you will find that you are surrounded by only untruth.

When you identify that which appears to you as untruth, then you will become free from it. When you do not identify the untruth, you cannot become free from it. Your own experiences in life make you identify your own untruth.

As you mature in life, you find everything is untruth - Events, situations, people, emotions, thoughts, opinions, concepts, your body - Everything is untruth. It is only then that *Satsang* (the company of truth) happens in the real sense. For example, a mother cannot see the child as untruth until the child becomes an adult. For a baby, sweet is not untruth, and for a teenager, sex is not untruth.

Question: Is knowledge also untruth?

Gurudev: Yes, if it is words, it is untruth. But as existence, it is truth. Love as an emotion is not truth; as existence, it is truth.

✍ *News Flash:*

After an enchanting Satsang on a boat in Paris, Gurudev has arrived for a brief and busy stay at the European Ashram in Bad Antogast, Germany.

The Art of Living in Shimla, India has undertaken a "Clean Shimla" project and a polyethylene bag-free city project.

258. I Am Neither Honest Nor Humble

A lady: I want an honest and humble man in my life.

Gurudev: I am neither honest nor humble. (Everyone is shocked.) I cannot tell everyone I am God, as not everyone will understand. So I am not honest. I am not humble - How can God be humble?

If I am humble, I am not honest.

If I am honest, I cannot be humble! *(Laughter)*

Hide your dispassion and express your love. By expressing dispassion you lose enthusiasm in life. And by not expressing love you feel stilled. Expressing dispassion may bring ego. Hide dispassion in your heart like the roots of a tree and express love like ripe fruit.

✍ *News Flash:*

Gurudev had given perfume to Mr. Salim, a devotee from Kollam. He called back to say that though he sprayed the perfume on many people, to everyone's amazement the bottle stayed full.

259. How To Deal With Humiliation

Know that humiliation does not weaken you - It strengthens you.

When you have a sense of belongingness, you do not feel humiliated. The more egotistic you are, the more humiliation you feel. When you are childlike and have a greater sense of kinship, then you do not feel humiliated.

When you are committed to truth and not to your ego, then you also do not feel humiliated.

If you are afraid of humiliation, you can neither make progress in your material life nor in your spiritual life.

When you stand above humiliation, you get closer to the Self - to God. When you are steeped in love, with the Existence, with the Divine, nothing whatsoever can humiliate you.

So the way out of humiliation is:

- Get humiliated.

- Be childlike.

- Be crazy.

- Get steeped in love with the Divine.

- Totally commit yourself to truth, to knowledge.

✍ *News Flash:*

There was an Advanced Course of 115 people and a Teacher Training Course with 70 people at the Bakal Ashram in Siberia. Divya Samaj Nirman (DSN) - Creating a Divine Society - Courses in Europe are keeping everyone on a high.

As people poured into the Montreal Ashram to join Gurudev for the summer programs, there was no space left, not even for the mosquitoes.

260. LEGENDS

Legendary is the love that withstands rejection. It will be free of anger and ego.

Legendary is the commitment that withstands humiliation. It will be one-pointed and will reach the goal.

Legendary is the wisdom that withstands turbulence. It will be integrated into life.

Legendary is the faith that withstands a million chances of doubt. It will bring perfection (*Siddhis*).

Legendary are the events that withstand time. They will become morals for the millions.

✐ *News Flash:*

The first Art of Living Basic Course was held in Bangladesh.

261. ARGUMENTS AND WRONG ACTION

A person who argues should not be given knowledge. An argumentative mind is not receptive to knowledge. When someone is in an argumentative mood, then giving knowledge or advice is in vain. In an argumentative mood you feel you know it all. Then you are not ready for knowledge. That is why wise people do not give advice when they are in an argumentative environment.

Argument has a purpose. It can bring out the truth if there is no emotion or sense of "I" attached to it. Argument can also have a disadvantage. It can make untruth appear to be truth.

A wise man will not take arguments seriously; he will just have fun with them. Wisdom is beyond all arguments.

Both a worldly person and a spiritual person will tell you not to do wrong, though the reasons they give are totally different. A worldly person will tell you not to do wrong because it hurts or causes him pain. A spiritual person will tell you not to do wrong because it would only harm you more.

Exercise

Identify any one specific virtue or good quality you would like to have. Ask for it on Guru Purnima day (the full moon - July 15-16) and know that you have it.

✍ *News Flash:*

Gurudev received the highest commendation from the mayor's office of the city of San Francisco for his contributions to society and for the indelible impression he has left on the community of San Francisco and the world.

July 19, 2000
Lake Tahoe, California, United States

262. VIRTUES

Virtues cannot be cultivated. You have to assume that they are there.

In the *Gita*, *Krishna* said to *Arjuna*, "Grieve not *Arjuna*, you are born with virtues."

The seeker should remember that he is born with virtues; otherwise he could not have been a seeker.

If you think you do not have virtues and then try to cultivate them, you will fail.

You often compare yourself with others on the basis of virtues. Do not compare yourself with them. Simply recognise all the virtues you appreciate in others, and realise that they are already present in you in seed form. You only have to nurture them.

When you think you do not have a virtue; then you come from a space of lack or deficiency.

Caroline: *Aho!* That is why we don't need positive affirmations!

Alice: Affirmations really don't work anyway.

Gurudev: Affirmations do not work because you think you do not have those virtues, and with affirmation you try to have them.

And so Caroline affirms: You are the home of all virtues. *(Laughter)*

✐ *News Flash:*

The Guru Purnima celebrations started with the divine sound of the Guru Puja being chanted by hundreds of devotees from all over the world who travelled here to be in the presence of their beloved master. The next evening, all gathered around Gurudev for a cruise to the middle of Lake Tahoe for a celebration of music and sweet silent meditation as the full moon rose over the surrounding peaks of the Sierra Nevada Mountains of eastern Kapillaranya (California).

263. ACTION AND REACTION

Action comes out of conscious decision. Reaction comes out of impulsiveness. Impulsiveness creates a chain of *karma*. Reaction and non-action both create *karma*, but conscious action transcends *karma*. Although conscious action does not create new *karma*, non-action can. For example, a soldier in war and a policeman using tear gas do not create *karma*, but a doctor who does not give medicine to a patient in need incurs *karma*.

Through knowledge and devotion, transcend all *karma* and be free.

✍ News Flash:

The Youth Training Program at the Bangalore Ashram is in progress with 150 participants from southern India. Meditation sessions are being conducted in the Indian Pavilion at the international Expo 2000 in Hanover, Germany. The European Ashram is bustling with activity and joy. A sudden thundershower had ecstatic devotees giggling and running down the slopes along with our mischievous master!

264. TECHNOLOGY

The purpose of technology is to harness nature to bring information and comfort to human beings. When Spiritual values - Human values - are ignored and neglected, instead of bringing comfort, technology brings fear and destruction.

Technology without human values considers nature a dead object. Science gives insight into the life of nature, and spirituality makes nature come alive. In the eyes of children there is nothing dead in the world - animals, trees, the sun and the moon - they all have life, they all have emotions, they all have feelings. But in the eyes of a stressed and ignorant person, even human beings are like robots - objects!

Technology without spirituality is destructive. Spirituality is the technology of consciousness, and the whole world is the play and display of consciousness.

✍ *News Flash:*

The first Art of Living Course was held in Kosovo.

The Bangalore Ashram has 250 enthusiasts in teacher training.

Every inch of the European Ashram is filled with smiling faces.

Gurudev was welcomed with much fanfare at the Indian Pavilion at Expo 2000 in Hanover, Germany with the traditional Aarti and a Manipuri dance. From there he walked through the Avenue of Trees, with devotees sprinkling rose petals in his path, and then to the Christ Pavilion where he was welcomed by African drummers. Accompanied by the melodious strains of a harp, he held a powerful meditation and spoke on the theme of the Expo: Humankind-Nature-Technology. The depth of silence was felt even in the prayer service, which ended with Gurudev being taken ceremoniously to sign in at the special gallery - the glass facade of the church!

265. Love - The Question of an Answer

In a congregation, Gurudev asked, "How many of you feel strong?" Many people raised their hands.

Gurudev then asked, "Why?"

"Because you are with us," they answered.

"Only those who feel weak can surrender," Gurudev responded.

All those who were feeling strong were taken aback; they suddenly felt weak!

If you are in love, you feel weak because love makes you weak. Yet there is no power stronger than love. Love is strength. Yet love is the greatest power on earth. You feel absolutely powerful when you are with the Divine.

Someone asked: But why do we keep alternating between strength and weakness?

Gurudev: That is the fluctuation in life.

When you feel weak - surrender.

When you feel strong - do *Seva*.

✍ News Flash:

This News Flash cannot contain all the reports from the 1,500 villages adopted by the 5H Program (Health, Homes, Hygiene, Human Values and Harmony in Diversity) in India. In New Delhi, Gurudev was busy appreciating all the good work, attending to problems, consoling grievances and correcting lapses.

266. CONFLICT AND INNOCENCE

Fights can only happen among equals. When you fight with someone, you make that person equal. But in reality there is no one at par with you. When you keep people either above or below you, then there is no fight.

When people are above you, you respect them. When they are below you, you love them and you feel compassionate. Either submission or compassion can take you out of a fight in no time. This is one way to look at a situation when you are tired of fighting. But when you are well rested, just fight and have fun.

The same is true of the mind. When the mind is caught up in the senses or thinks it is equal to the senses, there is constant conflict. But when the mind is smaller than the senses, as in animals, there is no conflict. And when it realises that it is bigger than the senses, there is no conflict. When the mind transcends the senses, it comes back to its true nature, which is innocence - "in no sense."

Does this make sense? *(Laughter)*

✍ News Flash:

Malawi, in central Africa, became the newest country to join the Art of Living family.

The jubilant Teacher Training Course and about 100 youth leaders have completed their training programs and will be serving 1,000 additional villages in the southern states of India for the 5H Program.

The Discovery Channel discovered the bliss in the ashram.

267. PROBLEMS? ONE MORE

The first solution to a problem is not to have the problem at all. *(Laughter)*

The second solution is to willingly accept the problem and see it as a challenge.

The third solution is to know that the problem is a bogeyman; it is not real.

The fourth solution is to know that nature has provided you the solution even before giving you the problem. First you met me and then you had a problem. *(Laughter)* When it snows, there are no bacteria since herbs to heal you do not grow in that season. In the spring, the herbs come first and then the bugs. In the summer, the shade comes before the summer sun gets strong. So, nature takes good care of you.

Sabya: What if longing is a problem?

Gurudev: Longing ripens you. Do not solve all your problems. Keep at least one of them. You need something to munch on - and life goes on.

✍ *News Flash:*

Another 100 youths moved on to 5H projects in Andhra Pradesh, Karnataka and Tamil Nadu in a moving graduation. Gurudev met with the Shankaracharya of Kanchi before flying to Mumbai where a Satsang, which was supposed to be quiet and secret, included 4,000 people.

Krishna's birthday was celebrated in the European Ashram.

268. Do Not Make a Mistake by Pointing Out Mistakes

A lady came to Gurudev and said that her husband lied to her. She was very upset. Gurudev asked, "Why does your husband lie to you?" He lies to you because he loves you, and is afraid to lose your love or to hurt you. If he did not love you, he wouldn't lie to you.

Do not tell a person a mistake he knows that he made. What is the use of pointing out a mistake that he knows he has committed? By doing this, you will only make that person feel more guilty, defensive or resentful and this will only create more distance.

You should only point out the mistake of a person who does not know, but who wants to know. Also do not point out the mistake of a person who knows but does not want you to know about it. Often people know the mistakes that they have committed, but they do not want you to tell them.

Think about the usefulness of your comments. Before pointing out a person's mistake, see whether your comments in any way will help to improve the situation, foster love or bring harmony. A magnanimous person does not pick on the mistakes of others and make them feel guilty. Instead, they correct other's mistakes with compassion and care, not through words but through their attitude.

✍ *News Flash:*

Washington, D. C. had big Satsangs and a lovely boat ride with Gurudev. The D.C. Mayor's office honoured Gurudev by proclaiming that henceforth August 26th would be celebrated as Gurudev Sri Sri Ravi Shankar Day. Senator Paul Strauss presented this honour to Gurudev at the elegant ball room of the Capitol Hilton in the presence of 1,500 people.

In the United Nations in New York City, Gurudevs speech was by far the best, and he was given a standing ovation. Among other wonderful things, he talked about how spirituality was the fruit of the banana and religion was the banana peel. At the end of the talk, people were asking each other, "Are you the banana, or are you the peel?" One person was heard commenting, "I am the monkey, I get both the banana and the peel!"

269. WISE ARE THE ONES WHO MAKE YOU CRAVE FOR THE DIVINE

Unfortunate are those who crave for the world.

Fortunate are those who crave for the Divine.

Unwise are those who make you crave for the world.

Wise are those who make you crave for the Divine.

The source of conflict is the notion of "mine" and "yours." Self-knowledge eases the sense of limited belongingness and resolves this conflict.

When knowledge dawns in you, there is no stranger in the whole world! At the same time you realise that you know very little about even the nearest one.

Suchak: Yes, our nearest one often remains a stranger.

Gurudev: You cannot understand anyone totally, for life is a mystery!

Marcy: But Gurudev, you understand us totally! *(Laughter)*

Gurudev: Wake up and see. All these distinctions, "Me, mine, others," simply dissolve.

✍ News Flash:

During the United Nations Millennium World Peace Summit in New York, the elders of the last of the Incas of Peru spotted Gurudev and recognized him as The Man Of Light. They bestowed their highest honour upon him to the sounds of their ancient conches and flutes.

At the Montreal Ashram, Katherine called and "complained" that Gurudev would not leave her digital camera. Each time she downloaded the pictures and tried to erase them from the camera, one particular picture of Gurudev always remained in the camera!

After the "mini" Advanced Course over the Labor Day weekend, Gurudev gave informal talks to packed halls in Montreal and Ottawa.

Sixteen fortunate devotees rose in Divine Love with the master - in a hot-air balloon! When they were asked how they had felt being "in space" with him, they gleefully replied, "Absolutely at home!"

270. Do You Have to be Thankful and Feel Obliged?

When you are on a spiritual path, you are not thankful or obliged to anybody. In the *Gita, Krishna* says, "He is dear to Me who neither goes on thanking people nor hates anyone (*Na abhinandati na dveshthi*)."

Thanking and feeling obliged indicates that you believe in someone else's existence rather than in the Divine who rules everything. When you feel obliged, then you are not honouring the principles of *Karma* or the Divine Plan.

Appreciate people for what they are; do not thank them for what they do. Otherwise your thankfulness is centred around ego. Be grateful, but do not be grateful for an act. Be grateful for what is. As every individual is nothing but a puppet of the ONE, thanking and being obliged is simply an exhibition of ignorance. Everything is ruled, controlled and managed by one Divinity. That consciousness has to shine forth in every act of yours; you do not need to make a mood of it.

Question: *Guru*dev, we are so grateful to you, what should we do?

Gurudev: When you have a total sense of belonging, then gratefulness does not become an obligation. Such gratefulness is for the Divine only, and this gratefulness enhances your strength.

✍ *News Flash:*

Gurudev addressed members of the Indian Association at Staten Island, N. Y. along with the Prime Minister of India. He also graced the Ayurvedic Conference and enlivened the discussion by giving Ayurveda a spiritual dimension that was otherwise hidden.

Many solutions for the tourism industry emerged when Gurudev delivered his wisdom at the Confederation of Indian Industry at Agra, India. At dawn, the minarets of the Taj Mahal seemed to bow in reverence welcoming Gurudev and his entourage. Despite Gurudev's repeated instruction to look at the Taj Mahal, the devotees' attention remained focused on him.

271. DIVINE LOVE AND THE COMPLAINING FACE

How would you like to see yourself - happy and bubbling with enthusiasm, or dull and difficult to please?

Sometimes you like to be pleased, appeased and cajoled, so you put on a tough, upset face and act difficult to please. If a person has to appease and please ten people all the time, it is so tiring. People who keep a long face and expect others to cajole and appease them, make others run away. Lovers often do this. They expend a lot of energy in cajoling and this reduces the joy and celebration of the moment.

It is okay for you to show your upset mood or tendency once in a while, but doing it repeatedly is taxing for you and the people you love.

If you feel down, appease and please yourself. Your need to be appeased by someone else is a sign of grossness. This is the root of ignorance. If you want attention, all you get is tension.

Become one whose enthusiasm never dies, come what may.

It is not possible to attain Divine Love with a complaining face. The complaining face is a sign of an unaware mind. If you want to complain, complain to God or your *Guru* because both have their ears covered. *(Laughter)*

✍ *News Flash:*

From a village near Alwar in Rajasthan, India, a nine-year-old girl, Uma, who was dumb from birth started speaking after her ART Excel Course. The same was reported of a twelve-year-old boy from Vallabh Vidyanagar in Gujarat.

Talakatora Stadium in Delhi was aptly decorated for a grand Satsang. Thousands who could not enter the stadium could still fully participate thanks to the big screens provided by the organisers. Gurudev went to Rishikesh to inspire and to get inspired by the 108 youth leaders who were beginning their service work for the 5H Program.

272. The Devotee Becomes God

When a river meets the ocean, the river no longer remains a river. It becomes the ocean. A drop of the ocean is part of the ocean. In the same way, the moment a devotee meets or surrenders to the Divine, the devotee becomes God. When the river meets the ocean, it recognises that it is the ocean from the beginning to the end. Similarly, the individual "I... I..." dissolves in one Divinity.

Question: What about backwaters?

Gurudev: Sometimes the ocean goes into the river to greet it. Sometimes it seems that the ocean is pushing back the river. Similarly, the Divine puts many questions and doubts in the mind or provides an amazing experience to bring you back home.

✍ *News Flash:*

Construction activities for the meditation hall, the water tank and more residential facilities are in full swing at the Bangalore Ashram to enable more devotees to participate in future celebrations.

273. Devotion is Steeped in Mystery

One who is not amazed by the magnificence of this creation - his eyes are not yet opened. Once your eyes are opened, they close and this is meditation. *(Laughter)*

Tell me, what in this creation is not a mystery? Birth is a mystery; death is a mystery. If both birth and death are mysterious, then life is certainly a greater mystery, isn't it?

Being completely immersed in the mystery of life and this creation is *Samadhi*.

Your knowing or believing does not really matter to what Is.

This creation is an unfathomable secret, and its mysteries only deepen. Getting steeped in mystery is devotion. The "Scene" is a mystery; the "Seer" is a mystery.

Deepening the mystery of Creation is science. Deepening the mystery of the Self is spirituality. They are the two sides of the same coin. If neither science nor spirituality can create wonder and devotion in you, then you are in deep slumber.

When a materialistic person tells you a secret, it will only create doubts and spread malaise.

When a wise or spiritual person tells you a secret, it will uplift your consciousness and spread benevolence.

News Flash:

Every day poor people were fed at the Bangalore Ashram during the Navratri Celebration. More than 5,000 people in the slums were given clothes. Gurudev has just emerged from his week-long silence looking more resplendent than ever. News about healing experiences continues to flood in from all over the world.

274. PERFECTION IS THE NATURE OF THE ENLIGHTENED

In a state of ignorance, imperfection is natural and perfection is an effort.

In a state of wisdom or enlightenment, imperfection is an effort but perfection is a compulsion and is unavoidable.

Perfection is taking total responsibility, and total responsibility means knowing that you are the only responsible person in the whole world. When you think that others are responsible, then your degree of responsibility diminishes.

When you are in total *Vairagya* - dispassion - you take care of even trivial and insignificant things with such perfection.

Swamiji: For example, during the *puja* every morning, Gurudev decorates the *puja* table using flowers with such great care, choosing different colour combinations and patterns every day, fully knowing that the decoration will not last even 10 minutes.

After the *puja* he himself removes the garlands from the *puja* table or showers people with flowers from it. Yet even while he is in a deep state of *Samadhi*, he effortlessly and lovingly decorates the *puja* table every day. It is obvious that it does not matter how the flowers are arranged - attention to such a trivial thing with such keen awareness can only come through utter dispassion.

Perfection is the very nature of the enlightened one.

News Flash:

Celebration continues as always.

275. Ignorance of Your Capability Can Expand You

Always know that the Divine never gives you a responsibility you cannot fulfil. No one ever expects you to treat them if you are not a doctor. No one will ask you to fix their wiring system if you are not an electrician.

Your responsibility is only what you can do. And you do not know what you can do. Always accept that you do not know what you can do.

Ignorance of your capability can expand you.

When you know what you can do, you can progress. But when you do not know what you can do, you can grow by leaps and bounds.

When you know what you can do, you can do things. When you do not know what you can do, you can do things even better!

News Flash:

Priyansh, a two-and-half-year-old boy, was playing with his friends on his eighth floor balcony. A while later his sister came running in shouting that her little brother had fallen from the balcony and was lying flat on the ground below. When everyone went down, his father thought that the boy was dead. To their surprise they found the child was blissfully lying down without even a tooth broken. Barring a small injury to his leg, everything was fine. When asked, Priyansh told his father that Gurudev had saved him.

276. Love is the Shadow of the Self

When you love something, you have a sense of belongingness with it. You can only love something when it belongs to you. If it is not yours, you cannot love it. Love is the shadow of the Self.

The bigger the Self, the bigger the shadow, and the bigger the love. When love is cast over all of creation, then you are the Big Self. That is Lordship.

When Lordship dawns in the Self, there is perennial celebration.

*Today is Deepawali, the festival of lights. There are many stories associated with this day.

It was on this day that the demon Narakasura was killed. King Narakasura - Naraka means hell - had been granted a boon that he could only be destroyed by a woman. Lord Krishna's wife Satyabhama was the one to destroy him.

Why could only Satyabhama kill Naraka? Satya means truth and bhama means the beloved. Untruth or lack of love cannot conquer hell. It cannot be removed by aggression. Hell can only be erased by love and surrender. Non-aggression, love and surrender are the inherent qualities of a woman. Hence only Satyabhama, the true beloved, could remove hell and bring the light back. And Narakasura's last wish was that every house should celebrate his demise with lights to mark the end of darkness. This is Deepawali.

It was also today that Lord Rama returned to Ayodhya, his kingdom, after his victory over Ravana, the demon king. Ayodhya means that which cannot be destroyed, that is, life. Ram means the Atma - the Self. When Self rules in life, then knowledge lights up. There is life everywhere. But when the spirit is awakened in life, Deepawali happens.

277. ARE YOU A TOURIST OR A PILGRIM?

What is the difference between a tourist and a pilgrim?

Both are on a journey. Where a tourist satisfies the senses, a pilgrim is in a quest for truth. A tourist gets tired and tanned, while a pilgrim sparkles with spirit. Every move a pilgrim makes is done with sacredness and gratitude, while a tourist is often preoccupied and unaware.

A tourist compares his journey with other experiences and places and thus is not in the present moment. But a pilgrim has a sense of sacredness so he tends to be in the present moment.

Most people in life are just tourists without even being aware of it. Only a few make their life a pilgrimage. Tourists come, look around, take pictures in their minds, only to come back again. But pilgrims are at home everywhere - they are hollow and empty.

When you consider life as sacred, nature waits on you.

Are you a tourist or a pilgrim?

✍ *News Flash:*

Diwali was celebrated in the Bangalore Ashram. With the Festival of Lights setting in, 50 people got back their sight, while thousands received insights. On the first anniversary of Amma's mahasamadhi, Gurudev related the meaning of Amma's name, Visalakshi - "one with broad vision."

"Broad vision gives you your guru and in turn your guru gives you broader vision."

Gurudev was a State guest in Orissa where he arrived after a brief Satsang in Chennai. Though it was the first time in Odissa, the arrangements and the enthusiasm were simply unmatchable as Gurudev mesmerized a crowd of more than 35,000 people. Gurudev went to Jagannath Puri, the Eastern seat of wisdom, where Vishnu Yagna was performed. Puri had a great Satsang, where many people reported miraculous healing experiences.

A report from Argentina tells us about the stunning experience of a medical team on the miraculous disappearance of a malignant tumor after their patient had been given 48 hours to live.

November 9, 2000
Bodh Gaya, India

278. THE BODHI TREE

Buddha was enlightened under the *bodhi* tree. He then stood up and watched the tree from a distance for seven days. He took sixteen steps towards the tree and under each step blossomed a lotus flower. This is the legend.

The *bodhi* tree is symbolic of both *sansara* - the world -and *dharma*. The lotus flower symbolizes clarity, dispassion, love, beauty and purity.

It is only when you are detached in life that you can watch the *sansara* and all of its plays. When you witness the *sansara*, every step you take is benevolent and impeccable. When every action of yours is preceded by witnessing, then every move you make in this *sansara* becomes perfect and significant.

✍ *News Flash:*

Gurudev's entourage moved to Jamshedpur where a crowd of more than 20,000 was enthralled by the master. Then on to Ranchi where another 60,000 were soaked in his grace. Later in the night, Gurudev met with more than a thousand villagers who came just to have a glimpse of him.

The City of Joy - Kolkata - was full of enthusiasm. Gurudev addressed the Confederation of Indian Industries. Gurudev's program in Kolkata was three Satsangs back to back over two days. Hundreds and thousands of people enjoyed the hospitality of West Bengal. Devotees were doubly stunned when an aggressive heckler was instantly transformed into a seeker who danced in joy.

Then Gurudev moved on to Gaya to offer tribute to his most beloved mother, our Amma, on the first anniversary of her death. And once again the bodhi tree had another date with the enlightened.

279. NIMIT - INSTRUMENT OF THE DIVINE

When you are neither clear nor confused, only then can you be a perfect instrument of the Divine. How would an instrument know what is going to be, and when? How can an instrument be confused, and how can an instrument be clear?

This state is called *Nimit* - just being an instrument of the Divine. Being very clear means not opening up to new possibilities; this can lead to limitations. But unlimited possibilities are open to one who is neither clear nor confused.

Your mind swings from clarity to confusion and from confusion to clarity. But the state in which there is no doership and no inertia is the most creative and progressive state.

Sharmila: Will this not lead to lethargy?

Gurudev: No. A sharp instrument does its job perfectly, effortlessly.

Sharmila: What about focus?

Gurudev: Focus is natural to a dynamic consciousness.

Confusion arises when new information flows in and clarity is lost. Then confusion again seeks clarity. Clarity constricts the possibility of new information. A confused consciousness seeks clarity and every confusion breaks away from clarity.

If there is only confusion, there is frustration. If there is only clarity, there is rigidity.

After giving contradictory knowledge, *Krishna* tells *Arjuna*, "Just be *Nimit!*" And to be an instrument, the prerequisite is to be madly in love. That is why in love there is neither confusion nor clarity; or there are both confusion and clarity simultaneously.

Nazreen: Is truth more important than love?

Gurudev: I'm confused! Is it clear? *(Laughter)*

✍ News Flash:

Allahabad, the city of the Kumbha Mela, had thousands blissed out at its first Satsang with the master.

Under the full moon, the meditation at the Sangam - the confluence of the main rivers - took the rowboats full of devotees beyond time - an amazingly mystical experience. High Court judges had the privilege of meeting with the master. Enthusiastic villagers greeted Gurudev when he visited the 5H model villages.

Delhi bustled with activity - so many Seva projects, so many meetings. Gurudev also gave the keynote address at a U.N. program for promoting tolerance among religious leaders.

The performance of our school at Bangalore has startled educators - sixteen prizes and seven first prizes! An amazing record from a rural school of first generation literates competing against established institutions in the state.

280. THE PROBLEM'S SOLUTION

Whenever there is a problem, we either deny it saying there is no problem or we sit to solve the problem and make it a big issue. Neither of these help. A problem does not disappear when you deny it. And it does not get solved when you sit to solve it. The five steps to solve a problem are:

- Acknowledge the problem - it is there.
- See it as a small problem, and do not say it is big.
- If it concerns people, keep in touch with them instead of avoiding them.
- Talk less and give time a chance.
- Get together and celebrate. When you celebrate and put the problem on the back burner, you will see that the problem gets solved in time.

So it is wise not to sit to solve a problem. Most of the meetings to solve problems end up in disaster.

If you do not have any problem, you will create problems for others! *(Laughter)* If you have a small problem in your pocket to solve, it will give focus to your mind. If you do not have any problems, you may be a problem for others. It is better to have a problem than to be a problem.

✍ *News Flash:*

The south zone organisers of India who came to solve problems finally found out that they had only one problem: they had no problems.

In New Delhi, the Imam Maulana Illyasi, who is the president of the organisation of Imams in India met with Gurudev along with the Turkish delegation and participated in a Satsang. Back in Bangalore, Gurudev gave the concluding address at the Confederation of Indian Industry.

Before leaving for Frankfurt, Gurudev made a brief stopover at Chennai, where he spent the two hours there going into the city to motivate the twenty-five 5H youth leaders, the Yuvacharyas.

December 1, 2000
European Ashram, Germany

281. SACREDNESS AND YOU

Throughout the ages, in all cultures, certain places, times, persons and symbols were considered sacred. The Native American Indians and the tribals in India consider the earth, sun, moon and all the directions to be sacred. In the ancient tradition, the *Rishis* considered all the rivers, mountains and even animals, trees and herbs to be sacred. And what of people? They are definitely sacred.

In different parts of the world, certain symbols, certain places and different times of the year are considered sacred. Various cultures honour certain people and consider them to be sacred. For Christians the Cross, Jerusalem, Christmas and the Pope are sacred. For Muslims, the crescent moon, Mecca and the month of Ramadan are sacred. The Hindus consider the river Ganges, the Himalayas and the Swamis to be sacred.

When you consider a symbol, place, time, person or act sacred, your attention is undivided and whole. When things are ordinary and the same, you tend to slip into unawareness and inertia. The moment you consider something sacred, your inertia disappears and you become more alive. There is nothing as fulfilling as a sacred act. You put your heart and soul into a sacred act. When every action of yours becomes sacred, you have become one with the Divine. Then every minute of your life, every place you go, every act of yours is sacred and every person you meet is only your reflection.

Question: Why does an act when performed repeatedly lose its sacredness?

Gurudev: This happens when your memory overpowers your consciousness and you lose your sensitivity. For example, people living in *Benares* do not feel that it is a sacred place. That sensitivity is just not there.

Question: How can we preserve that feeling of sacredness in our acts?

Gurudev: Through living in the present moment and through *Sadhana*. Your *Sadhana* will not allow your memory to overpower consciousness. Then repetition is not a hindrance.

It is good to feel that some symbols, places, time and people are sacred so that you can be awake and alive. But eventually you need to transcend and feel that the entire creation and your whole life are sacred. For the man of God, the whole world, with all its symbols, places and people are sacred at all times.

Be a man of God!

✍ *News Flash:*

Gurudev was the star attraction and the public magnet at the PSI Conference in Basel, Switzerland.

Gurudev presented the Human Values Award 2000 to Max van der Stoel, the OSCE (Organisation for Security and Cooperation in Europe) High Commissioner on national minorities, at the International Association for Human Values Conference in Amsterdam, Holland. The conference was attended by several dignitaries including the former prime minister of the Netherlands, who was one of the keynote speakers. Gurudev left an indelible mark in Amsterdam. A well-organised Satsang with many intelligent questions and knowledge flowing from the master left the packed hall spellbound and asking for more.

Gurudev's entourage walked in no-man's land between Germany and Switzerland!

282. I am God

It was thought that to say "I am God" is blasphemy. I tell you, to say "I am not God" is blasphemy. When you say, "I am not God," you deny God His omnipresence.

You are made up of love. If you say, "I am not God," you are denying that God is love. If you are love and you say, "I am not God," you are saying God is not love, and that is blasphemy.

"I am" is your consciousness. If you say, "I am not God," you deny that God is aware, alert and awake. You exist. When you say, "I am not God," you deny God a portion of existence, and that is blasphemy. You are denying the scriptures that say, "God made man in His own image." If you say, "I am not God," you are denying God.

Question: If God is omnipresent, why is there hatred and suffering in this world?

Gurudev: Just as in a movie, it does not matter whether it is a tragedy or a comedy, or one with a happy ending; in the Absolute there are no opposites. All the opposites are part of relative existence.

Relative existence is not the complete picture. Good and bad, right and wrong, everything is relative. For example, milk is good, but too much milk can kill you. A drop of poison can save a life - most medicines have "Poison" written on them. These are neither absolutely good nor bad; they just are.

Truth transcends duality, and God is the absolute and only truth. In a movie, when light passes through the film, it does not matter to the light what the film is. Tragedy or comedy, hero or villain, the light is always there.

In the same way, no matter what is happening in your mind, you are God.

As soon as Gurudev landed in Mumbai there was a Mahakriya for 15,000 people followed by a Satsang of 50,000!

Art of Living was the most "happening" thing in all of Northern Kerala. The largest grounds and stadiums in every city were brimming over with jubilant faces. In Thrissur, 1 lakh (100,000) people turned up for Satsang, in spite of a "bandh" and a complete transportation strike! On to Palghat, where two lakh of devotees eagerly welcomed the master. Calicut, with over two lakh people, was next, and then came Kannur, a politically disturbed small town. All the different religious and political factions forgot their differences for a day, and sang united and strong in a Satsang of over two lakh of people!

And then on to Mangalore for an intimate Satsang.

Gurudev visited five major cities in five days, and many other cities in 10-15 minute stopovers. Each of these places had enthusiastic Satsangs with huge crowds. Nearly one million people in Kerala participated in Satsang and meditation in the presence of the master in the last five days!

283. ATHEISM IS NOT A REALITY

It is difficult to see God as formless and it is difficult to see God as having a form. The formless is so abstract and God in a form appears to be too limited. So some people prefer to be atheists.

Atheism is not a reality; it is just a matter of convenience. When you have a spirit of inquiry or when you search for truth, atheism falls apart. With a spirit of inquiry, you cannot deny something that you have not disproved. An atheist denies God without first disproving God's existence. In order to disprove God, you must have enormous knowledge. And when you have enormous knowledge, you cannot disprove it! *(Laughter)*

To say that something does not exist, you must know about the whole universe. So you can never be one hundred percent atheistic. An atheist is only a believer who is sleeping!

For a person to say, "I don't believe in anything," means he must believe in himself - so he believes in a self that he does not even know.

An atheist can never be sincere because sincerity needs depth - and an atheist refuses to go to his depth. The deeper he goes, he finds a void, a field of all possibilities and he has to accept that there are many secrets he does not know. He would then need to acknowledge his ignorance - which he refuses to do - because the moment he is sincere, he seriously starts doubting his atheism. A doubt-free atheist is next to impossible! So you can never be a sincere and doubt-free atheist.

When the atheist realises his ignorance, what does he do? Where does he go? Does he go to a *Guru*? What does a *Guru* do to him? *(The answer next week.)*

*✍ **News Flash:***

Gurudev addressed a packed auditorium of prominent scientists and researchers at the Indian Institute of Sciences, Bangalore - the premier institute of India - where he praised the students for initiating a dialogue on "Bridging Science to Humanity. "Dr. AbdulKalam, scientific advisor to the Prime Minister, expressed immense admiration for Gurudev.

Then Gurudev left on a whirlwind trip to Vishakhapatnam where 10,000 children, who are a part of our 5H Program, received blessings.

Hyderabad had been promised a surprise visit which was a four-hour stop with only 24 hours notice. There were still hundreds queuing for darshan at Gurudev's departure.

The 109th country to become a part of the Art of Living map is Mozambique, Africa.

284. ATHEISM

Atheism is when you do not believe either in values or in the abstract. When an atheist comes to the *Guru*, what happens? You start experiencing your own form and discover that you are indeed formless, hollow and empty. And this abstract non-form in you becomes more and more concrete.

The *Guru* makes the abstract more real and what you thought was solid appears to be more unreal. Sensitivity and subtlety dawn. Perception of love, not as an emotion, but as the substratum of existence, becomes evident. The formless spirit shines through every form in creation and the mystery of life deepens, shattering atheism. Then the journey begins and it has four stages.

The first stage is '*Saarupya*' - to see the formless in the form - seeing God in all the forms. Often, one feels more comfortable seeing God as formless rather than with a form, because with a form, one feels a distance, a duality, a fear of rejection and other limitations. In life all of our interactions are with a form, other than in deep sleep and in *Samadhi*. And, if you do not see God in the form, then the waking part of life remains devoid of the Divine. All those who accept God to be formless use symbols, and perhaps love the symbols more than God himself. If God comes and tells a Christian to leave the Cross or a Muslim to drop the crescent, perhaps he may not do it. To begin with, loving the formless is possible only through forms.

The second stage is '*Saamipya*' - closeness - feeling absolutely close to the form you have chosen and reaching out to the formless. This leads to a sense of intimacy with the whole creation. In this stage, one overcomes the fear of rejection and other fears. But this is bound by time and space.

The third stage is '*Saanidhya*' - feeling the presence of the Divine by which you transcend the limitations of time and space.

Then the final stage - '*Saayujya*' - is when you are firmly entrenched in the Divine. It is then you realise you are one with the Divine. There is a total merging with the Beloved and all duality disappears.

This is that and that is this.

Vinod: Does a believer also go through these four stages?

Gurudev: Certainly, whether an atheist or believer, he goes through the four stages.

✍ News Flash:

The power of knowledge is obvious when impossible becomes possible. All arrangements for a mega event in Bangalore were made in just four days time, where Gurudev and His Holiness the Dalai Lama addressed 150,000 people. His Holiness the Dalai Lama visited the ashram and addressed the Advanced Course participants and praised the Art of Living Foundation for its work towards enriching human values around the world.

The Satsang was an historic moment. As Buddhist monks and Vedic pundits chanted, thousands, from the stillness of meditation, started singing, dancing and celebrating with lit candles held in their hands.

Waves of love, light and joy permeated the atmosphere. Five thousand peace balloons were sent up in the air. As the crowd pleaded for more, Gurudev led them through a second round of meditation. As if this was not enough, Gurudev granted everyone one wish and the next day thousands of grateful calls were received.

Youth Training Program camps are happening at many places in India.

285. To Say "Sorry" is a Good Mistake

Often, in establishing your righteousness, you are insensitive to others' feelings. When someone is hurt, arguing with them and establishing your righteousness will be in vain. By simply saying "sorry," you can uplift the other person and take away the bitterness. In many situations saying "sorry" is better than establishing your righteousness - it can avert much unpleasantness.

This one word of five letters, when said sincerely, can remove anger, guilt, hatred and distance.

Many people feel pride in hearing "sorry" from others - it boosts their ego. But when you say "sorry" to a wise man, it evokes compassion at your ignorance. And when you say "sorry" to your *Guru*, he will get angry and say, "Go! Listen to *Ashtavakra*!" *(Laughter)* Your saying "sorry" indicates doership - you feel that YOU have MADE a mistake.

A mistake is part of an unconscious mind. An unconscious mind cannot do right, while a conscious mind can do no wrong. The mind that makes the mistake and the mind that realises the mistake - saying "sorry" - are entirely different, aren't they? The mind that says "sorry" cannot be an unconscious mind.

Therefore, saying "sorry" sincerely is a big mistake.

Did you get it or are you confused? If you did not get it, do not feel sorry or... you can feel sorry! *(Laughter)*

How strange - truth is paradoxical!

✍ *News Flash:*

Gurudev was the chief guest at the 86th birthday celebration of Swami Satchidananda (of the Lotus Temple, Virginia) in Coimbatore. This was followed by a Satsang. He also inaugurated the K.G. Eye Hospital and addressed the doctors and computer professionals.

The European Ashram was all set to welcome the master for the Christmas Advanced Course. On looking at the beautifully decorated Christmas tree, Gurudev reminded everybody to be like a Christmas tree, evergreen and full of gifts. The Advanced Course at the European Ashram ended with full hearts, warm smiles and cold snow.

On to Canada for the New Year.

286. Kick the Ball and Be in the Goal

Do you know why the earth is shaped like a globe?

(Silence....)

So you can kick it and it will roll away! From the moment you wake up in the morning you are always with people and your mind is caught up in worldly thoughts. So sometime during the day, sit for a few minutes, get into the cave of your heart with your eyes closed and kick the world away like a ball.

But as soon as you open your eyes, hold onto the ball because you need to kick it again in the next session. *(Laughter)* During the day be 100 percent attached to the work; do not try to detach yourself. But when you sit for meditation, then totally detach yourself. Only those who can totally detach can take total responsibility.

Eventually you will be able to be both attached and detached simultaneously. Kick the ball and be in the goal! This is the art of living, the skill of living.

✍ News Flash:

Two hundred and fifty people "kicked the ball" and welcomed the New Year in deep meditation with Gurudev. The North American Ashram, deep in snow that sparkled like diamonds, seemed suitably decked out to receive Gurudev on this first winter visit. The frozen lakes provided great "skating" on afternoon walks (runs!) through the snow.

The City Council in Alpharetta, Georgia, U.S.A., planned to remove several 150-year-old oak trees as part of a street-widening project. The engineering firm, cable company, and phone company made their studies and gave approval. Local people who wanted to save the trees were told, "There's no hope; it's finished." A devotee - Juanita Rocca - put Gurudev's picture on each tree and phoned the city officials to tell them the trees were protected by a saint. Word spread through the town and 300 protestors, along with full media coverage, showed up at the City Council. Plans were abandoned, and the trees are happily standing.

287. "Important" and "Unimportant"

To many people are stuck with what is "important," always caught up in thinking about what is important. Why do you always have to do only that which is important?

For something to be important, there needs to be many things that are unimportant. So you cannot eliminate unimportant things. It is important to have unimportant things to make something else important. *(Laughter)* Things are either themselves important or they make other things important. So that means everything is important, and everything is unimportant.

When you realise this fact, you become choiceless.

When you say something is important, you are limiting your vastness.

A journalist asked me, "Why is it important to breathe?" "Why is it important to be happy?" "Why is it important to have peace?" These questions are not relevant at all. Why should you always look for what is important? Something that is unimportant can contribute to something that is important. And what is important and unimportant changes with time and space. Food is important when you are hungry and unimportant when you are full.

When something is inevitable, you do not categorize it as important or unimportant. It is beyond choice.

"Everything is important" is *Karma* Yoga. "Nothing is important" is deep meditation.

✍ *News Flash:*

Two African countries, Benin and Togo, have entered the Art of Living family - bringing the total number of countries to 112.

A Montreal devotee who is a cab driver by profession picked up a passenger one night who appeared overcome by drugs and alcohol. The passenger demanded to be taken to his destination for half-fare, and when the driver protested the passenger pulled a gun. At first the driver was afraid, but when he looked at the photo of Gurudev on the dashboard he felt completely protected. During the drive the passenger put the gun away. Eventually he asked who the person was in the photo. When they reached the destination, the passenger bowed to the picture and paid the full fare to the driver along with a handsome tip.

288. Worship - A Sign of Maturity

For a flame to rise up, you need space above it. In the same way, for a man to rise up in his life, he needs an ideal, he needs something to adore and worship. In worship, a sense of belongingness, love, honour and respect all come together. However, without a sense of belongingness, worship or idealism can bring low self-esteem. The ancient people knew this so they insisted that people should feel a part of what they worship. They encouraged people to worship the sun, moon, mountains, rivers, plants, animals and people. Worship is the culmination of love and appreciation. Worship prevents love from turning into hatred or jealousy, and prevents appreciation from becoming low self-esteem. In life, if you do not adore or appreciate anything, you will be filled with negativity. And a person who has nothing to worship or adore is sure to fall into depression.

Lack of adoration has led to many emotional, psychological and social problems in society. If you have nothing to hold high in life, selfishness, arrogance and violence are sure to follow. Adoring and honouring each other in society eliminates stress and fosters compassion and love.

In the previous century, it was thought that worshiping was an uncivilised and unintelligent thing to do. Worship was thought to rise from a slavish mentality. In fact it is just the contrary. Worship can only happen through gratefulness and not through subservience.

Worship in a true sense is a sign of maturity and not of weakness.

Question: You said worship is the culmination of love. Does worship also have a culmination?

Gurudev: Culmination of worship is self-knowledge, *Samadhi*.

News Flash:

Gurudev stopped at the European Ashram on his way to the Khumbha Mela in India, where 80 million people are assembled to worship the river Ganges and Mother Nature.

289. THE KUMBHA MELA

Once every 12 years, all the seers, saints and aspirants of spiritual knowledge congregate at the confluence, or *sangam*, of the three holy rivers - *Ganga*, *Yamuna* and *Saraswati*. The *Ganga* is a symbol of knowledge and self-inquiry. It is on the banks of the *Yamuna* that events of love have been immortalized. When knowledge and love come together, when the head meets the heart, *Saraswati*, symbolic of wisdom and the fine arts, emerges.

When a tiny atom explodes, the radiation lasts for a long time. The mind is more subtle than one millionth of an atom. When the mind explodes, that is enlightenment.

Over the centuries, thousands of sages who have meditated, done penance and have been enlightened come to the *Kumbha Mela* and relieve themselves of the burden of the merits gained through *Sadhana* by bathing in the rivers. The water can absorb the energy that they radiate. The seekers, who come from all corners to be in the company of seers and saints, gain that merit when they take a dip in the rivers.

Space by itself cannot be bought, and a lump of clay has no value, but when space is enveloped by clay it gains value, this is a *Kumbha* - a pot. Spirit is everywhere in nature, but when it dawns in the human body as an elevated state of consciousness, then it gains immense value. An embodied and elevated spirit is usually referred to as *Kumbha*. This is why the enlightened age is also called the Aquarian age. *Kumbha* denotes a pot, which is symbolic of fullness and perfection.

The *Kumbha Mela* is an ancient version of a spiritual expo.

✍ *News Flash:*

Gurudev was in Prayag for the Kumbha Mela. Many very touching incidents happened that show the depth of devotion of the people who had gathered there. Here are two of them.

One morning, Gurudev noticed an 80-year-old woman who had been separated from her family. She looked tired and hungry. Gurudev sent someone to give her some money, which she refused to accept saying that she had come here to give, not to take! Gurudev himself had to go to her and tell her that the money was prasad, which she then took from him.

It was very cold there every night, the temperature dropping to 2 or 3 degrees Celsius, and many people had no accommodations whatsoever and would just sleep in the sand on the banks of the rivers, most of them without even a shawl to cover themselves. Gurudev along with some yuvacharyas and other devotees would go and distribute many blankets every night to these people. Thousands of blankets were distributed each night. One night, they came across a teenager who was shivering with cold and gave him some blankets to cover himself with, which he refused to take saying, that he could bear this cold, and that there were so many others who would need them much more.

Gurudev later told everyone to note the devotion and the total surrender of these people who even in such desperate circumstances had such absolute faith in the Divine and knew that He would provide for them.

Our Ashram was bustling with activity all day long and attracted many people; food was being served continuously throughout the day. The community of saints there was overjoyed to meet with Gurudev and lauded the work of the Art of Living.

Back in Delhi Gurudev had very fruitful meetings with various leaders including the leader of Jamma Masjid.

January 31, 2001
From Davos to Zurich, Switzerland

290. THE OTHER SIDE OF FRIENDLINESS

Secretaries, police, judges, accountants and people in key positions should not be friendly!

The main disadvantages of being friendly are:

- You come under obligation.

- You lose your freedom.

- Your perception cannot be free and fair. Your thoughts and actions may not be impartial.

- Your focus, commitment, creativity and above all your time will be wasted.

- You become prone to picking up bad habits and negative moods.

It takes wisdom to be free from the burden of obligation and not be influenced by your friends' opinions and feelings.

On many occasions, it is better to be unfriendly than friendly. Being unfriendly does not mean being aggressive and inimical. The best secretaries, personal assistants, security personnel, and judges have to be unfriendly.

Those who are aloof and indifferent get centred more quickly than those who are too friendly. A certain degree of aloofness in every relationship will strengthen your personality and connect you to your source.

Vinod Sethi: It's very easy to be very aloof or very friendly. But to be friendly and aloof is a *Sadhana*.

Harish: Be an unfriendly friend!

From the Kumbha Mela, where he was one with even the poorest of the poor, Gurudev descended on the beautiful Alpine ski resort of Davos where the richest of the rich had gathered to participate in the World Economic Forum. Gurudev was invited to the World Economic Forum to participate in a dialogue with other spiritual and religious leaders from the Vatican, Israel, Egypt, Bosnia, South Africa, France and the United Kingdom.

It was a rare opportunity for the extremely busy créme de la créme of global business to interact with an even busier Guru!

Gurudev was the guest of honour at a reception hosted in his honour by a leading media magnate of Europe. In his welcoming speech, the host felicitated Gurudev and praised his beautiful energy. Other dignitaries who attended the reception included Shimon Peres - ex-prime minister of Israel, Peter Gabriel - pop singer, Reinhold Messner - mountaineer, Michael Dell - CEO Dell Computers, members of the European Royalty and CEOs of Fortune 50 companies. In the jam-packed hall, Gurudev was the centre of attraction, as all the guests lined up to greet him personally. Several guests were heard commenting that they could feel Gurudev's energy in every corner of the room!

In the concluding session of the meeting, Gurudev addressed the conference and said, "Globalization was pioneered by religious and spiritual leaders long ago. Whether you like it or not, you are all our followers!"

In India, hundreds of Art of Living volunteers are busily engaged in the relief efforts in the state of Gujarat. Within hours of the earthquake, our volunteers provided shelter and food to 1,500 people. Our Satsang groups are arranging food, clothing, water and funds.

291. Longing Itself is Divine

Longing itself is Divine.

Longing for worldly things makes you inert.

Longing for infinity fills you with life.

When longing dies, inertia sets in. But longing also brings along a sense of pain. To avoid the pain, you try to push away the longing. The skill is to bear the pain of longing and move on. Do not try to find a shortcut to overcome longing. Do not make the longing short - that's why it is called loooonging. *(Laughter)*

True longing in itself brings up spurts of bliss. That is why in ancient days longing was kept alive by singing and listening to *kathas* (stories).

When longing transcends relationships, judgments, jealousy and all other negative feelings drop off. It is only with wisdom and self-knowledge that you can transcend relationships. People often think wisdom is devoid of longing - No! Such wisdom is dry. The longing that comes in true wisdom makes life juicier. Divine is certainly juicy!

Longing gives you the power to bless. Bless the entire creation. For the longing in you is God.

✍ News Flash:

Gurudev's whirlwind tour of the state of Kerala, India began with hundreds of thousands celebrating at the Trivandrum Satsang. At Punaloor, over 50,000 people braved heavy rains for a "standing Satsang" throughout which Gurudev also stood. Hundreds of thousands rejoiced at Cherokolpuzha and Kottayam Satsangs.

Gurudev met with His Holiness Basilius Marthoma Matthew, the second Catholic Baba, and a descendant of St. Thomas. Gurudev was the chief guest at a meeting attended by Mr. George Fernandes, Defense Minister of India, and inaugurated homes for the aged at Suttur, near Mysore.

On to the Southern Kumbha Mela where he blessed hundreds of thousands taking the holy dip in the water at a confluence of rivers.

The intense longing of phase 2 teacher training graduates and ashramites pulled our precious Gurudev by helicopter from the Southern Kumbha Mela to reach the Bangalore Ashram just in time for a juicy Satsang.

292. Back to Space

From time to time the earth shakes and in its shaking wakes up the man who is in slumber, who not only misuses Nature but puts his faith in bricks and mortar. Your true security is in the Self, not in bricks and mortar. Perhaps this is what Nature wants to convey to you. Earthquakes, floods and volcanoes all drive home the truth that nothing is permanent and you can find no security in that which is impermanent. Disasters come to you as a shock and wake you up.

When such calamities occur we try to understand their cause so that we can blame someone. Strangely, when you find someone to blame you feel comfortable, but with natural calamities you cannot blame anyone. They come to you as a shock. With wisdom, shocks can make you grow in leaps and bounds. Without wisdom a shock can only lead you to negativity and depression.

Question: Why should nature destroy small innocent children?

Gurudev: Nature just does its job. It does not discriminate between young and old. Do you think that all those who eat bamboo shoots and eggs or pluck flower buds are not compassionate? Maybe, maybe not! *(Laughter)*

Instead of questioning Nature, wake up and see the opportunity for *Seva* or service. See what is happening in Gujarat now. Today, hundreds and thousands are engaged in service activities which would not have happened otherwise. One positive thing coming out of destruction is the reconstruction of Gujarat which would not have happened if not for the earthquake. Another interesting outcome is a fresh water spring that has appeared in a region that has been continuously drought prone.

Wisdom is considering the earth as your Valentine. Whether it shakes or breaks, it is dear to you. You always see good coming from it.

The four elements, other than space, create turbulence from time to time. If you depend on them for support, they will shake you and lead you back to space.

Finding security in inner space is spirituality.

Gurudev was a state guest in Andhra Pradesh. His talk to the government officials was greatly appreciated by the Chief Minister. Gurudev was invited to come and deliver more programs in that state. That evening there was a mammoth Satsang.

The Art of Living Foundation has adopted 26 villages in Kutch-Bhuj, the earthquake-hit area of Gujrat.

Twenty-five-year-old Rajani from Bangalore all of a sudden completely lost her hearing (sensorineural hearing loss) on the 9th of December, 2000. The world had become silent to her. Medical experts, after diagnosis and treatment, declared no possibility that she would regain her hearing. After attending the first day of the residential basic course at the Ashram on the 19th of January, 2001, she miraculously regained her hearing. Where medical science had failed, her Guru's grace transformed her life.

Research at the All India Institute of Medical Science showed significant changes in the brain wave patterns of the Art of Living teachers who participated in the study. All 18 subjects were found to maintain high integrity and awareness during activity.

293. PASSION AND SELF-RELIANCE

Passion makes you weak. Dispassion is strength.

For your passion to be fulfilled, you have to depend upon so many things. Passion and self-reliance do not appear to go together. If you are passionate, you have to forget about being self-reliant. If you want to be self-reliant, you have to drop your passion. This is generally true.

That which brings together these two completely different aspects in you is your spirit. The same spirit that wants to be self-reliant is also passionate. It is only in spirituality that passion and dispassion can happen together. This is the rarest combination.

When you are dispassionate, you have strength, and strength is self-reliance. True self-reliance is realising that nothing is excluded from the Self. And when you realise everything is part of the Self, then you can be passionate about everything! Even to fulfil your passion, you need to only rely on the Self, for Self alone is non-changing.

In Truth, there is neither reliance nor passion. In one state, you can either be passionate or you can be self-reliant. But in an elevated state of consciousness, you can be neither, or both!

✍ *News Flash:*
Shivratri - From every corner of India, and from all over the world, devotees came for Shiva's blessings!
Despite the Ashram overflowing with thousands, there was absolutely no chaos as the volunteers of the YLTP (Youth Leadership Training Program) did wonderful Seva and won everyone's hearts. It was celebration all round; even the ice creams sold like hot cakes. During the morning Rudra-puja, even the windows of the meditation hall were filled to capacity. Huge screens were laid out in the amphitheatre for the evening puja, which was followed by a spellbinding Satsang with Gurudev truly Bholenath - Lord of the Innocent! The celebrations continued until early morning as devotees queued for darshan.

294. THE OTHER SIDE OF FEAR - THE USEFULNESS OF FEAR

Nature has put an amount of inbuilt fear in all living beings. This fear makes life defend itself, protect itself. Like salt in the food, a little bit of fear is essential for people to be righteous.

Fear of hurting someone makes you more conscious.

Fear of failure makes you more keen and dynamic.

Fear moves you from carelessness to taking care.

Fear moves you from insensitivity to sensitivity.

Fear moves you from dullness to alertness.

Total lack of fear may lead to destructive tendencies - a distorted ego knows no fear. Neither does one with expanded consciousness! Whereas the ego dismisses fear and moves in a destructive manner, the wise one acknowledges fear and takes refuge in the Divine.

When you are in love, when you are surrendered, there is no fear. Ego, too knows no fear. But there is a difference, like that of heaven and earth, between these two types of fearless states.

Fear makes you righteous; fear brings you close to surrender; fear keeps you on the path; fear keeps you from being destructive. Peace and law are maintained on the planet because of fear.

A newborn child knows no fear - it totally relies on its mother. Whether a child, a kitten or a bird, when they start becoming independent they experience fear which makes them go running back to their mothers. This is inbuilt by nature to sustain life.

So, the purpose of fear is to bring you back to the source!

✒ *News Flash:*

Gurudev's entire journey from Mumbai to Surat was punctuated by darshan. Enthusiastic devotees, in hundreds, thronged every station. 40,000 attended the live Kriya in Surat setting off a wave of energy, culminating in a 'high-voltage' Satsang of over 300,000 people.

On to Ahmedabad, where Gurudev's meeting with the Chief Minister and bureaucrats proved extremely useful. Gurudev suggested drastic changes in the layout plan of the 900 quake-hit villages which are to be rebuilt. His ideas were greatly appreciated and immediately incorporated.

Gurudev wondered whether he was awakening people or not, but devotees who showed up all night at different stations between Ahmedabad and Udaipur, armed with musical bands, definitely kept waking up everyone with their fervor!

Gurudev's first ever visit to the city of Jheels (lakes), Udaipur, saw a grand Satsang. He also met with other NGOs and gave a highly illuminating talk on Integrated Social Development. Gliding softly over the moonlit waters in a boat to the glittering Jagmandir, he was given a royal reception and the Satsang happened in regal splendor!

"When the Divine dwells in your heart, the whole world appears to you as a temple."

Gurudev's entourage decided that it was high time he stopped traveling by train. On the last leg of this wonderfully eventful trip from Udaipur to Delhi, there was a brief stopover for 20 minutes at Jaipur where a welcome stage and over a thousand devotees compelled Gurudev to deplane and give darshan right there, even at the airport, where Satsang happened spontaneously!

295. THE OTHER SIDE OF EGO

Ego is an impediment for a leader, a wise man, a merchant or a servant, but it is a necessity for a warrior, a competitor. A warrior is one who takes on challenges and commitments and stands by them.

Ego makes one sacrifice oneself for a cause. Ego gives strength and courage, brings valour to meet the challenges with endurance and perseverance. A strong ego will counteract depression. Often ego is thought to be selfish but it is the greatest motivating factor for creativity and generosity.

Ego propels one to venture into the unknown.

There are three types of ego - *sattvic, rajasic* and *tamasic.*

1. *Tamasic* ego is barbaric and blind, and has self-destructive tendencies.

2. *Rajasic* ego is self-centred and causes misery to oneself and others.

3. *Sattvic* ego is creative and has protective tendencies.

If you cannot surrender, at least have a *sattvic* ego, as a *sattvic* ego is always ready to sacrifice.

Bhanu: This is very good! It gives many people relief. *(Laughter)*

✍ *News Flash:*

Rishikesh camp begins with the first Advance Course where joy and silence go hand in hand. Knowledge is flowing like the Ganges.

So far, 50 truckloads of materials have reached the areas severely hit by the earthquake in Gujarat. Our teachers are busy having courses to help people deal with their trauma.

296. THE PARADOX OF SACRIFICE

All the scriptures of the world glorify sacrifice. What is sacrifice?

It is giving up something that you value. You can only sacrifice that which you would like to keep for yourself; in other words, that which gives you pleasure and joy. You cannot sacrifice something that you dislike or disown. Sacrifice is always related to a higher cause for a greater good. At the same time, when your love for the greater good is so strong, nothing else assumes any value. Sacrifice here becomes irrelevant, because love alone is your strongest driving force. So when there is so much love there cannot be sacrifice. At the same time when there is no love, there is no sacrifice.

For example, if a mother has made plans to see a movie and she realises that her child is sick, she does not say that she has sacrificed the movie to nurse her child, because she simply did not want to go. Nothing else seems to charm the mother besides being with her child.

You do not sacrifice something for someone you are in love with. Sacrifice indicates that your pleasure has more value than the cause for which you are sacrificing.

When the love is lukewarm, then sacrifice assumes meaning. Yet sacrifice purifies the human mind and reins in selfish tendencies. It can also bring pride, arrogance, self-pity and sometimes even depression.

You can sacrifice only that which you value. For a wise man nothing is more valuable than truth, values and the Divine, and he will never sacrifice those. God is the greatest, and if someone values the greatest, then how can he sacrifice God? This is the paradox of sacrifice.

✍ News Flash:

Holi celebrations were simply memorable. With colours in the air, the celebrations transported people back in time on the banks of the Ganga.

Thousands got together in 43 cities all over the world to participate in the 5H Walk for Gujarat to rehabilitate the earthquake-destroyed areas of Gujarat, India. It was well covered by the media.

Pakistan is the latest addition to the list of countries where Art of Living Courses are conducted, bringing the total to 113.

297. Divine in the Form and Formless

Divinity is unmanifest, but man has an innate desire to perceive the Divine in the manifest creation around him. He creates idols, breathes faith into them and requests divinity to be present in the idol for a while, so that he can worship, express his love and play with it. At the end of his worship he requests divinity to go back into his heart from where divinity manifested. This is in all *puja* practices.

Participants in the *puja* are not actually worshipping the idols but are worshipping the unmanifest divinity which has the divine qualities. So, the idol worshippers of the East are not the same as the ones in the Middle East described in the Bible, because they are not just worshipping different gods and different idols, they are worshipping the ONE divinity in many different forms.

Paganism, Satan and animal worship, without the knowledge of the one divinity is very different from seeing the Divine in every form of the manifest universe. In the eastern tradition, gods and goddesses are part of the one divinity like the different colours of white sunlight, whereas in the Greek tradition, gods and goddesses are in themselves different entities.

Worshipping Satan and different entities is totally different from worshipping divinity in its various forms. Every form belongs to the Divine. When you adore the form, you are adoring the Divine behind the form.

With this knowledge, the very act of worship, which is more an inner phenomenon, assumes a more colourful and vibrant expression, indicating that both the form and the formless are all divine.

✍ *News Flash:*

Gurudev dashed to Delhi for a brief 48-hour visit where he rapped with the law students telling them that LAW stood for Love, Awareness and Wisdom. Human Resources stands both for Heart and Rational thinking, he emphasized while inaugurating an H.R. portal, and later converted a group of eminent scientists at the National Physical Laboratory to having both a scientific and spiritual temper by saying, "All discoveries are a product of consciousness." Provoking the leaders of business at the Associated Chambers of Commerce and Industry, he said, "If God can play man, why should man not play God?"

Ten schools have been opened in northeastern India and eleven school buildings are under construction in Gujarat.

298. Strength and Subordination

Many people do not want to work under someone else, be it in their profession, a company or even voluntary service. The general notion is that when you work under someone, you lose your freedom, you have to be answerable.

So, many people opt for business, wanting to be their own boss. But, in business, you are accountable to so many people. If you cannot be accountable to even one person, how can you be accountable to many? This is the paradox. In fact, being in business binds you more than the boss!

Refusing to work under someone is a sign of weakness, not strength. A strong person would not feel uncomfortable working under anyone, because he knows his strength. It is the weak and poor in spirit who do not like to work under someone else, because they are unaware of their strength. They can be neither successful in business nor in any profession.

And the same is true even in the field of social service - often volunteers do not want to work under someone else. This is merely an exhibition of their weakness. With such an attitude, they achieve very little.

One who is timid and weak in spirit would be uncomfortable to work even under the wise one; but one who knows his own strength can work effectively even under a fool!

Nityanand: But to work under a fool is frustrating!

Gurudev: When you know your strength, with skill and intelligence, you can turn every disadvantage into an advantage. A fool can bring out the best of your communication skills! *(Laughter)*

So watch out! If you feel uncomfortable working under someone, it clearly shows you need to strengthen yourself. Desiring freedom from circumstances, situations or people is no freedom at all. Knowing that nobody can take away your freedom - that is strength! And when you realise your strength is unshakable, you will not mind working under anybody.

✍ *News Flash:*

Over a thousand people took part in a 5H Walk at Muscat, in which the Royal family also participated.

Dehradun had a scintillating Satsang. The Advance Course in Rishikesh had knowledge, bliss and grace! The Hindu New Year was heralded with an early morning dip in the holy Ganges by Gurudev and all the devotees.

299. COMMITMENT AND CONVENIENCE

A commitment can only be felt when it oversteps convenience. That which is convenient is not commitment. If you just go on your convenience, your commitment falls apart causing more inconvenience! If you keep dropping your commitment because it is inconvenient, can you be comfortable? Often, what is convenient does not bring comfort, but gives an illusion of comfort. Also if you are too stuck in commitment, and it is too inconvenient too often, you will be unable to fulfil your commitment and it will only generate frustration. Wisdom is to strike a balance between convenience and commitment because both bring comfort to the body, mind and spirit.

A seeker of knowledge should forget about convenience, so should soldiers, rulers, students, seekers of wealth and all essential service providers. Those who want to be creative and adventurous transcend convenience. Those who are ambitious and have a passion for a goal do not care for convenience. To the wise their commitment is their comfort. Whenever their commitment is shaken, their comfort is also shaken. To the lazy, commitment is torture though it is the best remedy.

Commitment will always bring comfort in the long run.

Question: Are there any commitments that can be given up?

Gurudev: Yes. Sometimes when you are committed without a vision, you feel stifled when your vision expands. Such commitments made with shortsightedness can be given up.

* A smaller less important commitment can be given up for a greater commitment.

* Commitment to the means can be given up for the sake of the commitment to the goals.

* When your commitment brings misery to many in the long run, it can be given up.

✍ Knowledge Splash!

Gurudev held up a pistachio nut and asked, "What is this?"

Everybody said, "Pistachio."

Gurudev held up a pistachio nut without the shell and asked, "What is this?"

Everybody said, "Pistachio."

Gurudev then held up the shell and asked, "What is this?"

Everybody said, "Shell."

Gurudev then said, "As the nut with or without the shell is 'pistachio', similarly spirit with or without the body is God. But just as the shell without the nut is not pistachio, the body without spirit is not God. Spirit is certainly God because it is present everywhere. The body is certainly not God because it cannot be present everywhere."

When someone asks you, "Are you God?" - who is the question addressed to? As it is only the spirit that answers, you have no choice but to say, "Yes!"

When asked, "Are you God?"- the best answer is: God is within the body and God embodies the whole universe. Those who have eyes will see.

300. DEALING WITH BLAME AND ACCUSATION

When someone blames you, you feel a heavy load on your head, and when you talk about it you spread the unpleasant feeling all around you. At that moment wake up and see you are Being and nothing can touch you. This is all just a drama that you yourself have created. You have gone through this over and over again. All the accusations you face in your life are your own creation. Knowing this, you feel free and light.

Owning responsibility for all your experiences in life makes you powerful and will put an end to grumbling, planning counterattacks, explanations, and a host of negative tendencies. Owning full responsibility makes you free.

When someone blames you, directly or indirectly, what do you do?

- Do you lodge it in your mind and get emotionally upset?
- Do you dismiss it and the blamer altogether without taking a lesson from it?
- Do you talk about it with people and waste your time and other's time and money?
- Do you pity yourself and blame your shortcomings?
- Do you blame the other person?
- Do you generalise and eternalise the problem?

When this happens you are not living up to the knowledge. You need to do the basic course at least half a dozen times and read all the weekly knowledge.

- Do you laugh at it and not even take notice of it?
- Do you treat it as a non-event, not even worth talking about, let one taking any action?
- Do you treat comments and accusations as passing clouds and more of an entertainment?
- Do you discourage dwelling on unpleasant and negative moments?
- Do you remain non-judgmental and absolutely unshaken in your space of love?
- Outwardly you may be calm, but do you also remain centred and calm within you, not even taking pride in your growth or wisdom?

Then you are a pride to your tutor - the master.

✍ You cannot take credit for loving *Gurudev* or any wise person. You have no choice at all as it will happen against all odds!

To love someone whom you like is not a big deal at all.

To love someone because they love you, gets you zero marks.

To love someone whom you do not like, means you have learned a lesson in life.

To love someone who blames you for no reason, shows you have learned the art of living.

✍ *News Flash:*

A gentleman complained to Gurudev that some people have ganged up against him and blamed him. Gurudev patiently listened, adding a few comments. The person felt he gained some sympathy and as he started feeling righteous, Gurudev shot back saying, "You have already wasted enough of your time. Why do you want to waste mine also! You only get what you have sown!" Suddenly the whole atmosphere became serene and smiles returned.

301. SELF-CONFIDENCE AND AMBITION

Ambition indicates a lack of self-confidence!

When you know you can achieve something easily, you are not ambitious about it. You are simply confident that you can do it. Your ambition indicates challenge and uncertainty, which is contrary to self-confidence. So one who has total self-confidence cannot be ambitious! At the same time a person who lacks total self-confidence cannot be ambitious either! For ambition to be, one must have a little bit of confidence and total ignorance of the Self.

It is next to impossible to have total confidence without Self-knowledge. With the knowledge of the Self, there is nothing left to achieve, for the entire nature of existence is mere play and display of one's own consciousness.

People take pride in being ambitious. The wise man will only smile at them. Ambition can never be for something you know you can achieve effortlessly. You can only be ambitious about something for which you must put forth effort, which poses a challenge and which you are not even certain you will be able to achieve.

Moreover, ambition takes away the joy of the moment.

With Self-knowledge nothing is challenging to you, nor do you need to exert any effort. Nature is ready to fulfil your intentions even before they arise, giving you no chance to crave or desire. Nature does not allow the wise to have desires or ambitions, nor does it allow the unwise to fulfil or get rid of them.

Do you still want to be ambitious or is your only ambition to get rid of ambition? *(Laughter)*

✐ News Flash:

After a fantastic Satsang in Los Angeles, and a brief stopover in Apple Valley, California, Gurudev left for his Central and South American tour.

Gurudev is encouraging Satsang groups to read the Yoga Vasistha.

302. The Dangers of Belongingness and Advantages of Obligations

Belongingness can bring about a host of negative emotions like demand, jealousy, unawareness and lack of gratitude. Just look into your own life - you feel more grateful to strangers than the people you feel "belong" to you. Belongingness reduces gratefulness, awareness, and gives rise to demands which destroy love. This is the biggest problem in relationships. People are nice to strangers and give more attention to them but with a sense of belongingness comes a lack of attention and a sense of being carefree.

Belongingness can make you insensitive, dull, and take away the charm in life. Who belongs to whom in this world? Here you are a stranger and everyone is a stranger to you. Blessed are those who feel themselves a stranger.

You feel more obligation to a stranger than to the person you feel belongs to you. Obligation is very good for keeping a check on your ego. It makes you humble. There is no greater antidote to ego than humility. Being humble is the beginning of all virtues.

People have such resistance to obligations. They do not realise that they are always under obligation, whether giving or taking. Dull people think that one is obliged only when one takes. The wise know that even when giving, one is under obligations as the person has accepted what one gives. So whether you give or take you are under obligations. And if someone does not give or take, you are still under obligation, for they are freeing you from visible obligations. That is to say, you are obliged even to those who do not make you obliged.

Life renews itself constantly by becoming a stranger in this old and familiar world. You are simply loaded with obligations and you are a total stranger in this world every moment. How does it feel?

✍ News Flash:

In Suriname, the Vice-President, Speaker of the Parliament and other parliamentarians received Gurudev, and later the Army, Navy, Air Force, and the prison and police chief met with Gurudev. They were greatly impressed with the Art of Living programs and requested that they be offered continuously.

Gurudev was received at the chamber of the Vice-Governor of Bahia, Brazil. As Gurudev entered a great sense of calmness dawned on everyone. The Vice-President shared that there was a conflict going on over border issues, and suddenly within moments of Gurudev's arrival in the building, it was resolved.

At the Recife Airport, Gurudev played tricks on all those who were accompanying him, so everyone said they would not listen to him anymore.

303. Prestige and Honour - Your Golden Cage

Honour reduces freedom. Your fame, honour and virtue can limit your freedom.

Nobody expects a good person to make a mistake. So the better you are, the higher the expectations people have of you. It is then that you lose your freedom. Your virtues and good actions are like a golden cage. You are trapped by your own good actions, for everyone expects more from a good person and nobody expects anything from a bad person.

Most of the people are stuck in this cage of prestige and honour. They cannot smile. They are constantly worried about keeping up their prestige and their honour. It becomes more important than their own life. Just being good or doing good to retain prestige and honour is worthless. Prestige and honour can bring more misery in life than poverty.

Many desire fame but little do they know that they are looking for a cage.

It is an art to be dignified and yet not be suffocated by it. Only the wise would know this. For the wise one it is natural to be honoured, but he has no concerns even if it falls apart. Despite having fame or prestige, he will live as though he has none. A wise person can handle any fame without feeling suffocated for he too is crazy!

By doing good in society one gains prestige, then when enjoying the prestige and honour one's freedom is lost.

Question: Then how do you keep your freedom?

Gurudev: By being like a child, considering the world as a dream, a burden or a joke.

✍ *News Flash:*

The state assembly of Sao Paulo honoured Gurudev where he spoke and conducted a meditation. After a moving Satsang that evening, Gurudev left for Buenos Aires. In Argentina, Gurudev addressed the prestigious International Counsel for Cultural Relationships and then moved on to Panama, where he addressed a group of women government and business leaders and had private meetings with the mayor, the provincial governor and the Vice President. In the evening a huge Satsang was held at the local university. When the local driver got lost in Buenos Aires, Gurudev magically navigated the car to find one of the 7 by 3 meter billboards with Gurudev's picture.

304. LIFE IS A DREAM, A BURDEN OR A JOKE

Often when you are happy you feel life is a dream because you do not believe in the reality of it. When there is misery, you feel life is a burden, and we take trivial things very seriously. But one who has really gone through the pleasure realises that pleasure is also a burden. If you have undergone misery thoroughly you will realise that life is a dream. You have been walked or carried through every miserable condition and then you realise life is a dream. Only when you see life as a dream, a burden or a joke can you be centred.

When you have really gone through misery then you have really seen life is a dream, and in between the pain and pleasure life is all a joke.

Life is very uncertain. Before it takes you away, realise it is a dream, a burden or a joke.

Question: What about life is a joke?

Gurudev: You do not question a joke. If you question a joke, it is no longer a joke. Do not question burden either; it is a waste of time to question life and its events.

Burden makes you go deep. It gets you to the core of yourself. Realisation of a dream wakes you up and seeing life as a joke makes you light.

The only certainty is that life is a dream, a burden or a joke and only when you realise this can you be centred.

✍ *News Flash:*

Two of our dearest devotees, Nandita Judge and Nityanand Trehan who lived knowledge so deeply like Janaka returned back to the source this week. They were Seva warriors. They had filled the Art of Living family with love and laughter and in their departure they have deepen our dispassion and strengthened our commitment. This year the 13th of May will be a worldwide celebration and Satsang honouring Nityanand and Nandita.

305. REASON AND FAITH

Reason is reeling in the known.
Faith is moving in the unknown.
Reason is repetition. Faith is exploration.
Reason is routine. Faith is adventure.

Reason and faith are completely opposite, yet they are an integral part of life.

Not having faith itself is misery; faith gives instant comfort. While reasoning keeps you sane and grounded, miracles cannot happen without faith. Faith takes you beyond limitations. In faith you can transcend the laws of nature but your faith must be pure.

Faith is beyond reason, yet you need to have faith in your own reasoning! Faith and reason cannot exist without each other. Every reason is based on some faith. Whenever reason or faith break, confusion and chaos prevail which is often a step for growth.

There are two types of faith: faith out of fear, greed and insecurity; and faith born out of love like the faith between the mother and child, the master and disciple. Whereas faith out of love cannot be broken, faith out of fear and greed is shaky.

An atheist bases himself on reason and a believer on faith. A believer uses God as an insurance policy; he thinks he is special. In the eyes of God there is no "mine" and "others" - all are the same. An atheist rationalises to keep his eyes shut to reality. Death shakes them both. When someone close dies, an atheist's eyes are opened and a believer's faith cracks. Only a Yogi - a wise one - remains unshaken, for that person has transcended both reason and faith.

You need a balance between faith and reason.

News Flash:

On Gurudev's birthday, in a grand sea of memorial services throughout the globe, the world paid moving tributes to Gurudev's most beloved devotees, Nityanand and Nandita. Nityanand's parents cut the cake in Delhi, and thousands gathered in Satsang, soaked in knowledge, dancing and celebrating life as well as death.

The Canadian Ashram teacher's refresher course left the teachers astounded.

306. Doing Trivial Things

What can you do for eternity? Definitely not anything that is big or great because it needs effort and effort tires you. So, doing something great is a temporary state. If you can think of one thing that is well below your capacity to do and agree to do it for eternity, that becomes *puja*.

The readiness to consciously do trivial things for eternity unites you with eternity. This is an antidote to ego. Ego is always ambitious and wants to do the toughest job like climbing Mount Everest. But a simple act like watching a butterfly, watering the garden, watching the birds or the sky can bring deep relaxation; and relaxation connects you with your source. Not that you should do trivial things all your life, but consciously agreeing to do the trivial actions for eternity opens a new dimension and brings immense peace and restfulness.

To find rest in activity, choose an activity that is far below your capacity and agree to do it for all eternity. Doing a job far below your capacity and being satisfied with it will make it possible to do a job much beyond your capacity.

Know that all actions are born out of infinity and that which is born out of infinity can take you to infinity.

✍ News Flash:

A traditional South Indian welcome with Poorna Kumbha, garlands and the Vaadyam greeted Gurudev when he arrived at the Kodai Road station on the way to the South Zone Teacher's Meet at picturesque Kodaikanal. Devotees from the nearby areas thronged the platform, and the Satsang and celebration lasted for half an hour.

The entourage then proceeded to "The Nest" at Kodaikanal which was booked exclusively for the Art of Living Teacher's Meet. Nearly 160 teachers took part in this meet and had the privilege of having Gurudev exclusively to themselves for three days. They spent quality time with Gurudev and had uplifting knowledge sessions with the master. Interactive discussions among the teachers kept the meet lively.

Gurudev, with a few teachers, proceeded to Trichy where a Satsang had been arranged.

307. Joy and Sorrow

The inability to experience joy and sorrow is inertia. Experiencing joy and sorrow is a trait of consciousness.

Being happy in one's own joy and sad in one's own sorrow is a trait of animals. Being happy at another's joy and saddened by another's sorrow is a trait of humans.

If you are saddened by others' sorrow, then sorrow will never come to you. If you are happy at another's joy, then joy will never leave you.

Seeing that every relative joy is also a misery is a sign of dispassion. Seeing both joy and sorrow as just a technique is a sign of the wise.

Considering sorrow as mere illusion is divinity. Transcending joy and sorrow and being established in the Self is perfection.

As the late Swami Sharanananda said, "Pray for the strength to serve in joy and to sacrifice in sorrow."

✍ *News Flash:*

King Dasharatha had done the Nav Chetana Shibir (the Breath-Water-Sound Program) but Lord Rama had not taken the Art of Living Course! For clues read Yoga Vasistha.

June 7, 2001
Berlin, Germany

308. DEEP REST AND BLISS

Deep rest is bliss and bliss is the understanding that only God exists. Knowing that only God exists is the deepest rest possible.

This conviction or experience that "only God exists" is *'Samadhi.'* *Samadhi* is the mother of all talents, strengths and virtues. *Samadhi* is needed even for the most materialistic person because a materialistic person looks to gain strength and virtues. To be in *Samadhi* you do not need any effort or talents, strengths or virtues.

Withdrawing from all types of physical and mental activity is rest. That is built into our system as sleep, and sleep is the best friend of activity.

Samadhi is a conscious rest. *Samadhi* is the best friend of life. To be alive in your full potential, *Samadhi* is indispensable.

What obstructs *Samadhi* is restlessness. How many types of restlessness are there and what are the remedies? *(The answer next week.)*

✍ *News Flash:*

The Satsang wave moved on with Gurudev from Bangalore to Mumbai to Germany. In Baden Baden, Germany, Gurudev was the keynote speaker at the Rainbow Spirit Festival. Then on to a boat ride Satsang in Paris, and a moving Satsang in Lyon. Gurudev is now in Berlin.

The Art of Living Course has now been held in 156 countries. Last week the course was held in Jordan.

309. FIVE TYPES OF RESTLESSNESS

There are five types of restlessness.

The first type of restlessness is due to the place you are in. When you move away from that place, the street or the house, you immediately feel better. Chanting, singing, children playing and laughing can change this atmospheric restlessness. If you chant and sing, the vibration in the place changes.

The second type of restlessness is in the body. Eating the wrong food or *vata* aggravating food, eating at odd times, not exercising, and overworking can all cause a physical restlessness. The remedy for this is exercise, moderation in work habits and going on a vegetable or juice diet for one or two days.

The third type of restlessness is mental restlessness. It is caused by ambition, strong thoughts, likes or dislikes. Knowledge alone can cure this restlessness: seeing life from a broader perspective, knowing the Self and realising the impermanence of everything. If you achieve everything, so what? After your achievement, you will die. Knowledge of your death or life, confidence in the Self, in the Divine, can all calm down this mental restlessness.

Then there is emotional restlessness. Any amount of knowledge does not help here. Only *Kriya* helps. All the emotional restlessness vanishes after practicing *Kriya*. The presence of your *Guru*, a wise person, or a saint will also help to calm your emotional restlessness.

The fifth type of restlessness is rare. It is the restlessness of the soul. When everything feels empty and meaningless, know you are very fortunate. That longing and restlessness is the restlessness of the soul. Do not try to get rid of it. Embrace it! Welcome it! Usually to get rid of it people do all sorts of things - change places, jobs or partners, do this, do that. It seems to help for some time, but it does not last.

This restlessness of the soul alone can bring authentic prayer in you. It brings perfection, *Siddhis* and miracles in life. It is so precious to get that innermost longing for the Divine. *Satsang* and the presence of an enlightened one soothes the restlessness of the soul.

After a memorable Satsang in the biggest cathedral in Berlin, Gurudev moved on to London. In Westminster Abbey and the town hall of Brent Town, Satsangs exploded with enthusiastic devotees. Gurudev inaugurated our new centre in London. Excellent teamwork marked Gurudev's much awaited London tour.

On the 13th he arrived in Strasbourg to deliver a talk at the European Parliament. It was presided by Reinholt Messner, the famous mountaineer and Peter von Kohl, the President of the Organisation of Journalists of the European Parliament.

Gurudev is now in the European Ashram and on Friday he will address the biggest ever gathering of Christians in Germany.

310. TENDENCIES AND INFLUENCES

Life moves by dual factors: inner tendencies and outer influences.

Inner tendencies form your attitudes and behaviour, while external influences make strong impressions in your mind. Often your tendencies generate external situations, and situations around you can form tendencies within you. This is what is called *karma*.

Both these factors - the tendencies from within and influences from outside - can be either beneficial or harmful.

It is awareness that filters the outer negative influences and it is awareness that corrects and annihilates the unhealthy inner tendencies. This awareness is called *gyana*. The purpose of education is to develop this awareness so that you can be selective about your tendencies and influences.

It is practically impossible to resist the external influences and the inner tendencies without raising one's consciousness. This can be gradual or sudden. And that is how a human being has both free will and destiny.

Freedom is when you have a say about your tendencies and your influences. Only awareness and impeccable devotion can bring this freedom.

✍ News Flash:

Gurudev's address to the Protestant Christian Congregation in Germany was simply brilliant. Denmark, Sweden and Norway had enthralling Satsangs. He is moving on to the Advanced Course in Gotenborg.

311. AUTHENTICITY AND SKILFULNESS

Authenticity and skilfulness appear to be contradictory, but in fact they are complementary. Your intentions need to be authentic and your actions need to be skilful. The more authentic the intention, the more skilful the action will be. Authentic intention and skilful action make you unshakable.

Skill is required only when authenticity cannot have its way. Yet skill without authenticity makes you shallow. You cannot have an authentic action and a skilful intention. If you try to be authentic in your action but manipulative in your mind, that is when mistakes happen.

John: Is it possible to have a powerful intention, like greed, that is authentic?

Gurudev: If your intention is coloured by such things as greed or over-ambition, then your intention is not authentic. Whenever your intentions are impure, it pricks your consciousness, so it cannot be authentic. Authentic intentions are free from negative emotions. An action that is not skilful leads to negative emotions and an intention that is not authentic harbours negative emotions.

Gayatri: If our intention is authentic and yet our actions are not skilful, what should we do?

Gurudev: Carry a handkerchief. *(Laughter)*

Question: What is the best skill to deal with intention?

Gurudev: Do not keep any *sankalpas*, or intentions, to yourself. Offer them to the Divine.

Actions can never be perfect but our intentions can be perfect. Actions always have room for improvement. Action means growth and movement, and that needs space.

The depth in you and the freedom in you bring out the skilfulness in you. *Krishna* was the most skilful because his silence was so deep.

✍ News Flash:

Gurudev arrived in the U.S. after a wonderful Advanced Course in Scandinavia. At the airport he set off the security alarms to the amazement and delight of the security staff.

The Mayor of Franklin Township, New Jersey declared June 24, to be "Ravi Shankar Day" in honour of our founder's achievements. After grand Satsangs in Raleigh, North Carolina and Richmond, Virginia, Gurudev ended the East Coast portion of his tour at the historic Constitution Hall on the National Mall in Washington, D. C., just one block from the White House. The mayor of Washington, D. C. declared June 27 as the "Art of Living Day" in the US capital.

312. Time, Space and Mind

Become God to each other. Do not look for God somewhere in the sky, but see God in every pair of eyes, in the mountains, water, trees and animals. How? Only when you see God in yourself will this happen. Only Gods can worship Gods. To recognize divinity, there are three dimensions: time, space and mind.

For a seeker, it is necessary to honour time and space so he or she can experience sacredness in his or her mind. When you honour time and space, your mind becomes alert. But for the one who has transcended the mind, either sacredness has no meaning, or all time, every place and every mood is sacred.

Precious moments are few in life. Catch them and treasure them. Place, time and the mood of your mind are factors that influence celebration.

Snatch every opportunity to celebrate; then you will feel great and full. Then celebration infiltrates your mind in all moods and space, and celebration is inevitable.

Celebration reminds you of the fullness of the moment. The moments you are in the company of knowledge - the master - are the most precious moments in your life.

Treasure them. In treasuring them you transcend the mind, time and space, and that is true celebration.

News Flash:

Guru Purnima was celebrated surrounded by the majestic mountains and magnificent skies of Lake Tahoe. All heads were crowned by our beloved Gurudev in the presence of eight Swamis of various mutts from India, the world's foremost Ayurvedic physician, Dr. Trigunaji, and Dr. Trigunaji's son.

Weeklong Seva activities and slum cleanup projects were begun in Bangalore. Medical camps were set up, and clothes and food were distributed from many Art of Living centres.

While compiling this weekly knowledge, Marcy lost her mind in time and space.

July 12, 2001
Lake Tahoe, California, United States

313. MISTAKES

Mistakes happen all the time. You often get irritated by mistakes and you want to correct them, but how many can you correct? You correct others mistakes for two reasons. First is when someone's mistake bothers you, and second is when you correct someone for their sake so that they can grow, not because it bothers you. Correcting mistakes in the first case, when the mistake bothers you, does not work.

To correct mistakes you need both authority and love. Authority and love seem to be contradictory but in reality they are not. Authority without love is stifling and does not work. Love without authority is shallow. You need both but they need to be in the right combination so that you can be successful in correcting others' mistakes. This can happen if you are totally dispassionate and centred.

When you allow room for mistakes, you can be both authoritative and sweet. That is how the Divine is – the right balance of both. *Krishna* and Jesus had both. People in love also exercise authority with those they love. Authority and love exist in all relationships.

Abhay: The husband just loves and the wife has the authority.

Mikey: Is that a mistake?

Gurudev: I don't want to correct it! *(Laughter)*

✍ *News Flash:*

Gurudev was resplendent rafting down the river, with all the course participants following and chanting bhajans.

314. THE GREAT PLEASURE OF REST

There is pleasure in rest and pleasure in activity. The pleasure in activity is momentary and causes fatigue, while the pleasure in rest is magnanimous and energising. So to the one who has tasted pleasure in rest (*Samadhi*), the pleasure in activity is insignificant. All activities that you do, you do so that you can have deep rest. Activity is part of the system. However, the real pleasure is in *Samadhi*. In order to have deep rest one must be active. The proper balance of both is essential.

Many seek pleasure in this or that, but the wise man just smiles. The real rest is only in knowledge.

✍ *News Flash:*

At 46,000 feet, on the flight from Lake Tahoe to Montreal, 2+1 really did become 0! After 11-1/2 years, the beautiful "I don't know" became a reality, with numerous devotees finally getting it. If you "don't know" what this means, listen to *Bhakti Sutras Tape 12.

Preparation for the yaj-nas is already underway. Nine pundits from India have arrived at the North American Ashram to begin the yaj-nas, which are ancient ceremonies for creating beneficial effects in the environment.

*Available to the reader through the Divine Shops

315. WORRY & FEELINGS

The head worries and the heart feels. The two cannot function at the same time. When your feelings dominate, worry dissolves. If you worry a lot, your feelings are dead and you are stuck in your head. Worrying makes your mind and heart inert and dull. It steals your energy and prevents you from thinking clearly. Worries are like a rock in the head. They entangle you; they trap you in a cage. Worries are uncertain since they are about the future.

When you feel, you do not worry. Feelings are like flowers, they come up, they blossom and they die. Feelings rise, they fall and then disappear. When your feelings are expressed, you feel relieved. When you are angry, you express your anger and the next moment you feel fine. Or when you are upset, you cry and you get over it. Feelings last for some short time and then they drop away, but worry eats at you for longer periods of time and eventually consumes you.

Feelings make you spontaneous. Children feel so they are spontaneous, but adults put brakes on their feelings and start worrying. Worry obstructs action while feelings propel action. Worrying about negative feelings is a blessing because it puts brakes on those feelings, preventing you from acting on them. Worries about positive feelings usually never occur. Often you start worrying about your feelings when you think you are feeling too much.

Offering your worries is prayer and prayer moves you in feelings.

316. WHO IS PLEASING WHOM?

God created man and the whole world with so many varieties, so many good things. God made so many types of vegetables, fragrances, flowers and thorns, dragons and horrors, to please man and keep him entertained. But man became more and more depressed.

God then acted tough and man had to start pleasing Him. So man kept himself busy pleasing God and he became happier since he had no time to get worried or depressed. When you have someone to please, it keeps you on your toes and you are happier. But if your goal is just to please yourself, depression is sure to follow.

Pleasure simply brings more craving. But the problem is that we try to get contentment through pleasure. True contentment can only come through service.

✍ *News Flash:*

People from 29 countries are gathered in the European Ashram for an enlightening Advanced Course.

317. TWO PERSPECTIVES OF THE *GURU*

In the Orient, having a Master is considered a matter of pride. A Master is a symbol of security, love and a sign of great wealth. Being with a *Guru* is like being with one's higher self. Not having a Master was looked down upon as being an orphan or poor, or a sign of misfortune. Those without a Master were considered to be orphans, but not those without parents. But in the Occident having a Master is considered a matter of shame and a sign of weakness, for there Masters are known for enslaving people.

In the Orient people take pride in having a *Guru* for every discipline – a religious *Guru* (*Dharma Guru*), a family *Guru* (*Kula Guru*), a *Guru* for the kingdom (*Raj Guru*), a *Guru* for a particular discipline (*Vidya Guru*), and a spiritual *Guru* (*Sad Guru*).

In the Orient, Masters make their disciples feel powerful, while in the Occident, Masters are thought to make people weak. In the Orient, there is a deep sense of belongingness that enables people to dissolve their limited identity into infinity. But in the Occident, a Master is considered to be a motivator and one who provokes competition.

✍ *News Flash:*

The social welfare minister, Shiv Kumar, inaugurated the Institute for Rural Development in Bangalore.

Art of Living leaders are leading U.N. conferences in Geneva this week.

Bad Antogast is overflowing with various courses. Preparations for yaj-nas are on at the European Ashram.

318. LOVE & AUTHORITY

Love and authority are totally opposite values yet they co-exist.

The grosser the consciousness, the more pronounced the authority must be. The more refined and subtle the consciousness, the less need there is to exercise authority.

When you are unrefined, you demand authority and when you demand authority, love recedes. Asserting authority indicates lack of confidence and love. The more evident one's authority, the less sensitive and effective it will be.

A sensible person will not demand authority at all but will assume it. The most effective CEO'S will not make you feel their authority, for authority can never bring inspiration.

Your sincere servant has more authority over you than your boss, isn't that so? A baby has full authority over his mother. Similarly, a devotee has complete authority over the Divine, though he never exercises it.

The subtler you become, the more authority you gain. The greater the love, the subtler will be the authority. The lesser the love, the more pronounced will be the authority.

✍ *News Flash:*

Yaj-nas were performed for world peace in the European Ashram, and Krishna's birthday was celebrated with gaiety.

The Bangalore Ashram is buzzing with blissful faces as Gurudev arrives for his hectic program.

319. GANESHA

The lord of the diverse universe is called *Ganesha*.

The whole universe is nothing but groups of atoms, groups of qualities, of energy. '*Gana*' means group and a group cannot exist without a lord. Like the queen bee, whose mere existence brings forth the honeycomb, this diverse universe in itself is enough evidence for *Ganesha's* presence.

Ganesha, or Lord, was born from the unmanifest transcendental consciousness, the Self, called *Shiva*. Just as when atoms bond, matter comes into existence; so when all the fragmented aspects of human consciousness bond, Divinity happens effortlessly and that is the birth of *Ganesha* from *Shiva*.

✍ *News Flash:*

The Ganesha Festival was celebrated in the Bangalore Ashram. The Ashram school has been accredited as the best school in Bangalore because for the third time in a row the school students achieved 100% on their test results. Being a first generation school (i.e. the children are the first generation in their families to get an education) this feat is truly remarkable!

This week 2,400 prison inmates in the Tihar Jail, New Delhi, are taking the Art of Living Course. This is the largest ever Art of Living Course, requiring 20 teachers.

Recent research conducted by Dr. H. Geetha, professor of biochemistry at the Bangalore Medical College, shows a marked improvement in cholesterol levels after practicing Sudarshan Kriya.

320. HUNGRY FOR POWER

Why are people hungry for power?

People are hungry for power because they want attention and recognition. Power is a means, just like money. Passion is for an end. People who do not see power or money as a means but as an end in itself do not live, they simply exist. If you do not realise that you are THE power, that you are enlightened, then you crave for power.

You crave for attention and recognition if you do not have any talents, love or passion, or if you are not innocent and childlike.

If you do not have any talents and you are not contributing anything substantial to society, like an artist, a scientist, an Art of Living teacher or a volunteer, then you are hungry for power.

If you do not have a love or a passion to bring about a transformation in society, then you are hungry for power.

If you are not innocent and childlike and do not have a sense of belongingness with the whole world, then you are hungry for power.

Those who do not have any of these four, like some politicians, also crave for power.

True power is the power of the spirit; real confidence, strength and happiness all spring from the spirit. And one who knows this and has this is not hungry at all for power.

News Flash:

Kerala Day, the Onam Festival, was celebrated in the Bangalore Ashram.

Art of Living members are leading the Educational Caucus and the Spirituality and Religion Causus at the U.N. conference in Durban.

September 13, 2001
Bangalore Ashram, India

321. YOU & OWNERSHIP

Man has a tendency to own things. When he owns something small his mind stays small, his life gets stifled and his whole consciousness is immersed in his house, car, spouse, children and such. A recluse leaves his home and goes far away. There also he starts owning his *asana*, rosary, books, concepts and his knowledge.

Owning has simply shifted from objects and people to ideas and practises. But a wise one knows that he owns the sun, the moon, the stars, the air, all of space and the Divine in its entirety. When you own something big then your consciousness also expands, and when you own something small then small negative emotions start coming up, such as anger and greed.

I wonder why people do not feel connected to the sun? The very existence of life depends upon the sun. Perhaps it is lack of awareness that causes people to refuse to acknowledge and own their connectedness to the macrocosmic universe. The *rishis* in ancient India, the Native Americans and the Aboriginals from all over the globe have insisted that you can feel connected to the sun, the moon and the directions.

When you own something magnanimous your consciousness also becomes magnanimous.

✍ *News Flash:*

Thousands of people arrived from Kerala to celebrate the festival of Onam in the Bangalore Ashram. A big feast was served for the celebration.

Dean and Shirley Harmison, Werner Luedemann and the entire South African team participated in the Durban UN. Conference on Racism. The Art of Living provided the chairperson for leading the conference and for the educator caucus.

The U.K. and U.S.A. teams of musicians are taking the college students in Bangalore, Chennai, Vizag and Kolkata by storm. The West Zone Teacher's Meet in the Bangalore Ashram was simply stupendous. The teachers left with more zeal and enthusiasm.

There was a rousing welcome for Gurudev in Pune.

322. REVERENCE & OWNERSHIP

Often you do not have reverence for that which you own, and losing that reverence happens unconsciously.

Whatever you revere becomes bigger than you. When you have reverence in all your relationships then your own consciousness expands. Then even small things appear to be significant and big. Every little creature appears to be dignified. It is the reverence in every relationship that saves the relationship.

When you have reverence for the whole universe, you are in harmony with the whole universe. Then you do not need to reject or renounce anything.

Reverence in ownership frees you from greed, jealousy and lust. Cultivate the skill of having reverence every moment in your life.

✍ News Flash:

En route to Himachal Pradesh, the hill state of India, Gurudev had a lively Satsang in Delhi. Gurudev was given a red-carpet welcome at Kalka as a State Guest of Himachal Pradesh.

After brief Satsangs in Purwanoo and Solan, Gurudev arrived at Simla, a famous hill station, where he received a moving traditional welcome with horns, music and dances. At Simla, Gurudev addressed the senior bureaucrats of the State Government at the State Guest House. A Maha Kriya and a big Satsang attended by thousands were held the following day.

On to Uttar Pradesh, the largest state of India, where Gurudev was again invited as a State Guest to the state capital, Lucknow. He was received there by an enthusiastic crowd of several thousand people. His address to the prominent people of Lucknow was laced with wit and humour. Gurudev gifted cycles, wheelchairs and hearing aids to 500 physically challenged. Several thousand were blissed out in the evening Satsang.

Gurudev returned to Delhi for yet another blissful Satsang with thousands of devotees. Also on the agenda was an inspiring address to over 5,000 village youth at a conference attended by Uma Bharati, Minister for Youth in India.

It was a whirlwind tour, and it was as if an Art of Living wave swept across all the cities that Gurudev visited.

323. WAR : THE WORST ACT OF REASON

The worst act of reason is war.

Every war has a reason, and the reason justifies the war. Those who engage in war reason it out. But reason is limited. As reason changes, the justification falls apart. All the reasons for every war appear to be justifiable to some limited minds and for a limited time. Hence, war becomes inevitable on this planet.

War is limited to human beings. No other species in creation engages in war or mass destruction, as they have no reason. Animals have their prey and let everything just be. But mankind, from time immemorial, has engaged in war because man lives on reason. Man gives reason to every act of his and justifies it. As reasons change, his justifications fall apart.

Man has to transcend reason, and only then can he realise Divinity. Then he will not engage in war. Only when people become sensible, rise above hatred and have heightened consciousness can war be stopped.

✍ *News Flash:*

Gurudev arrived in Shillong to a tumultuous welcome by the Governor and the Chief Minister. For the first time ever Shillong had huge gatherings as thousands were rapt in meditation and high in spirit during Satsang.

Gurudev was the state guest of four different Indian states – Meghalaya, Assam, West Bengal and Tripura! Estimated crowds of over 250,000 people came for darshan and blessings from Gurudev, and over 35,000 people did Sudarshan Kriya with Gurudev!

At Kolkata, Gurudev and His Holiness the Dalai Lama addressed delegates of the Kolkata Chamber of Commerce. The evening Satsang had 30,000 people rapt in meditation and blissfully singing bhajans. Memorable yajñas were performed at Kolkata and Guwahati for harmony in the world. Guwahati welcomed Gurudev with beautiful tribal folk songs and dances. Gurudev emphasized the need to protect the rich and diverse tribal culture. Thousands braved the rains to be in the evening Satsang. Gurudev inaugurated the Gurudev Sri Sri Ravi Shankar Vidya Mandir (school) in Guwahati by ringing a bell. After a cruise on the river Brahmaputra, the entourage left for Siliguri for a stay of less than 24 hours.

Siliguri, a town in the foothills of Darjeeling, celebrated his arrival with all roads leading to the mega Satsang. Gurudevs entourage had no risk of getting lost, as any resident of the town could guide them to Gurudevs residence and the Satsang. Thousands attended the morning MahaKriya where they did Sudarshan Kriya with Gurudev, and over 50,000 people were singing, dancing and celebrating the grace of Gurudev at the mega Satsang. Gurudev graced the Gurudev Sri Sri Ravi Shankar Vidya Mandir and inaugurated the Rural Training Centre in the Siliguri Ashram. The entourage then headed to Agartala for the last leg of Gurudevs tour of Indias northeast.

324. Terrorism : the Cause & the Remedy

The act which is only destructive and inflicts suffering on both oneself and others, is terrorism. In such an act human values are lost in the process of achieving a goal.

Some of the factors that lead to terrorism are:

- Frustration and desperation in achieving a goal

- Confused emotions

- Shortsightedness and impulsive action

- Belief in a non-verifiable concept of heaven and merit; a childish concept of God where God favours some and is angry with others, undermining the omniscience and omnipotence of the Divine.

Terrorism induces fear psychosis in everyone, increases poverty, suffering and loss of life with no apparent gain. Instead of life-supporting solutions the terrorist chooses destruction as an answer. If you criticise without giving a solution, know that it comes from the seed of terrorism.

Although there are certain qualities you can appreciate in a terrorist such as fearlessness, commitment to a goal, and sacrifice, you must learn from them things that you should never do. These are valuing some ideas and concepts more than life, having a narrow perspective of life, and dishonouring its diversity.

The remedy for terrorism is:

- Inculcating a broader perspective of life.

- Valuing life more than race, religion and nationality.

- Providing education in human values – friendliness, compassion, cooperation and upliftment.

- Teaching methods to release stress and tension.

- Cultivating confidence in achieving noble aims by peaceful and nonviolent means.

- Weeding out destructive tendencies with spiritual upliftment.

Question: Can terrorism be more than physical violence, such as cultural or economic violence?

Gurudev: Yes. The solution for economic violence is to "Think globally, buy locally," and the solution for cultural violence is to "Broaden your vision, deepen your roots."

Question: How does one cope with the aftermath of terrorism?

Gurudev: Faith and prayer. When disaster happens, anger is inevitable. To take precautions that one does not react improperly, wisdom is needed not emotional outbursts. One mistake cannot be corrected by another mistake. Strive to have multicultural and multi-religious education and have spiritual upliftment reach every part of the globe, for the world will not be safe if even a small pocket of people are left ignorant.

✍ News Flash:

A record crowd, the likes of which has never before been seen in the state, listened in rapt attention to Gurudev at the Satsang in Tripura, a state in the remote northeastern region of India. Our school was opened in a part of the royal palace in Agartala - a symbol of the rich cultural heritage of the state. The Governor of the state and many dignitaries attended the inauguration ceremony. Leaders of various communities as well as government and non-governmental organisations came to pay their respects to Gurudev. Gurudev promised them that more schools would be started in the remote regions.

Satsangs and counselling to help reduce stress and post traumatic syndromes have been started in New York, where our senior teachers are busy.

Scientists engaged in research on Sudarshan Kriya are thrilled by recent findings. Their papers will be published shortly. At the United Nations in Geneva, the International Association for Human Values initiative was adopted, so that official meetings now begin and end with one minute of silence for peace and harmony.

325. How to Deal With Anxiety

Today many are anxious about how to deal with their anxiety! Here are some of the ways you can manage it:

- Sing, dance and celebrate. The very intention to celebrate will pull you to a more harmonious state.

- Think about what you can do for others rather than about yourself. Get energised with service activities.

- Practice yoga, breathing and meditation.

- Know the impermanence of the world.

- Have faith in and surrender to the Divine. Know that there is a supreme power who loves you, is behind you and accepts you totally. Feeling secure comes with the sense of belongingness.

- Be courageous and invoke the lion within you.

- Have an attitude of sacrifice.

- Remind yourself that you are committed to a greater goal.

- Be unpredictable for a while. Anxiety is always related to some anticipated action so do something completely irrelevant and unpredictable.

- Be ready to face the worst. This will leave you with stability in the mind.

- Remember a similar situation in the past when you were able to overcome your anxiety.

Chanakya: If none of these work, just come and be in the presence of the Master! *(Laughter)*

✍ **News Flash:**

The International Association for Human Values, based in Geneva, has been chosen as a member of the Swiss Peace Foundation, which is an office of the Swiss Federal Government.

Teacher Training Courses, Phase I and Phase II, were held at the European Ashram and culminated with Gurudev's visit.

The North American Ashram was blushing in fall colours to welcome Gurudev.

Several public Satsangs and post-traumatic stress relief courses are in progress in the New York/New Jersey area.

326. IS WAR VIOLENCE OR NONVIOLENCE?

Violence and nonviolence do not depend on an act but on the intention behind it. The basis of violence is anger, lust, hatred, jealousy, greed, frustration or aggression.

A surgeon cuts open a person's belly, so does a criminal. The action is similar but the surgeon's intention is to save and the criminal's is to destroy. Violence or nonviolence is determined by the attitude and not the act.

Even a war can be nonviolent if it is devoid of anger, hatred, jealousy or greed and it is for educating someone who cannot be educated in any other way. Even charity can be an act of violence if it takes away self-esteem and inflicts slavery, and a war can be an act of compassion if it helps to establish the right perspective.

Strange but true!

✍ *News Flash:*

The New York Fire Department has lauded the September 11 contributions of the Art of Living Seva team and has sent them a letter of appreciation.

327. HONEY

Let the wind that blows be sweet

Let the oceans flow honey

Let all the herbs and plant kingdom be favourable to us

Let the nights be sweet and let the days be sweet

Let the dust of this planet be sweet to us

Let the heavens and our forefathers be sweet to us

Let all the trees be laden with honey

Let the sun be sweet to us and let all the radiations be favourable to us

Let all the animals be sweet to us

Let our food be favourable to us

Let all our thoughts and our speech be sweet like honey

Let our life be pure and divine

Let it be sweet like honey.

✍ *News Flash:*

The one who has made our life sweet as honey is in silence!

328. DROP YOUR INTENTIONS

A strong tendency to keep doing something, whether important or unimportant, becomes an impediment to meditation.

"Doing" starts first with an intention and then translates into action. Though intention springs from Being, when it becomes doing it does not let you settle down. All intentions, good or bad, trivial or important, need to be dropped for meditation to happen.

Vijay: But isn't dropping all intentions itself an intention?

Gurudev: Yes, but that intention is the last and necessary one. Dropping intentions is not an act. Just the intention to drop them itself serves the purpose. Dropping all intentions even for a moment brings you in touch with your Self and in that instant meditation happens.

While you sit for meditation you have to let the world be the way it is. The repetition of meditation is to habituate your system to stop and start activity at will. The ability to consciously do this is a very precious skill.

✍ *News Flash:*

During Navaratri there was unmitigated joy from all over the world. Gurudev emerged from silence even more radiant, more profound Many saints visited the Bangalore Ashram during the pujas. A renowned saint from Rishikesh gave daily discourses on the Bhagavatam. Yajñas were performed for the health, happiness and well-being of people allover the world, and to establish peace everywhere. Blessings are always special, but the ecstasy experienced by one and all on Rishi Homa (the last day of Navarathri), as Gurudev enthusiastically rushed into the crowds, spraying all his devotees with holy water, was without parallel!

329. AISHWARYA & MADHURYA

Usually in places where there is *Aishwarya* (lordship) there is no *Madhurya* (sweetness), and where there is *Madhurya* there is no *Aishwarya*. Where life has blossomed fully, there is both.

Aishwarya means '*ishvaratvaa*' – lordship of that which "Is". Wealth, too, is referred to as *Aishwarya* because wealth does command a certain amount of authority.

Can love and authority co-exist? Only in a fully blossomed being is there both lordship and sweetness. There was *Aishwarya* in *Sri Rama*, but only glimpses of *Madhurya*. In *Parashuram's* life there is only lordship, but no *Madhurya*. *Buddha* manifested more *Madhurya* (the sweetness), and less authority. But *Krishna* manifested both and so did Jesus. There was lordship when they said, "I am the way!" And there was sweetness in their expressions of prayer and love.

✍ *News Flash:*

The Art of Living is the only nonprofit organisation that was asked to be a part of America Back On Track, a train that is going from Washington to New York, and then on to 20 other cities, as a way of encouraging Americans to return to normal.

Art of Living Courses have started in Uruguay, South America.

The South-East Teachers 'Meet ended in immense gratitude and heightened fervor! The Ashram is buzzing with the enthusiasm of more than 200 Teacher Training Course participants!

330. VOLUNTEER

Who is a volunteer? It is one who comes to help without being asked. One who is self-motivated and inspired becomes a volunteer.

It is possible for a volunteer's inspirational motivation to diminish, which can bring frustration. Usually a volunteer's attitude comes from demand rather than humility, diluting the quality of the service. Another downfall that can happen to volunteers is that they slip away from commitment, thinking there is no "boss"; thinking, "If I like it, I'll do it; if I don't like it, I won't do it!" It is like the steering wheel of a car – if all the tires say they do not need to be steered, then the car cannot move smoothly. If you want to construct a building, you have to accept the authority of the structural engineer, -"boss".

All these problems can only be overcome by being more grounded in spiritual knowledge. A volunteer devoid of a spiritual dimension is utterly weak.

- A volunteer needs to stick to his commitment.

- The integrity of a volunteer comes from his spiritual practices.

- The authority for the volunteer project needs to be acknowledged.

- The strength of a volunteer comes from the challenges he is ready and willing to face.

- A volunteer moves beyond boundaries when he finds he is capable of doing so much more than he ever thought of doing.

- A true volunteer does not expect appreciation or reward. He is thoroughly mistaken if he thinks he is obliging somebody.

- A person volunteers because he derives joy from it.

- That joy itself is the reward and it is immediate. It does not come on the first of every month in the form of a salary! When a volunteer realises this, he is filled with gratitude.

When a volunteer waivers from within, his support system is knowledge and good friends.

✍ News Flash:

In Delhi, Gurudev addressed the U.N. Conference on Volunteerism. Then on to Hong Kong, where he gave an inspiring talk at a beautiful Satsang in the packed Grand Ballroom of the Sheraton Hotel. Today Gurudev blessed the inauguration of the Museum of World Religions in Taipei, Taiwan, in the company of the Taiwanese Prime Minister.

The founder of the museum, Zen Master Hsin Tao, came and met with Gurudev the night before and expressed his gratitude. Tomorrow, Gurudev will speak on "The Preservation of Sacred Sites."

331. ADULATION

Adulation shows the magnanimity of the one who adores, rather than the one who is adored! Adulation is an indicator that the ego has become transparent. The best antidote for ego is adulation.

Adulation works in three ways. If it is for someone else, it is not palatable to an egoistic person. If it is for you, it boosts your ego. If you adore somebody, it dissolves your ego and makes you magnanimous.

Group: When *Guru*dev is adulated, EVERYONE adores it! *(Laughter)*

- A desire for adulation is a sign of immaturity.

- Aversion to adulation is small-mindedness.

- Lack of adulation in life is dryness and boredom.

- A healthy mind always likes to adulate, to elevate others.

- An unhealthy mind likes to pull everything down. Adulation indicates the trust, enthusiasm and richness in a culture.

- Lack of adulation indicates a self-centred, small-minded, fearful and culturally impoverished society.

Adulation does not sway the one who is great. The test of a person's greatness is that he is not shaken by any amount of adulation. Being indifferent to adulation when it comes to you and being magnanimous when it is to be given is the way of the wise!

✍ *News Flash:*

Gurudev returned to the Bangalore Ashram for a mega Diwali celebration. Twenty years of Ved Vignan Mahavidyapeeth coincided with Dhanvantari (Ayurveda) Day and Dhanteras, the day and of wealth! Teacher Training phase One and Two ended on an enthusiastic high, amid bursting of firecrackers and thousands of jyotis (lit candles). Fifty seven new teachers have taken off, committed to spreading the knowledge like warriors.

332. SEVA

There are five types of *Seva* (service).

- The first type is the *Seva* done when you do not even know that you are doing it. You do not recognise it as *Seva* because it is your very nature – you cannot but do it!

- The second type is the *Seva* which you do because it is needed for that situation.

- You do the third type of *Seva* because it gives you joy.

- The fourth type is done out of your desire for merit – you do *Seva* expecting some benefit in the future.

- And the fifth type is when you do *Seva* just to show off, to improve your image and to gain social or political recognition. Such *Seva* is simply exhausting, while the first type does not bring any tiredness at all!

To improve the quality of your *Seva*, regardless of where you start, you must move up to higher levels of *Seva*.

✍ *News Flash:*

The Prime Minister of India had an hour-long discussion with Gurudev in New Delhi.

- *It was all celebration in the steel township of Vijyanagar.*

- *The highlights of the week were:*

- *A mass marriage for the poor where 45 couples were wedded*

- *The 5H Program at work in neighbouring villages*

- *Grand Satsangs at Bellari and Hospet*

- *A whirlwind tour of the ancient temples of Hampi Kollur and Udipi including meetings with the pontiffs of these temple ashrams.*

333. Confidence With Humility: the Rarest Combination

One of the rarest character combinations is the coexistence of confidence and humility. Often people who are confident are not humble and people with humility are not confident. Confidence blended with humility is most appreciated by everybody.

Question: How can confidence be developed in one who is humble, and humility in one who is confident?

Gurudev: First, when you see your life in a bigger context of time and space then you realise your life is nothing. Second, those who are humble need to see that they are unique and dear to the Divine, which brings confidence, and when you realise you are insignificant, that also brings confidence. And third, by having a *Guru*, because he gives you confidence and cultures humility in you. When you have a *Guru* you cannot be arrogant. The weakness in humility and the arrogance in confidence are removed. You are left with confidence and humility!

✍ *News Flash:*

Gurudev had a captive audience while inaugurating the International Convention on Information Technology. He stated that information should be intuitive, communication creative and technology should bring comfort.

In a "flying" visit to Tirupati, Gurudev addressed all the Tirupati temple administrators and workers.

The 250 teachers at the Teachers' Refresher Meet in Rishikesh are blissed and blessed!

334. Dreaming the Impossible

Question: Gurudev, how can we control daydreams?

Gurudev: Dream in the night! *(Laughter)*

What is daydreaming? You have a desire but you do not have the faith that you can achieve your desire – that is what you call daydreaming. You can control daydreaming by having a strong goal and believing in it. Like the scientist who wanted to go to the moon and kept dreaming about it – for him it was the goal of his life but for others it was daydreaming.

Either you drop that it will happen or you believe it will! When you do not know yourself, your potentiality, you have no faith or confidence in your dreams. Once you have faith and confidence in your dreams, they are no longer day dreams!

✍ News Flash:

Yuvacharyas are conducting Navchetena Shibirs, Satsangs, "creating awareness through cleanliness" campaigns and tree planting drives, and are busy transforming naxalite-hit villages into "model villages." Within a year 3,000 villages in India were touched and there are now 500 Yuvacharyas. The confidence and commitment of the Yuvacharyas held everyone spell bound as they recounted Success tales of alcohol-free, tobacco free villages, where love and belongingness are being nurtured.

Many terrorists have also been transformed Immense numbers of legal cases have been withdrawn from courts, with warring factions agreeing to peaceful settlements, especially those involving underprivileged classes. Homes are being given to the needy, Sri Sri Ravi Shankar Vidya Mandirs opened where schools are not available. Tulsi, neem, genda and other trees are being planted around homes and throughout villages. Two hundred twenty four self-help groups have been formed and villagers are encouraged to practice savings. Villagers are celebrating festivals as one big family and human values are increasingly being nurtured.

Over a thousand participants are at the Advanced Course in Rishikesh where they were showered with blessings by a distinguished panel of swamis at the Samapan Samaroh (closing ceremony). The panel also lauded Gurudev's worldwide service projects.

335. RESPECT & EGO

There are two types of respect. The first is respect that comes to you because of your position, fame or wealth. This type of respect is impermanent. It can be lost once you lose your wealth or status. The second type of respect comes because of your smile and your virtues, such as honesty, kindness, commitment and patience. This respect no one can take away.

The less you are attached to your virtues, the more self-respect you have. When you get attached to your virtues, you look down upon everybody else and your virtues start diminishing. Non-attachment to virtues brings the highest self-respect.

Often ego is confused with self-esteem. Ego needs the other for comparison but self-esteem is just confidence in oneself. A gentleman claiming that he is skilled in mathematics or geography is an example of self-esteem. But to say, "I know better than you," is ego.

Ego simply means lack of respect for the Self. Your ego will often upset you but those with self esteem are immune to getting upset from external factors. In self-respect everything is a game, winning or losing has no meaning, every step is joy, every move is celebration. In self-esteem you simply realise you have it.

✍ News Flash:

This time all roads did not lead to Rome, but to Florence, where people from all over Italy flocked to meet Gurudev. The President of Tuscany, who has also done Art of Living Basic and Advanced Courses, organised the program.

Then Gurudev arrived in Lithuania to inspire the assembly of East European teachers and an Advanced Course.

On his return to Bangalore, Gurudev blessed 35 Yuvacharyas (youth leaders), who graduated on Sunday and will be taking care of 236 villages spanning four districts under the aegis of the 5H Program.

336. MAYA

What is *maya*?

Maya is that which can be measured. The whole world can be measured, that is why it is Maya. All five elements – earth, water, fire, air and ether – can be measured.

Question: Can space be measured?

Gurudev: Only in space can things be measured. Space is the first dimension of measurement.

Measurement is always relative and not absolute. For example, if something weighs six kilograms on earth, it will weigh only one kilogram on the moon. The light of the star you see today is not really today's light. It has taken at least four years for the light to reach you! Both size and weight change in air, water and earth. So "measure" is illusive and not dependable. Your bones, skin, body, environment and the five elements can be measured; you can put a value, a quantity, to them. So, the whole world is *maya*!

All measurements only provide a relative understanding. Einstein's theory of relativity correlates with the *Advaita* (non-dual) philosophy.

But what is not Maya? All that cannot be measured is not Maya. You cannot say one ounce of love, two ounces of peace, and five kilograms of happiness. Can YOU be measured? It is not possible. Your body has weight, but not you. Truth cannot be measured, *ananda* (joy) cannot be measured, and beauty cannot be measured. All these are part of consciousness or *Ishvara* (the Divine), and are not Maya.

✍ *News Flash:*

A huge Satsang in Malleswaram, Bangalore was attended by thousands of people. Gurudev's father, Acharya Ratnananda, well known as Pitaji, was felicitated on his 78th birthday.

December 27, 2001
European Ashram, Bad Antogast, Germany

337. LETTING GO OF CONTROL

Many have a problem with letting go of control. This causes anxiety, restlessness and soured relationships.

Wake up and see, are you really in control? What are you in control of? Perhaps a tiny part of your waking state! Isn't that so?

- You are not in control when you are sleeping or dreaming.
- You are not in control of the thoughts and emotions coming to you. You may choose to express them or not, but they come to you without your prior permission!
- Most of the functions of your body are not in your control.

Do you think you are in control of all the events in your life, in the world or in the universe? That is a joke!

When you look at things from this angle you need not be afraid of losing control, because you have none.

Whether you realise it or not, when you let go of your sense of control that is when you truly relax. Your identification of being somebody does not let you totally relax and it limits your domain.

✍ *News Flash:*

The highlights of Gurudev's Chennai visit were a MahaSatsang, a Maha Kriya, a Rudra Puja, free medical camps and more.

This year Gurudev deviated from his routine. He was in the Bangalore Ashram to celebrate Christmas where ashramites staged a play of the birth of Christ.

A white blanket of snow covered the Black Forest to welcome Gurudev to the European Ashram. The European Teachers' Meet is underway with full zest and vigour.

338. Memory: a Hindrance & a Blessing

Being forgetful of man's nature is the root cause of all problems and suffering in life. But the very remembrance of one's nature, which is godliness, brings freedom. Here memory is your best friend. The purpose of knowledge is to remind you of your true nature. In the *Bhagavad Gita*, *Arjuna* said to *Krishna*, "I got back my memory. Now I have realised my true nature and will do as you say."

Memory is a blessing and your best friend when it helps you realise your true nature. Memory is a hindrance when it does not let you be free of events, pleasant or unpleasant. Pleasant events create cravings and competition in the mind and do not allow fresh experiences, whereas unpleasant events bias perception and create paranoia. So the memory is both a blessing and a hindrance depending on whether you remember your nature or you are stuck with events in time and space.

✍ *News Flash:*

The year 2001 was given a fond farewell with an international feast. Participants at the European Ashram held a cultural evening filled with music and dances from several countries represented there. The new year was welcomed with silence and a beautiful meditation with Gurudev.

339. Don't be Perturbed by Foolishness

What really perturbs you? Is it the foolishness that goes on around you?

It is foolish to be perturbed by foolishness. Foolishness cannot overpower or annihilate wisdom nor does foolishness last very long. When you are not well-founded in wisdom then foolishness perturbs you, throws you out of balance. When you create space for foolishness you do not get perturbed by it, rather you will laugh and move on. Otherwise you get hateful or angry, or become stressed by foolish acts.

When you know that truth is eternal and invincible, you accept foolishness as a joke and remain unmoved by it. Those who are averse to foolishness or get irritated by it are members of the Fools Club.

Beware! Do not sign up.

✍ News Flash:

A great course in the great state of Texas! January 10th was declared "Gurudev Ravi Shankar Day" by the Honourable Mayor Garcia of Austin, the capital of Texas. In the past year 310,000 people have benefited from the 5H Program in 7,000 villages.

January 16, 2001
Cascade, Colorado, United States

340. GLORY & DISPASSION (VAIBHAV & VAIRAGYA)

It is often believed that glory and dispassion are contradictory and cannot co-exist. Glory and luxury without dispassion is a nauseating pomp and show. Such glory does not bring fulfilment for anyone; it is shallow. Alternately, the dispassion that is afraid of glory is weak. True dispassion is oblivious to glory.

The glory that comes with dispassion is something that is true; it is permanent and authentic. When someone chases after glory they are shallow. Movie stars, politicians and religious leaders who try to hold on to their status, to their glory, are certain to lose it. If you run after glory all that you get is misery. When you are dispassionate, glory comes to you.

If you are afraid of glory, that means you are not well-founded in dispassion. In India the *sadhus* run away from glory. They think they will lose their dispassion and get trapped in the web of the world, the circus. The dispassion is so blissful that they get attached to it. They are afraid of losing the dispassion, the centeredness and the bliss that comes along with it. This is weak dispassion.

Dispassion is a state of being and glory is the happening around it. True dispassion can never be lost or overshadowed by glory.

True dispassion is glorious!

Real glory is true dispassion!

✍ *News Flash:*

Colorado Springs and Boulder, both in Colorado, had overflowing halls of joy for Gurudev's public talks. The students and faculty of Naropa University were ecstatic and inspired finding Gurudev with them.

Gurudev visited the Garden of the Gods, a sacred site for Native Americans with towering red rock formations. Although the rocks were glorious all eyes were on Gurudev! For wherever Gurudev goes on this planet, glory follows.

341. WHERE DISPASSION IS DETRIMENTAL!

Karthik: Is there something we should not be dispassionate about?

Gurudev: Myself! *(Laughter)*

Do not put off the fire of longing for the Divine or for *Satsang* with dispassion. There is a little fire in you that propels you toward knowledge, *Sadhana*, devotion and service but sometimes you use knowledge to put off that fire. The so-called dispassionate people are often morose and unenthusiastic. Many times you hear people saying, "Oh never mind, God is everywhere, *Gurudev* is in my heart, I can do *Satsang* anywhere. My *Seva* is my *Sadhana*, so there is no need to meditate. Anyway I am doing *Sadhana* 24 hours a day. When God wills he will call me to *Satsang* and Advanced Courses again!" Such excuses should not be justified as dispassion.

When you want to do some service, the mind goes, "Oh it is all *maya* anyway, everything is an illusion. It is all just happening. Things will happen when the time comes!"

In this way knowledge gets misused and is quoted out of context to suit one's convenience or laziness.

Using knowledge like this you miss a lot.

In the name of dispassion do not lose that spark of enthusiasm and interest. Keep the fire of longing for the Divine and for service to society alive.

Dispassion here would be detrimental.

✍ *Old Flash:*

As Gurudev spoke on "time," we found the moment, this moment had passed and the news was already old. The "News" Flash can never be new, so Birjoo decided to call it Old Flash!

342. BUSINESS & SPIRITUALITY

Often business is looked down upon by spiritual people, and spirituality is put off as impractical by business people. The ancient people conceived that spirituality is the heart and business is the legs. An individual or a society is incomplete without both these aspects. Business brings material comfort and spirituality brings mental and emotional comfort. Spirituality brings ethics and fair practice to business.

In the body/mind complex, depriving either the body or the mind of comfort means depriving both of them comfort. You cannot talk of spirituality to the poorest of the poor people without taking care of their basic needs. They need to be supported materially. There is no spirituality in the world that is devoid of service and service cannot happen if material needs are ignored. Service cannot happen only through the lips, it needs legs to work.

Every system has its flaws. Capitalism exploits the poor while socialism dampens individual creativity and entrepreneurial spirit. Spirituality is the bridge between socialism and capitalism. Spirituality gives the capitalist the heart to serve and the socialist the spirit to innovate.

News Flash:

While Gurudev attended the World Economic Forum, the Art of Living Foundation was simultaneously being represented at the World Social Forum in Brazil and the U.N. Conference on Sustainable Development in New York.

343. THE SUBTLE TRUTH ABOUT VIRTUES

If you observe your behaviour, you will notice that you procrastinate when doing something good but hurry when it comes to doing something bad. For example if you are angry, you want to express it immediately.

Do you know why? Because virtues are your very nature and they will never leave you. Your vices are not your nature and they will leave you. Negative tendencies are transient and will leave you if you do not act on them. Frustration and crying cannot stay long, especially with the same intensity. Perhaps you are concerned that your vices will leave you if you do not act on them.

It is wise to postpone acting on vices, for they will not stay, and to act immediately for doing good, otherwise you will continue to postpone doing good for the next few lifetimes. *(Laughter)*

✍ *News Flash:*

There was an attempt during the World Economic Forum to divide the religious communities into monotheistic and polytheistic. This was given up at Gurudev's insistence and harmony finally prevailed. Leaders from all religious communities, including Archbishop of Canterbury, agreed to drop this draft resolution as Gurudev had desired.

An Advance Course with people from 37 countries is in progress at the Bangalore Ashram.

344. HUMOUR & HUMILIATION

Humour is the buffer that saves you from humiliation. If you have a good sense of humour you can never be humiliated, and if you refuse to be humiliated you become invincible. Humour brings people together while humiliation tears them apart. In a society torn with humiliation and insults, humour is like a breath of fresh air. A good sense of humour relieves you from fear and anxiety.

Humour should be coupled with care and concern. Mere humour without care and concern or appropriate action often irritates those who come to you with serious problems.

- Humour can keep spirits high, yet if overdone it leaves a bad taste.

- Humour without wisdom is shallow.

- Humour with wisdom creates an atmosphere of celebration.

- Humour without sensitivity is satire and it returns to you with more problems.

- The wise use humour to bring wisdom and to lighten every situation.

- The intelligent use humour as a shield against humiliation.

- The cruel use humour as a sword to insult others.

- The irresponsible use humour to escape from responsibility.

- The fool takes humour too seriously!

- To make an effort to be humorous is nonsensical.

Question: How does one cultivate a sense of humour?

Gurudev: Humour is not just words, it is the lightness of your being. Your sense of humour can grow by:

- Being cordial and lighthearted. This brings out authentic humour, which is not just repeating jokes.

- Not taking life too seriously, because you will never come out of it alive! *(Laughter)*

- Having a sense of belongingness with everybody, including those who are not friendly.

- Practicing yoga and meditation.

- Having unshakable faith in the Divine and in the laws of *karma*.

- Being in the company of those who live in knowledge and who are humorous.

- Having a willingness to be a clown.

✍ News Flash:

On Valentine's Day, jubilant and ecstatic participants of Teacher Training phase One and Two and the International Advanced Course (more than 700 in all) celebrated with a colourful multilingual cultural program that highlighted Gurudev's universal message of love.

After an intensive but blissful course, with nearly eight days of silence and deep meditation, the Advanced Course participants had a surprise picnic with Gurudev, visiting an ancient Shiva temple over 5,000 years old. The temple authorities were moved as they recollected the prophecies of two saints which were fulfilled by Gurudev's visit.

345. LOVE & TRUTH

Why would someone tell a lie to their close ones or to their beloved?

This is a question often asked by lovers. Love cannot stand untruth, causing relationships to break up when this happens. The answer lies in understanding the paradox of love and truth.

People tell lies just to save and maintain their love. The fear that the truth might damage their love causes lies to be told between husband and wife, boyfriend and girlfriend, parents and children and in other family situations.

In love you feel weak but truth brings strength. Yet why do people prefer love over truth, weakness over strength?

No one wants to sacrifice love. Thus people are ready to give up the truth for their love. Love takes the lustre out of truth. Sometimes truth can make love bitter while in love even lies can appear sweet, like *Krishna's* lies to his mother, *Yashoda!*

The truth that does not nourish love makes no sense, and the love that cannot withstand the truth is not true love. When one is assured that their love is so strong that the truth can neither break it nor cause bitterness, then the truth prevails and love shines.

With truth there are judgments, but true love is beyond judgments. Thus true love makes you weak and yet it is the greatest strength.

✍ News Flash:

Bliss reigned supreme in the beautiful South Indian state of Kerala. Over a million hearts were stolen by Gurudev during his tour of Kerala. Everywhere he went, the script was the same – overflowing stadiums, inspiring and scintillating discourses, deep meditations, tears of gratitude. No one could escape! All the events were highlighted in the media. The Chief Minister of Kerala State and most of his cabinet ministers hosted Gurudev at a special function and sought his advice on problems that they were facing.

In Thiruvananthapuram, when the participants opened their eyes after Sudarshan Kriya, they could not see Gurudev on the stage, though they could hear his voice. Later they found him sitting on the branch of a tree with a cordless microphone!

346. An Awkward Situation

Why do you feel awkward? How do you get out of it?

If you have always been the centre of attention and are suddenly sidelined, you may feel out of place. Similarly if you have always been on the sidelines and are suddenly pushed to centre stage, you may experience restlessness. A very busy person with nothing to do, or a laid-back person who is faced with responsibilities may also experience restlessness. If you are accustomed to ordering others and suddenly have to take orders, or if you usually follow orders and then are made to give them, you may feel out of place. Very often feeling out of place blocks reason and distorts logic.

If the situation you are in is inevitable, tolerate it.

If it is avoidable, walk away from it. If you feel that it can expand your abilities, smile through it.

Every awkward situation increases your comfort zone. Every awkward situation is a test for how deep you are in the knowledge.

Love something of an awkward situation. This will increase your comfort zone. When your comfort zone increases, no one will be able to push your buttons and you will become centred and unshakable.

✍ *News Flash:*

From Bangalore to Bihar, the Master has been busy bowling hearts, beautifying interiors and bestowing grace!

From the moment of his tumultuous arrival, Patna opened its heart. The Hathwa Palace brimming over with people, rapturously welcomed Gurudev. Evening Satsang was at the Beur Jail where the prisoners had a heart-to-heart chat with Gurudev. Later, hundreds of students had the benefit of an exclusive session with him. Over 150,000 people experienced his electrifying presence at the MahaSatsang.

The next morning Gurudev left for the village of Massauri which has been the target of numerous terrorist attacks. Thousands who have benefited from Navchetena Shibirs (Breath-Water-Sound Workshops) had been preparing for weeks for his visit. Most villagers shared that it was impossible to leave their homes after dusk because of the very volatile and dangerous situation there, but the Shibirs and Satsangs had transformed their lives.

Following the Gujarat tragedy, Gurudev requested that everyone observe two minutes of silence on Wednesday, March 6, 2002, at 9 a.m. local time throughout the world for communal peace and harmony and to pay respect to those who were victims of religious intolerance.

347. THE TRUE YAJÑA

Rage has no ears, nor does it have vision. It only leads to reaction. And reaction leads to regret. Regret causes frustration. Frustration clouds reason. Unreasonable acts provoke rage, starting a vicious cycle.

Self-knowledge and devotion alone can free you from this vicious cycle.

In the fire of knowledge, when rage and revenge are offered, the warmth of the blemishless Self shines forth. This is the true *Yajña*.

✍ *News Flash:*

Gurudev was exceptionally busy this week, meeting various leaders of the Muslim and Hindu communities late into the night to bring peace and harmony and a resolution of the Ayodhya issue. He convinced both the Muslim personal law board and the VHP (Vishva Hindu Parishad - a Hindu society) to come to the negotiating table.

There were remarkably interesting sessions at the AIIMS (All India Institute of Medical Sciences) symposium on the Science of Breath, some of which Gurudev chaired. An international team of doctors presented their research findings to more than 1,000 delegates. A synopsis and videos will be made available by May.

Gurudev also went to an impromptu Satsang that was organised for him at the Tihar Jail. More than 4,000 inmates who had already gone through the Art of Living Prison Program greeted him enthusiastically. He went among them and showered them with flowers of grace. He noticed that there were some very old women prisoners there who could barely sit or stand by themselves – utterly incapable of committing any crimes. He has made an appeal to the Governor to grant them amnesty.

348. Your Nature is Shiva

Peace is your nature, yet you remain restless. Freedom is your nature, yet you remain in bondage. Happiness is your nature, yet you become miserable for some reason or another.

Contentment is your nature, yet you continue to reel in desires.

Benevolence is your nature, yet you do not reach out.

Going toward your nature is *Sadhana. Sadhana* is becoming what you truly are! Your true nature is *Shiva.* And *Shiva* is peace, infinity, beauty and the non-dual One.

Ratri means "to take refuge." *Shivaratri* is taking refuge in *Shiva.*

✍ *News Flash:*

Gurudev was a state guest in Uttaranchal where he was welcomed by the Chief Minister. Mr. and Mrs. Mann hosted a beautiful Satsang in Dehradun.

Shivaratri celebrations in Rishikesh truly took everyone to the peak of bliss and to the silence beyond. Rudra pujas in the morning and evening cast a spell in the air, the chants reverberated through the ashram and stilled hearts and minds. The all-night Satsang included thousands, and it ended with an early morning Sudarshan Kriya with the master.

349. PRAISE THE FOOLS

Praising the fool is beneficial to society!

A fool when pleased might stop doing harm and start doing good work. In this sense it is wise to praise a fool; it helps to motivate him. So your praise is meaningful when it is directed toward a fool.

A wise man by his very nature will continue doing good work because his attitude does not depend on someone's praise or blame. So it serves no purpose to praise a wise man because your praise will have no impact on him.

There are three types of people – the wise, the crooked and the immature. The wise man continues doing good work even if he is scolded or praised. Crooked people need to be praised to get them to do good work. And from time to time the immature person needs to be both praised and scolded for them to do something good.

✍ News Flash:

A close associate of Osama Bin Laden, Mohammad Afroz, who is currently in the high security Bombay prison, was involved in the plan to blow up a London airport. He took the Art of Living Prison Program and was totally transformed. He wrote that he wished that all Al Qaeda members would do the course that brought forth such a transformation in him. His desire is to become an Art of Living teacher and bring peace and harmony to people!

At the same time Reverend Sri Shiva Muniji Maharaj, a proponent of nonviolence (ahimsa) and the head of the Jain religion, was on the Advanced Course and proclaimed the fulfilment of the Jain religion from what he found in the Art of Living.

The participants on the third Advanced Course are soaking in bliss on the banks of the Ganges River.

350. WHAT MAKES A REAL HOLIDAY?

Rest and happiness make a real holiday. Often people go on a holiday and they come back tired and tanned, but needing a few more days to recuperate! A real holiday is that which energises you and does not wear you out.

Nothing energises you like wisdom, so remember:

- Doubts and complaints are impediments to rest.

- The moment you set out on your holiday, know that it has begun. Often people expect to find a pinnacle of happiness. Enjoy every moment of the journey as children do, do not wait for the destination.

- If you cannot be happy in one place, you cannot be happy in any other place. If you do not know how to row one boat, you will not be able to row any other boat.

- To get maximum satisfaction out of your holiday you need to do something creative and to engage in *Seva*.

- Do not ever forget to make meditation and prayer a part of your holiday.

If your days are holy, then every day is a holiday!

✍ News Flash:

Holi the festival of colours, was celebrated with enthusiasm and jubilation. Over 5,000 people were awash with blessings, bliss and myriad hues of happiness. Satsang continued through the day as Gurudev showered colours and love on people's lives.

On to Delhi, where Gurudev addressed the Chamber of Commerce and several top Muslim leaders. Later Gurudev visited the Hazrat Nizamuddin Dargah Sharief and was given a reception at the Fatehpuri Masjid.

351. WAKE UP & SLOW DOWN

Often you are in a rush in life. When you are in a rush, you are unable to properly perceive things. This takes the charm, thrill and beauty from your life. You can never be close to the truth when you are in a rush because your perception, observation and expression become distorted.

The rush to enjoy robs the joy from life and only denies the happiness and freedom of here and now. Often you do not even know why you are in a hurry. It almost becomes a biological phenomenon to be in a rush. Wake up and become aware of the rush in you!

Anne Farrow: Wake up and slow down! *(Laughter)*

It is ridiculous to be in a rush to slow down. Just being aware of the rush itself will take care of it. Slowing down does not mean procrastinating or being lethargic, though it is easy to be at the extremes of either rushing or lethargy. Rushing is caused by feverishness, and feverishness arises out of deficiency, a need to achieve; whereas dynamism is an expression of fulfilment.

The golden rule is to be awake, and when you are awake you cannot help but be dynamic.

Right now realise that you are awake and cool.

✍ *News Flash:*

Gurudev was a state guest in Arunachal Pradesh where he addressed the ministers and NGO's, he inaugurated the Art of Living International School, and he addressed the intellectuals at the Arunachal Pradesh University in the scenic Rono Hills. On the way to a Satsang in Itanagar, Gurudev visited the local Nyishi tribe who pray to the sun god.

On to Guwahati, Assam, where the heavens held their rain for a Satsang and live Sudarshan Kriya attended by thousands of people. Gurudev inaugurated a model village near Tezpur and laid a foundation stone for a new technical school and ashram on the banks of the Brahmaputra River.

Thousands attended a Satsang in Siliguri, West Bengal, as Gurudev travelled northward to Sikkim.

352. COMMUNISM & SPIRITUALITY

Communism has three goals: To check the greed of feudal and capitalistic societies; to halt the fanaticism and fundamentalism of religious communities; and to care for and share resources with the needy.

Only spirituality brings fulfilment to communism. Only spirituality checks greed and opens the hearts of the rich to help the needy. Only spirituality stops the fanaticism and fundamentalism of religious groups and creates a sense of belongingness with the whole world. Only spirituality cultures the tendency to care and share. Only spirituality brings about open-mindedness and a progressive attitude.

Communism cannot fulfil its goals without spirituality. It is impossible and time has proved it. Spirituality nourishes communism.

KNOWLEDGE NIBBLE!

Question: If you have a *Guru* do you need luck?

Gurudev: You need luck to have a *Guru*! *(Laughter)*

✍ *News Flash:*

Gurudev was in Sikkim for a huge Satsang. He later visited the Rumtek Monastery where he was given a traditional Buddhist welcome. Thousands thronged the largest stadium in Kolkata for a rousing Satsang and a deep rejuvenating meditation with Gurudev.

For the first time, 700 people boarded the Enlightenment Express from Mumbai to Bangalore for a wonderful Advanced Course with Gurudev.

353. WAS BUDDHA AN ATHEIST?

A pure atheist is impossible to find. An atheist is one who does not believe in anything that is not concrete and tangible, but life is not all concrete and tangible, nor is this universe. Whether it is business, science or art, all involve a certain amount of guesswork, assumptions, imagination and intuition. All of them are ethereal in nature and are not tangible.

The moment an atheist accepts, even remotely, a field that is unexplainable, he ceases to be an atheist. An intelligent person cannot rule out the mysteries in life and the universe, and hence cannot honestly be an atheist! The so-called atheists are perhaps only denouncing certain concepts of God.

Question: Was *Buddha* an atheist?

Gurudev: No, in one sense, because he professed emptiness, which is very hard for an atheist to accept. And yes, in another sense, because he did not profess concepts of God.

Jim: An atheist believes only what he can see, but *Buddha* said all that you see is not real.

Gurudev: If only an present-day atheists could be *Buddhas*.

354. THE STRENGTH OF COMMITMENT

Question: Why is it easier for some of us to commit to our own welfare rather than that of others?

Gurudev: Because you do not know that whatever you are committed to brings you strength.

If you are committed to your family then your family supports you. If you are committed to your society, you enjoy the support of society. If you are committed to God, God gives you strength. If you are committed to truth, truth brings you strength.

Often people are not aware of this and that is why they are hesitant to commit to a greater cause. There is also a fear that commitment would weaken people or take away their freedom. Your commitment to a cause is bound to bring you comfort in the long run.

Commitment in life grows toward a higher cause. The higher the commitment, the greater is the good for all.

Noah: Why don't we take any vows in the Art of Living?

Gurudev: When the path is charming, commitment is effortless and is part of your nature.

Mikey: In the Art of Living we don't take vows, we have wows! (*Laughter*)

✍ *News Flash:*

Gurudev's visit to Saarbruken and Stutgaart in Germany was extensively covered by the media. Three more universities in Berlin have made the Art of Living Course a part of their curriculum, for a total of five universities officially offering the course.

Hundreds of participants were graced by Gurudev's presence at the one-day Advanced Course in New Jersey. Following an intimate Satsang in New York, Gurudev gave a surprise public talk in Washington, D. C.

Hundreds of students were inspired by Gurudev's talk in Amherst and Boston.

355. Two Types of Knowledge

There are two types of knowledge. The first one is pure knowledge and the second one is applied knowledge. Applied knowledge may benefit you directly and immediately, but pure knowledge benefits you indirectly and in the long run.

If there are some things that you have studied or understood that you are unable to put into practice, do not get disheartened. Sometime in the future, if you do not discard the knowledge you have as impractical, it will be of use to you.

Often people discard pure knowledge for its lack of immediate application. In fact these two types of knowledge complement each other. Applied knowledge without pure knowledge remains weak. And pure knowledge without application will remain unfulfilled.

Do not discard or label the knowledge as impractical, and do not label yourself as weak or unworthy because you are unable to apply the knowledge in your day-to-day life.

Sometimes when you are alone in nature, silent, taking a walk, looking at the sand on the beach, a bird in the sky, or while meditating – suddenly the knowledge will emerge and you will recognise the knowledge dawning in your life.

✍ *News Flash:*

Gurudev went to Venice, Italy, where he inaugurated the international conference entitled "World Peace Through Prayer and Meditation."

In Switzerland, Art of Living Courses will be offered to high school teachers as part of their continuing education.

Mera Lee Goldman, the Mayor of Beverly Hills, California, officially proclaimed May 9, 2002, to be "Gurudev Sri Sri Ravi Shankar Day. On May 6, the Mayor of Los Angeles, California, James K. Hahn, formally recognized the activities of the Art of Living Foundation for "outstanding efforts and accomplishments which have been of great benefit to the City of Los Angeles.

An Advanced Course is being held now in the San Francisco Bay area.

356. FRIENDSHIP FOR A CAUSE

Examine your friendships for their cause. Here are the reasons:

- You make friends because you have common enemies. Fear or a threat to survival brings people together.

- You make friends because you have common problems such as sickness or job dissatisfaction.

- People get together and become friends because they have common interests. Examples are business people or professionals such as doctors, architects or social workers.

- You make friends because of common tastes. Examples of this are common interests in sports, movies, music and hobbies.

- People become friends with those for whom they have compassion or provide service.

- People become friends merely because of a long term acquaintance.

Brave are those who nurture friendships for only friendship's sake. Such friendships will never die nor become soured for they are born out of one's friendly nature. Only through wisdom is one friendly by nature.

✍ News Flash:

On Gurudev's birthday, May 13, Seva projects and Satsangs were held all over the world. Thousands of poor and needy were fed and received clothes.

From San Jose, Gurudev travelled to Bali with a brief stopover in Japan. In Bali an Advanced Course was held for South East Asia and Australia. Then Gurudev went to Yogjakarta, Indonesia, to visit one of the seven wonders of the world After Satsangs in Jakarta and Singapore, Gurudev will leave for Bangalore.

357. THREE TYPES OF DISPASSION

There are three types of dispassion:

- The first type is the dispassion that arises when you realise the misery in the world and you fear misery. The events in life – the pain and suffering you experience or see – bring dispassion.

- The second type of dispassion is born out of your desire to achieve something higher. Some consider dispassion as a path to enlightenment by renouncing something here to gain something out there. They engage in austerities and take vows to have a better place in heaven.

- The third type of dispassion comes from wisdom or knowledge. A broader understanding of the transient nature of things cultures a state of non-attachment to events, objects, people or situations which lets you remain calm and unperturbed.

Divine love does not let dispassion manifest. The attainment of love brings such bliss and such intoxication that it not only takes away your passion, but dispassion as well.

This is the problem with many Art of Living members. They feel they have attained the highest and remain blissed out!

✍ News Flash:

The YLTP (Youth Leadership Training Program) trainer's meeting concluded last week with great enthusiasm and celebration.

A huge contingent from Kerala came to the Bangalore Ashram for an Advanced Course with Gurudev.

A teacher training program is in progress for those who will be teaching in the Sri Sri Ravi Shankar Vidya Mandir schools all over the country.

358. Faith & Alertness

Faith and alertness appear to be completely opposite in nature. When you are alert there usually is no faith, and you feel restless and insecure. When you have faith your mind is secure and in a restful state, and you are not alert.

There are three types of faith:

- *Tamasic* faith is caused by dullness. An example is when you do not want to take responsibility or action and you say, "Oh, it doesn't matter, God will take care of all these things!" *(Laughter)*

- *Rajasic* faith is brought on by an intense compulsion of desires and ambition. The ambition keeps your faith alive.

- *Satvic* faith is innocent and is born out of fullness of consciousness.

Faith and alertness, though apparently opposite in nature, are actually complementary to each other. In the absence of faith there can be no growth, and with out alertness there can be no correct understanding. Faith can make you complacent while alertness makes you tense. If there is no faith, there is fear. And when there is no alertness you cannot perceive or express properly, so a combination of both is essential.

In *gyana* (a state of wisdom) there is alertness with out tension and faith without complacency. The purpose of education should be to remove the element of dullness from faith and the element of fear from alertness. This is a unique and rare combination. If you have faith and alertness at the same time, then you will become a true *gyani* (wise one).

359. ENTHUSIASM & DISPASSION

What is enthusiasm? Enthusiasm means to be connected to God within. When you are with your source, you can only be enthusiastic and you cannot be but enthusiastic when your mind is totally in the present moment. Apathy is when you are away from the source of life.

You should know that dispassion is not apathy; it is simply a broader perspective of reality. Dispassion is moving toward the source. Dispassion simply means the way back home. It is the journey toward the source, which is a reservoir of enthusiasm.

When dispassion and enthusiasm co-exist, that is the secret of perennial enthusiasm and profound dispassion. Though they appear to be opposite, they are actually complementary.

✍ *News Flash:*

An 11th century temple rose from ruins in Gurudev's birth place of Thayagasamudram, thanks to the sole effort of one of our Art of Living teachers, Setu Mamy. Though about 80 years old, her enthusiasm was that of a teenager. Single-handedly she overcame all hurdles to bring this temple back to life. It was a grand celebration in the village. Gurudev promised to build homes for needy people there.

360. *Guru* Tidbits

What to do if your commitment is boring?

Commitment has value when things are not so charming. When things are interesting you do not need commitment at all. You never say you are committed to doing something that is very interesting or charming.

Learning :

Learning is inevitable. By doing things right you learn, and by doing things wrong you also learn. From every situation, from everybody, you learn either what to do or what not to do. Either by mistakes or by doing things correctly, you cannot but learn. Learning is inevitable.

It is only when you sleep that you do not learn. And if you are asleep in your life, there is neither pain nor pleasure nor learning. Most people are in such deep slumber. That is why many people do not even make an effort to get out of their pain.

Question: How do I improve my patience?

Gurudev: Can I tell you next year? *(Laughter)*

Question: How do I improve my memory?

Gurudev: Ask me this question later. *(Laughter)*

✍ **News Flash:**

Gurudev went to Kumbakonam where there was a huge Satsang of several hundred thousand in the biggest temple city of Tamil Nadu.

Then on to Heidelberg and Berlin in Germany where people came in large numbers to attend talks and Satsangs. While there, he was received at the Indian Embassy and met with several senators from the German Congress.

361. NIGRAHA, AGRAHA, SATYAGRAHA & DURAAGRAHA

'Nigraha' means control. *'Agraha'* means insistence. *'Satyagraha'* means steadfast determination. *'Duraagraha'* means blind adamancy, reckless stubbornness.

These four allow you to progress when practiced for just a limited period of time and will give limited results, positive or negative. But if practiced for a long period of time, they will eat away the potential of life. You have to transcend all four to attain peace.

Freedom is when you transcend all four. They are inevitable to streamline life but you need to transcend them to be free.

Exercise: Give your own examples and discuss

Nigraha, Agraha, Satyagraha and *Duraagraha.*

✍ *News Flash:*

Gurudev's North American tour began in Chicago, where he was the keynote speaker at the meeting of the American Association of Physicians of Indian Origin. He also received a letter of appreciation from the United States Congress and one from Mayor Daley of Chicago. June 28 was declared "Gurudev Sri Sri Ravi Shankar Day" in Chicago.

362. Wake Up & Transcend

The foolish one uses spiritual power to gain material comfort.

An intelligent one uses the material world to rise high in the spirit.

When you transcend the intellect you allow your self to be used by the spirit.

One who is awake neither uses anything nor loses anything.

Become intelligent, transcend and wake up.

✍ News Flash:

Gurudev gave the inaugural address at the American Telugu Association Conference in Dallas on July 5. His inspiring words left the audience wanting more. A group of hecklers tried to stop Gurudev's public talk but mysteriously dispersed as his car approached. He charmed the Texas crowd with his humour and knowledge.

The first ever North American YLTP (Youth Leadership Training Program) took place in Brownsville, Texas. These college students and their friends are now Breath- Water-Sound teachers and are traveling in Belize and Mexico offering this fantastic course to people in impoverished villages and barrios.

July 17, 2002
North American Ashram, Montreal., Canada

363. KNOW YOUR GROUP TYPE

Normally in the world people with similar tendencies group together; intelligent people group together, fools get together, happy people get together, ambitious people get together and disgruntled people also group together to celebrate their problems! (Laughter) There is a saying, "Birds of a feather flock together."

The disgruntled people get together, they complain and pull each other down. A frustrated person cannot be with someone happy because the other is not dancing to their tune. You only feel comfortable when the other person is in tune with you. Intelligent people do not feel at home with foolish people. Foolish people feel that intelligent ones are not humane. One with wisdom feels at home with the disgruntled as well as the happy, foolish and intelligent. Similarly, people with all these tendencies also feel at home with the wise.

Just turn around and look at what goes on in your group – are you grateful or grumbling? Take responsibility to uplift the people around you. That is Satsang, not just singing and leaving.

The wise person is like the sky where all birds can fly.

✍ *News Flash:*

Gurudev traveled to the Canadian North American Ashram to greet a joyous TTC.

364. CREATIVITY

Creativity brings a new beginning for "time". When you are creative, you break the monotony of time. Everything becomes fresh and alive. Creativity brings along with it a new round of enthusiasm. Both creative and procreative impulses in nature are associated with enthusiasm. When you are enthusiastic you are closer to the creative principle of existence.

Deep silence is the mother of creativity. No creativity can come out of one who is too busy, worried, over-ambitious or lethargic. Balanced activity, rest and yoga can kindle skills and creativity in you.

✍ *News Flash:*

The chief of 12 million Native Americans (the indigenous people of the Americas) signed a Memorandum of Understanding with Gurudev in a moving ceremony, wherein Gurudev was formally invited to North America and requested to work in close co-operation for the betterment of the indigenous people.

Guru Purnima was celebrated at the North American Ashram with over 2,000 people participating.

365. FREE WILL AND DESTINY

When people consider the past as free will they are filled with remorse and regret.

When they consider the future as destiny, lethargy and inertia set in.

A wise person will consider the past as destiny and the future as free will.

When you consider the past as destiny, no more questions are raised and the mind is at ease.

And when you consider the future as free will you are filled with enthusiasm and dynamism.

Of course there will be some uncertainty when you consider the future as free will, and some anxiety, but it can also bring alertness and creativity.

Consider the past as destiny, the future as free will and the present moment as Divinity.

Question: How do we remove the anxiety?

Gurudev: By having faith in the Divine and doing sadhana.

✍ *News Flash:*

The Art of Living played a leading role in the World Sustainable Development Summit 2002 held in Johannesburg, South Africa. Dean Harmison and his team were greatly appreciated. (More news to come)

More than 100 Art of Living volunteers from seven European countries came together to help flood victims in Dresden, Germany where huge floods have destroyed all that people once had. Many volunteers worked through the night to free houses from the mud. The mayor of Pirna/Dresden and the leading military officer there have expressed their gratitude to the Art of Living volunteers.

Currently, free Art of Living Breath-Water-Sound and ART Excel courses are being conducted for the victims.

And finally, Gurudev celebrated Lord Krishna's birth in Hyderabad with a grand satsang. He then proceeded to Nagpur.

Message For The New Millennium

The sun rises and celebrates
The sky embraces and celebrates

Winds blow and celebrate
Rivers flow and celebrate

Birds sing and celebrate
Peacocks dance and celebrate

Trees flower and celebrate
Buds bloom and celebrate

We smile and serve
Meditate and celebrate

Gurudev Sri Sri Ravi Shankar

Wisdom For Organisers

Knowledge has organising power. Only knowledge can organise. The more steeped you are in knowledge, the better you can organise.

Never underestimate your organisation. If you underestimate your organisation, you will not be able to build it.

Defend your intentions, not your actions. Often people defend their actions and lose sight of their intentions. Then they feel sorry and weak. There is no need to feel sorry. Defend your intention to do right.

Teamwork. In teamwork, you achieve more than you do individually. Certain work is best done alone and other work is best done with a team. Find the balance between walking alone and working with a team. In either case, alone or with a team, you will face obstacles. For your growth, both are essential. Each has its disadvantages and advantages. Drop any one, and you will be at a loss. The skill is not to have an aversion to either and to focus on the goal.

Defending friends. Suppose you have introduced a friend to a job and they make a mistake. Do not try to defend them. That is where the team breaks up. When you defend a friend, you are not friendly to everybody.

Defending someone's mistakes does not do justice to the teamwork and stops the person from learning. Soft-heartedness and compassion in an organisation can be detrimental to both the teamwork and the organisation.

Never justify a mistake with intimidation or logic. Raising your voice, intimidation, anger, shouting and applying erroneous logic makes a wrong appear right. Do not give in to that. Do not give into assertiveness, intimidation, wrong logic and soft-heartedness.

Working with volunteers. Volunteers often act as though everyone's a boss and not a worker. When working with volunteers, be calm and quiet. Ask, "Have you finished your work?"

Solutions will always be ad hoc. The more dynamic an institution is, the more the solutions will be ad hoc. Its not like a nine-to-five company job where roles are designed and planned for a year. With volunteers, the productivity is more intense. The more dynamic a group, the quicker things happen. Maintaining a margin for confusion and chaos can prevent stress.

Jai Guru Dev

The Art of Living
&
The International Association
for Human Values

Transforming Lives

The Founder
Gurudev Sri Sri Ravi Shankar

Gurudev Sri Sri Ravi Shankar is a universally revered spiritual and humanitarian leader. His vision of a violence-free, stress-free society through the reawakening of human values has inspired millions to broaden their spheres of responsibility and work towards the betterment of the world. Born in 1956 in southern India, Gurudev was often found deep in meditation as a child. At the age of four, he astonished his teachers by reciting the Bhagwad Gita, an ancient Sanskrit scripture. He has always had the unique gift of presenting the deepest truths in the simplest of words.

Gurudev established The Art of Living, an educational and humanitarian Non-Governmental Organisation that works in special consultative status with the Economic and Social Council (ECOSOC) of the United Nations in 1981. Present in over 156 countries, it formulates and implements lasting solutions to conflicts and issues faced by individuals, communities and nations. In 1997, he founded the International Association for Human Values (IAHV) to foster human values and lead sustainable development projects. Gurudev has reached out to more than 300 million people worldwide through personal interactions, public events, teachings, The Art of Living workshops and humanitarian initiatives. He has brought to the masses ancient practices which were traditionally kept exclusive, and has designed many self development techniques which can easily be integrated into daily life to calm the mind and instill confidence and enthusiasm. One of Gurudev's most unique offerings to the world is the Sudarshan Kriya, a powerful breathing technique that facilitates physical, mental, emotional and social well-being.

Numerous awards have been bestowed upon Gurudev Sri Sri Ravi Shankar which includes Padma Vibhushan (India's second highest civilian award) and the highest civilian awards from Paraguay, Mongolia and Colombia. Gurudev has addressed several international forums, including the United Nations Millennium World Peace Summit (2000), World Economic Forum (2001, 2003), World Summit On Ethics In Sports at FIFA Headquarters, Zurich (2014, 2016), UNESCO (2015), Parliaments of France, Britain, Norway (2016) and others.

Gurudev has played a key role in conflict resolution across the world including Colombia, Kashmir, Iraq, Ivory Coast, Naxal inhabited regions of India, and many other places.

Follow Gurudev on:

Twitter - @srisri

Facebook - www.facebook.com/SriSriRaviShankar

Website - www.srisriravishankar.org

YouTube - www.youtube.com/srisri

Instagram - www.instagram.com/srisriravishankar

LinkedIn - www.linkedin.com/in/srisriravishankar

The Art of Living

In Service Around The World

Founded in 1981 by Gurudev Sri Sri Ravi Shankar, The Art of Living is engaged in stress-elimination programs and service initiatives. The organization operates globally in 156 countries with one of the largest volunteer bases in the world and has touched the lives of over 370 million people.

The organisation works in special consultative status with the Economic and Social Council (ECOSOC) of the United Nations, participating in a variety of committees and activities related to health and conflict resolution.

In 1997, Gurudev Sri Sri Ravi Shankar also founded the International Association for Human Values (IAHV) to coordinate sustainable development projects, nurture human values and coordinate conflict resolution in association with The Art of Living. In India, Africa and South America, the two sister organizations' volunteers are spearheading sustainable growth in rural communities, and have already reached out to 40,212 villages.

The Art of Living movement has spread peace and transformation across communities through diverse humanitarian projects.

- Conflict Resolution
- Alleviating pain in War Zones
- Relieving trauma in Post Terror Attacks
- Disaster Relief
- Environment
- Education
- Empowerment of Women
- Prisoner Rehabilitation
- Rural Transformation

The Art of Living Programs

The Art of Living programs are guided by Gurudev Sri Sri Ravi Shankar's philosophy of peace: "Unless we have a stress-free mind and a violence-free society, we cannot achieve world peace." To help individuals get rid of stress and experience inner peace, The Art of Living offers stress-elimination programs which include breathing techniques, meditation and yoga. They cater to every age group - children, youth, adults and every section of society – rural communities, governments, corporate houses, etc. These programs have helped millions around the world to overcome stress, depression and violent tendencies. Emphasizing holistic living and personal self-development, the programs facilitate the complete blossoming of an individual's full potential. The cornerstone of all our workshops is the Sudarshan Kriya, a unique and potent breathing practice.

Introductory Programs:

• **The Happiness Program (Age 18+):**
  The 3-day program equips participants with practical knowledge and techniques to unlock their deepest potential and bring fullness to life.

• **Sahaj Samadhi Meditation (Age 18+):**
  Meditation technique that deeply relaxes the mind and rejuvenates the system.

• **Utkarsh Yoga (Age 8-13):**
  Introduce your children to spirituality, nurture human values, inculcate self-discipline, and develop their personality to be healthy and well-rounded.

• **Medha Yoga (Age 14-18):**
  Dynamic and innovative educational program for both high school and college students.

• **Prajñā Yoga (Age 5-18):**
  Helps children tap into the inherent intuitive abilities of the mind.

For more information please visit: www.artofliving.org

International Centres

INDIA
21st km, Kanakapura Road, Udayapura,
Bangalore - 560 082, Karnataka
Telephone: 0091 - 80-67262626 / 27 / 28
Email: info@srisripublications.com

GERMANY
Bad Antogast 1, 77728 Oppenau,
Baden-Württemberg
Telephone: 0049 - 7804-973-90
Email: info@artofliving.de

CANADA
13 Infinity Road, St. Mathieu du Parc,
Quebec G0X 1N0
Telephone: 001 - 819-532-3328
Email: artdevivre@artofliving.org

USA
639 Whispering Hills Rd,
Boone, NC 28607
Telephone: 001 - 828-263-4910
Email: info@artoflivingretreatcenter.org

www.srisriravishankar.org
www.artofliving.org
www.iahv.org